The Immortal Patriot

Frederick Channell

The Immortal Patriot

Frederick Channell

Published in the United States by Sugar Run Books

ISBN-13: 978-0615776866
ISBN-10: 0615776868

1. United States--History--18th century. 2. Canada--History--Emigration and immigration--19th century 3. Revolutionary War--War of 1812. 3. Constitutional history.

Visit the website at www.immortalpatriot.com

First Printing, 2013

DEDICATION

To my mother, my wife, and my wonderful daughters

TABLE OF CONTENTS

Prologue

The old man stood and stared down at his appearance in the lake. His reflection resembled an apple which had dried in the sun and shriveled up with age. In spite of his appearance he was quite active for a centenarian, and with a burst of determination he had come down to the lake shore from the steps of his tavern. He had called this lake home for many years. Even now in his advanced age a fire burned within him and he considered taking a ride in a skiff, or having a swim in the cool clear waters of the northern lake the Natives named Memphremagog. He paused and stood at the base of a large pine tree. While he looked up into the highest point of the pine, the aged man imagined the tall mast of a ship, and men in the crow's nest pointing off excitedly to a sail on the horizon. As he imagined the sounds of the ship, he grabbed hold of the tree firmly for support when he stumbled suddenly after he remembered his age. Most of the trees that now caused the sunlight to dapple on the ground around his feet had been seedlings on an ancient forest floor when he was born.

The voice of his son roused him from his contemplation.

"Sir, I have been looking all over for you and was quite worried when you could not be found."

Abraham looked at the younger man.

"Have you nothing to do but look after me? I am fine."

His son took his arm and politely helped him back up to the porch of the inn.

"I do not want you to take a fall father, please stay here in the chair."

"Can I get you anything?" He asked.

"No son, I am content. Please go tend to the patrons in the tavern," the old man replied.

The son looked at his father. He had known him his whole life and yet there was so much he did not know. So many secrets that lay cloaked behind the wrinkled facade. How many events pass by in a century, those to be proud of, some that must remain hidden, and others that may haunt us in our later years?

Out of the corner of Abraham's eye came his wife, Wealthy. A shawl was tied about her head and she wore clothing meant for working, not for entertaining guests. She took her place in the chair beside her husband as she had for the past forty years. Taking his hand she gazed into her husbands face.

"Did we go on another adventure down to the lake dear?" She asked.

"Yes" he replied, "if only I were a few years younger I would jump in and have a swim."

Wealthy chuckled and replied with a gleam in her eye.

"Will you never begin acting as your age dictates you should?" Abraham looked off to the mountains in the distance, watching somber clouds glide over the summits.

"I put on the knit cap you made me yesterday and went on an adventure to get my image taken, and I needed another adventure today."

Wealthy looked at him and replied, "has the world not changed in these many years; have you not had more than your share of adventure?"

"Yes Wealthy, it has been a grand adventure, but the biggest one still awaits me" said Abraham.

"Someone should write a book about you," Wealthy declared.

"Perhaps someday one of my children will," Abraham said, thinking of his many descendants; children, grandchildren, and great grandchildren that he had lived long enough to lay his eyes upon.

"That would be a grand book Abraham," said Wealthy, "a grand one indeed."

They looked off at the lake together as the steam boat *Mountain Maid* plied through the lake water as it approached the dock at Georgeville to load up with firewood and to let off more guests. The foaming lake lapping at the hull reminded him of a journey on a frigate he had taken so very long ago.......

My alarm clock rang out and I abruptly awoke from my dream. I looked about and stretched out on an old iron bed in Fayston, Vermont. Today would be the day I confronted my past. This would be the day I began the journey to discover my ancestor. I gathered my camera and notebooks and got ready for the long drive north.

Georgeville, Canada *Belden Illustrated Atlas of the Dominion of Canada* 1881

Welcome to the King's Navy

The early September sun started to rise in the bright blue Vermont sky as the trees blurred by my window. I traveled on a small country road along the Mad River in Vermont. The water from the rocky stream slowly flowed through the land that was a second home to me. The river was quiet now but is called the Mad River for a reason: when it overflows its bank, as it sometimes does, it leaves a vast path of destruction behind it. For now it lay quietly flowing with the river well contained within its rocky banks. The fog slowly lifted from the valley and the mist rose off the river as I began a journey to the final resting place of my ancestor, Abraham FitzJohn Channell.

I hoped the fog over his life would lift for me as I traveled north along the northern section of Route 89 to the international border. This is roughly the same route of direction that Abraham had taken in his day; two hundred years ago. The old turnpike roads and rural paths that he traveled are now long gone and I may have crossed over his route many times. Unknowingly stepping into the footprints of the past. I was going north in the correct direction, and with a little luck my vehicle might just make it. My old Toyota was not very luxurious, and its worn tires rumbled out a rough ride, but it was certainly more comfortable than the horse or wagon that my ancestor had ridden across the small paths in the northern forest of New England two hundred years before. I hoped the veil of secrecy created by the past might just fade a bit with a trip to his former home.

So with a full tank of gas and my U.S. passport safely tucked in my pocket, I went north in search of him and his final resting place. This would be a trip across an international border that hardly existed when my ancestor first crossed it. I thought of the faded old family tree my mother had left me, and the loss of both my parents that had made me feel disconnected from my past. As if with their loss a link to my ancestors and past had been broken. Although forgetful by nature, I had somehow not misplaced but kept that family tree safe in the decades since my mom had given it to me. For some reason she had entrusted it to me. They say that one person is entrusted in each family to understand its past.

I did not realize it, but I had become the chosen one the day that my mother passed the tree on to me. My mother had left me with a fabulous story I needed to validate-to pick up the tale where she had left off. Now decades later I was skeptical of the short description of my ancestor's life that I had been given. The story seemed too far fetched to me to possibly be true. I was to find out it was all true and more, but at that moment, I did not have any idea what I would discover. With the help of modern computer search technology and with my training as a historian, I hoped his story would become clearer to me. When a history book is read, the reader relies on the writer to interpret history for them. I had no such luxury. When the evidence piled up it became my responsibility to piece the puzzle together.

Little of this evidence was available to my mom before her death. I really knew nothing about the side of my family that I had received my surname from. My grandmother and grandfather on this side of my family had both died before I was born, and my father never spoke to me about his father or their family story. For some reason my mother had taken an interest in it, and passed on what she had been able to discover to me. What began as an interest in my family's past became an obsession.

Searching through my ancestor's past would eventually propel me forward and help me to discover myself through my country's history. As I drove along the seemingly endless road north I wondered just what I would find there in Canada. I gazed out my window at the changing landscape as the day warmed and I neared the Canadian border near Derby Line, Vermont. The tall green mountains of Central Vermont leveled out to the rolling hills of the Northeast Kingdom area, and the leaves had not yet begun to change their color. I turned off before the border and approached the crossing at Derby Line.

Crossing the border is a more serious undertaking in a post 9/11 world. A decade ago all you needed for identification to cross was your driver's license. People who lived on the border used to be able to cross back and forth all the time with just a familiar wave to the border guards: all that has changed since the terrorist attack on the Twin Towers. The guard there asked me what my plans were after taking my passport. I told the official I was going to visit Georgeville to do some historic research. The border guard looked at me a little oddly. People go to the sleepy town of Georgeville to vacation or fish if they go at all. Most Americans are not interested in Canadian history, no wonder I got an odd look. The guard handed me back my passport and waved me through to a country my ancestors had left a century before. I was not far from the border when the road turned to gravel farm roads, and I left the two lane blacktop behind me.

The modern navigation device suspended from my windshield took me down lots of rural back country roads. The influence of the French culture that had later moved into the area after my ancestor's death was suddenly all around me. The change was only on the surface, the land and mountains were much the same on either side of the border. Only the politics and language of man divide the land. The *Quebecoise* culture was in contrast to where I grew up in the English speaking suburbs surrounding Boston. It seems like a slower pace of life. People were friendlier and more relaxed.

I finally arrived in Georgeville, Quebec, just north of the international border that separates Vermont from Canada. It had been a long and lonely ride. It was the kind of journey that allows a person to spend a lot of time thinking. I did my share of thinking of all that had brought me here. Curiosity, and the unquenchable need to add one more piece to the puzzle. A puzzle that began at one end with his birth and the other end with his death. After climbing out of my car, I walked down to the shore of the lake that my ancestor had spent his last fifty years gazing upon. It had been almost one hundred and fifty years since he had taken his last breath, here.

As I walked along the quiet backstreet on my way back from the lake, I listened to the children playing in the playground to hear if I could ascertain what language they spoke. Many of the original homes from his time survived. The rural setting preserved the small town from too much development. The area was absent of the urban sprawl of strip malls, shopping areas, and traffic lights, that are a part of my life in Massachusetts. I then went into a small *magasin* and bought a soda. It was a delightful little old country store with a front deck and white clapboards. I paid in U.S. currency and received Canadian in return. They greeted me with *bonjour* but thanked me in English after they realized I was from the United States, my origin deduced from the paper currency I handed them. The English legacy that Abraham and the other settlers had planted there had not yet completely faded. The French language is gradually taking over the area town by town. Georgeville had once been an English speaking town, but was now bilingual.

I strolled down to the lake front and took in its natural beauty. I felt an odd feeling of familiarity as I stood on the dock. I had read as much about the lake as I could in spite of having never traveled there. I was drawn to the lake by some unknown force that I could not resist ever since I first read about it. Now here I was finally standing on its shore. The vast body of water spread out before me in either direction. Trees have branches that spread out and roots that do the same. A family is no different. Ancestors are the roots and descendants are the branches that reach and spread out into the future. In a small way I expected someone or something to be there at the lake shore waiting for me. A friendly familiar face from the past welcoming me perhaps, but of course nothing was.

The past is never there waiting for us in its entirety. Even going back to the place where we once played childhood games in our own more recent past is never the same. It never survives quite as we remember it. Streets seem busier and noisier; the large park you once played in as a child that seemed to go on forever is now just a small patch of grass with a few rusty swings. The clues from the past remain the same, but the way we interpret them changes with each generation. All these clues I later discovered, remain shrouded in a cloak of history, and the interpretation of other historians. I wanted to bring out the zeitgeist of Abraham's time, but can his story ever be fully understood? I decided to begin this journey and try to tell it as best as I could. I will try to interpret the echoes of his past life to the best of my ability. I will try not to judge him or his actions but travel through his success and failure as much as the records of the past will allow me.

I pondered this thought while I felt the September sun on my back turn cold as storm clouds took charge there by the lake. I could see why Abraham chose to spend so much of his life here. What joys and hardships he must have experienced in his life just waiting to be discovered by me I thought. I was within walking distance of the location where my ancestor's tavern had been. In fact, I later found, I had been standing on his former land and property without knowing it.

As I stood there in this largely unspoiled quaint town, I imagined through my knowledge and love of history how his story may have begun over two hundred years ago......

London Fall of 1775

From the Authors antique postcard collection.

The colonies of New England were in full revolt following the battles at Lexington and Concord. An order to prepare ships was given by Lord Sandwich, John Montagu, the man in overall command of the British Navy, to the Secretary of the Admiralty, Philip Stephens. The orders that Sandwich gave were quite urgent.[1] In response to these orders, on July 29, 1775, Stephens put British Under-Secretary John Pownall in charge of preparing five frigates and crew to be sent to Boston to defend the British supply ships that had recently come under attack. The British were shocked; they did not expect the outbreak of a full military rebellion, or that their ships would be set upon. The leadership had made no plans for it. The King and his military needed to act quickly. King George III wanted to strike convincingly to put down the Rebellion that was beginning to foment in his Empire at land, and now at sea.

The North American colonies sent a document known as the Olive Branch Petition, in hopes to reconcile with the king. The King refused to accept the document when it arrived on August 23, 1775. King George III, as can be seen from his order to ready more warships, had already decided to ignore the petition and to try to bring the colonies to their knees with his empire's military power. The king would not bargain with rebels and pirates.

Time was of the essence in fitting out these ships for service in the colonies. Many were in desperate need of repair, and getting them fitted out and ready to be sent to the colonies took time the British did not have. Only four frigates out of the five desired were found and readied to be sailed to the colonies to support those already there. The repair of the ships and the impressment of men to serve on them began. The difficulty in preparing the ships was increased by a dock strike that raged in the shipyard. The king wrote to Lord Sandwich, "I am sorry the shipwrights are not yet returned to their work, but doubt not you will soon bring them to their senses."[2] This seems to have been a subtle warning to end the strike and get his ships in order. Two days after the Olive Branch Petition was received, and ignored, the king proclaimed that the American colonies were in full rebellion, and the struggle known today as the American Revolution was begun.

The British Navy, for all of its glory and greatness of the past had been caught with its "sails down" at the beginning of the conflict. John Montagu, the head of the Admiralty and the 4th Earl of Sandwich (Lord Sandwich), had been appointed to his political position in 1770. Since then he had been accused of corruption and defrauding the public.[3] He may well have gambled away the money that was supposed to go towards repairing and keeping the British Navy afloat in his twenty-four hour gambling sessions. To sustain himself during these card games he is attributed with the culinary creation of putting two slices of bread and a slice of meat between them to eat without needing to leave the gaming table.[4] He was later often blamed for the loss of the colonies.   It was not his fault alone. During the war he found himself "sandwiched" between a stingy Parliament and an underpowered naval force. The Parliament did their own bit of gambling, by overlooking the experience of seafaring in the colonies. The colonists did not lack any experience in privateering, boat building, or smuggling. The Parliament failed to fully comprehend or understand the American threat. This mistake made the British unable to secure the upper hand. By not spending the money to expand their fleet right away, the Royal Navy later found themselves at a considerable disadvantage at sea.[5]

On September 29, 1775, Vice Admiral Samuel Graves received thirty press warrants from Philip Stephens to help outfit British Navy ships with their essential crew.[6] The press warrants authorized men to be taken into the Kings naval service with or without their willingness to join the Navy. The process of impressment had been used to gain and secure men for naval service for hundreds of years in Britain and its colonies, and was now begun once again. The issuance of the press warrants greatly changed the course of many lives. The warrants forced men into service and carried them three thousand miles across the Atlantic in service of the king. Whether they wanted to serve or not.

The plan was to have seventy-nine British warships in total serve in the colonies. Many were already there, after having been sent the previous year to close off the ports due to the embarrassment of what the Rebels called the Boston Tea Party. These ships were not enough muscle to accomplish the mission of closing down the ports that they had been sent to the colonies for. When the situation was debated in the British Parliament, it was felt by one admiral to be too weak a force for war, and too much to establish peace.[7] The British Secretary of War, Lord Barrington, wanted to stop the Rebellion by destroying the American sea trade.[8]

It was felt that by doing this the colonies would suffer economically and call off the Rebellion. This would take a powerful fleet of ships to achieve. The ships to accomplish this were not available and the problems with the readiness of the Royal Navy were blamed on Lord Sandwich. The Parliament did not think he would succeed and told him, "your ships will be wrecked upon that frozen coast."[9] Patrolling off the coast of New England would be no pleasure cruise in the winter of 1775-

1776, for those men, like Abraham, that were to be pressed into service to close off those ports, while clinging to icy and frozen decks.

The Army of Britain was no better prepared than its Navy. At the beginning of the conflict it consisted of a total strength of less than nineteen thousand men. The king then reached out to other members of his family for help. King George III was first denied troops by his cousin Czarina Catherine, the Empress of Russia. The King then turned to his family in Germany, where he was the Elector of Hanover. Here King George III was able to acquire more troops to fight in the struggle. These troops had no stake or interest in the war other than their measly pay. These troops needed to be brought across the ocean from Europe, requiring even more sail power. It should have been more apparent that this struggle would be won or lost with sea power. Later, his wise cousin the Czarina recommended that he try to end the conflict through peaceful negotiations. Unfortunately for both Abraham and Britain the King ignored her advice.[10] British leaders did not respect American soldiers in any case. In their opinion the more Americans there were, the easier they would be beaten.[11]

After the press warrants were released, the press gangs set out in London to find the men who were urgently needed to outfit the hastily repaired frigates. The press gangs were small groups of local toughs led by a lieutenant from the British ship. This gang looked for men to help fill out and complete their crews. The gangs captured men for the service in any way possible, including getting them drunk or outright kidnapping them. Men of wealth and property were able to buy themselves out of the situation. They used family connections to get officers commissions if they had any interest in a career in the military service. With the present desperate need for men, the navy had to use equally desperate measures to outfit them. The impressed men could also be used to load, repair and get the ships ready to sail to put down the Rebellion in the colonies. The ships needed to sail, and needed men to sail them.

Pressman only impressed unskilled men to sail in times of great need. The fall of 1775, in London, was one of those times. In times of peace, unskilled young men like Abraham were likely to be rejected by the officers of the ship. the role he would serve as servant, did not require much skill anyway. In this time of desperation in Britain, all the men that could be found would be needed on board the ships. There were not enough men, ships, or supplies, for any of these necessities to be ignored. After being outfitted and prepared to sail, the ships and newly impressed men and sailors were to be sent in support of the Boston Station in Massachusetts. They were to operate along the coast of the New England States and suppress the Rebellion that was escalating along there at breakneck speed.

The Strand

One cold fall day in London, Abraham FitzJohn returned from errands that he was sent on by his master, Uncle Varney. London was the biggest city in the world, with a population of just under one million. In many respects it was the center of the world due to its colonies and extensive shipping and trade.

Like a lot of the young men that lived there who were not fortunate enough to be part of the wealthy class he just tried to make the best of it and carve out his piece of the pie. Abraham had been apprenticed as a tailor to his uncle for a few years. He had become an accomplished clothier, and did much of the work in the shop. By this time he had learned enough to be useful and productive. It is estimated that ten percent of the male population of London were apprentices. In London, an apprentice's family usually paid a fee to their child's future master. The apprentice received room and board while they gradually grew more and more useful from experience.

The master normally gained some benefit from them cleaning, opening the shop, making deliveries, and the performance of other basic tasks. The apprentice gained no wages until the end of the contract. As their skills grew they also became a potential rival for the business, and knew all the businesses contacts and clients. It may have been safer to apprentice family members rather than strangers. Uncle Varney may have had no sons of his own, and so he contracted to apprentice Abraham for the customary seven years of training with Abraham's father Robert. Varney could then recoup the cost of training him in the final few years of the contract by having a skilled worker with no wages needing to be paid. This is at least how it should have been...

Abraham slowly walked along the back streets of London on the

Strand,[12] a major thoroughfare and the center of debauchery in the city of London. He was not considering the business of cloth and needles, Abraham was deep in thought regarding the attractive young servant girl he had just met as he delivered the waistcoat and breeches he had mended for a customer. The last thing on his mind was international politics and rebellion. Around him there on the Strand were young pickpockets, bagnio's, and bawdy houses. Abraham took in the sights and sounds of the busy yet dangerous center as he strolled back to the shop along the cobbled streets, ignoring the establishments sordid invitations. A young man had to be careful of all manner of threats as he walked the streets of Georgian London. Perhaps he will stop by tomorrow to see if the master of the house was pleased with his garment? It might give him another opportunity to see the girl, and ask if he could call on her sometime.

To quench his growing thirst, and to kill time before he returned to his work, Abraham quickly darted into a pub and ordered a pint of ale, since water was then unfit to drink in London. The murky water from the Thames River was both the source of their drinking water and the means by which sewerage and filth washed out of the city. Abraham wisely chose to be careful what he drank. Ale was fine, provided he did not drink too much of it. He took out some of the tip money he had been given, which he usually hid from his uncle, and ordered his brew. While deep in thought about the lovely young maid he'd met, he stared down into the golden ale through the clear glass bottom of the pewter mug. He was totally unaware of several men that were beginning to rise up the stairs from the basement. Abraham took up a magazine from a table in the pub and began to read a poem about London by Samuel Johnson:

> Here malice, rapine, accident conspire,
> And now a rabble rages, now a fire;
> their ambush here relentless ruffians lay,
> and here the fell attorney prowls for prey;
> here falling houses thunder on your head,
> and here a female atheist talks you dead....
> This mournful truth is everywhere confessed,
> Slow rises worth, by poverty depressed.[13]

Abraham considered the words of the poem and the many dangers that existed in his urban life. These dangers included prison, the pillory, public flogging, press-gangs, and footpads, armed men who stole anything of value while they prowled the streets. All of these dangers offered "moral instruction" and entertainment to the masses in the street.[14] As Charles Dickens would later write in the Christmas Carol, they served to "decrease the surplus population" of the great city. Violence in the city of London was an everyday hazard of life. The young tailor rose from his seat to answer the call of nature and empty his water behind the pub in the alley.

Down In the basement room of the pub, men gambled the outcome of rat baiting in the pit. The winner was the one who correctly guessed the number of rats killed by an angry dog when it was put in the pit with the varmints. The lieutenant and his pressmen had run out of money, but all they needed was to press one man to furnish them with the income they needed to continue with their entertainment. So while the rat catcher went to the docks to get more rodents for the evening matches, the press gang rose from their seats and went in pursuit of their own prey.

Many patrons of the pub had became alarmed when the gang started moving about, and they quickly filed out as they saw the opportunists climb the narrow stairs. They knew trouble, and not ale, was brewing in the pub. Abraham failed to notice the other patrons leaving out the front door as he returned to his table for his refreshment. The young tailor settled back down in his seat to quench his thirst. He lifted his pewter mug and swiftly drank down the ale from the tankard as he continued to read his poem. Setting the tankard down on the table he heard an odd tinkling sound. Looking inside the vessel he saw a shiny shilling coin with the head of the king stamped on it.[15] The light shone through the bottom of the tankard and illuminated the coin inside. That is odd, he thought to himself. He raised his gaze up from the cup and was stunned to see several burly members of a press gang sneering at him.

"Congratulations Lad and welcome to the Kings Navy," a rather large, ugly, brute of a man said.

Abraham could now see that he was in trouble. As he glanced about the pub he saw at least six men surrounding him.

"I did not join any navy," Abraham said in return as he boldly stood up. "I cannot even sail," he said in an effort to bide some time. The man smirked and his cohorts closed in more on the young tailor.

Abraham quickly formulated a plan to make a run for the door. Once outside, he surmised, they might never be able to catch him. He was a fleet footed young man and would not be easy to catch. He had eluded press gangs in London before in this way, as did many young men who also had to avoid being dragged into the service. The gangs were a well known scourge in the city, especially now with the coming need for sailors to put down the rebellion in the colonies. The rebellion was none of Abraham's concern and he wouldn't go without a fight.

When Abraham stepped quickly forward to seek his escape, one of the men roughly grabbed his shoulder, and he struck the crimp in the face while another grabbed at the apprentice's leg. The young tailor jumped up with his left knee and kicked another with his right foot as high up as his own shoulder and knocked the crimp over a chair and against the wall. Coming down from this kick Abraham felt once again he might manage to escape. The young tailor was just nearing the door and saw his escape at hand when a club struck the back of his head, he quickly lost consciousness and slumped to the floor.

The leader strolled over and took the shilling out of the tankard and slipped it back into his pocket. The shilling paid good dividends when slipped into the tankards of the unsuspecting. Abraham was roughly brought to his feet and led to the warship that was scheduled to depart soon after its final preparations for the colonies. No one came to his aid. Abraham had become just another victim of the streets of London.

Others that were impressed fled from their situations through one of the only avenues available to them; the sea. Often those on the fringe in society such as thieves and murderers were impressed into service. For some it was the best and only option. The lure and mystique of the sea may have been irresistible to many of them, and with a strong pull of wanderlust they sought to leave and seek their fortune in the world. The press gangs told young men like Abraham great tales of adventure on the never ending sea that spurred their imagination and enticed them to enlist. If they did not enlist, they were then forced to anyway. It is hoped that Abraham was not among this group, and there is no evidence to support it, but others that were impressed were.

In telling his story it is hard not to think of my own father and how he had signed on to fight in the Pacific during World War II at the tender age of sixteen. What had made him sign up may not have been that much different from men like Abraham. Young men do dream of adventure and travel to foreign places to meet new people. Although many of these re-creations told in the book are drawn from my imagination, if hair color, facial features, and mannerisms are inherited through DNA and passed down in the family, perhaps some obscure knowledge of past events from your ancestors is also inherited. In telling the story of an interesting ancestor it may be okay to allow the imagination to wander, and perhaps touch the past and bring it into the present. The poet Mandelstam once said, "The word I forgot, which once I wished to say, a voiceless thought, returns to shadow's chambers." So in the cases when the thought of what occurred overwhelms me; they will be released into the tale, and saved from the "palace of ghosts."[16]

The reality of life on board ship for Abraham was quite different from the romantic tales told by the old sailors at the pub. It was like serving a prison sentence at sea. The British Navy used its sailors like slaves or dogs. Discipline on board the ships was severe, and so were the punishments. Sea water or rain poured into the hammocks of the sailors through the tar sealed decks above, and disease quickly spread from sailor to sailor. Unwashed men lay sleeping-stinking side by side in their hammocks for months before they could wash. If Abraham actually tried to defend himself as he did in the previous fictional account, he was not alone. There were many violent acts against press-gangs recorded in the British courts.

There had been many acts and riots against impressment in the colonies as well. There was one violent protest and riot that occurred in the streets of Boston in 1747. Later in 1769, Boston attorney and future United States President John Adams represented a sailor in a little known impressment case. While out to sea an American sailor was approached by a British officer for impressment when the merchant ship he was on was boarded by a British Navy ship. When the British officer failed to heed his warning to back away, the sailor thrust a harpoon through the officer's neck. Adams argued on the man's behalf in court that "self preservation is [the] first law of nature," and John Adams won his case.[17] John Adams was unfortunately an ocean away from London and neither he nor any other lawyer was there to help free Abraham from his predicament.

The Immortal Patriot

The successful Impressment of Abraham meant that he lost his freedom and became a slave to the British Navy, regardless of the exact way that it occurred. To truly understand and appreciate freedom, there is no better teacher than to first be enslaved. Tea taxes and stamp acts may have led the Colonies to revolt in 1775, but there can be no better example of the tyranny of Britain and the King than the impressment that Abraham and other men in the colonies suffered. Impressment, as we have seen, did occur in all the port cities of the British colonies in conflicts prior to the American Revolution, and did create outrage that helped fuel revolutionary ideas and discontent. After running through the streets of the Strand and fighting men in the pub in London, Abraham had no doubt as to whom his enemies were. At that time it became Abraham's own government and king that stole his liberties and took away his freedom, much as they had in the colonies.

Abraham arose the next day in the ship with a pounding in his skull that reminded him of the prior day's events. He heard the crew as they sang a song above decks while they prepared the ship to sail to America:

> Come cheer up, my lads, 'tis to glory we steer,
> To add something more to this wonderful year,
> To honour we call you, not press you like slaves,
> For who are so free as the sons of the waves?[18]

Waking up in the lower deck of the warship the young tailor tried to accustom himself to the foul odors of the boat. Around him were other men between the ages of fifteen and fifty-five who had also been captured by the marauding press gangs. Another of Samuel Johnson's writings may describe Abraham's thoughts at that moment:

> No man will be a sailor who has contrivance enough to get
> himself into a jail; for being in a ship is being in a jail,
> with the chance of being drowned.... A man in a jail has more
> room, better food, and commonly better company.[19]

The British courts overlooked impressment due to the pride in their navy and the necessity of these methods to supply seamen to work the ships.[20] They needed men, and even though impressment conflicted with their view of Britain being a place where the liberties of men were respected, the process of impressment were nonetheless still allowed to be carried out.

When the boatswain's pipe sounded the new watch the men were brought up on deck. Some were sick from the wounds they had received in their impressment, others sought to argue against their impressment for various reasons, and still others resigned to their fate. Those who argued too much were flogged; discipline on board the ship was severe. The officers had full disciplinary control over the sailors and other members of the crew. Get to work boys, "dig out, dig out blind!" they shouted. Overhead the sails were being installed and new rigging was put in place. Men were hard at work bringing supplies up on deck and stowing them away in the holds. Abraham, not wanting to taste the "crack of the cat-o'-nine" got quickly to work himself.

The young man rubbed the stinging lump on his head and followed the instructions he was given by the mates to the best of his ability. He watched the officer's stride about the deck in their fine cerulean colored uniforms adorned with gold trim. Abraham mended his share of those uniforms in his coming months at sea. He looked over at the docks in the hope of seeing his father coming to get him; but it was no use. He was asked to sign the muster roll to receive his pay from the ships purser; then referred to as a slop.[21] He needed to do this so he could purchase clothing and other articles he needed such as a hammock. He received a little income, however, the only place to spend any of it was on-board.

Without signing as a volunteer he remained pressed, and could not receive the money, or credit, to purchase the basic essentials he needed.[22] Abraham had no choice but to sign the muster on October 6, 1775, on board the warship. He did sign the book, but he used an alias, and he quickly wrote Channel for his surname. The reason for this choice of name remains a mystery. Could he have anticipated his trip through the English Channel? Abraham would go on with a new life and a new name from his beginnings in London. His past he thought, remained forever behind him. The young tailor would never see Britain, London, or any of his family there again.

The ship Abraham found himself impressed on was the *HMS Milford*. A class six, twenty-eight-gun Man-of-War frigate built in 1759, during the Seven Years War (1756-1763).[23] That war took place over a decade earlier in both Europe and in the Colonies between the French, their Native allies, and the British and American Colonists. In North America it was known as the French and Indian War. The ship was now laid up in "rotten row," and needed to be repaired and restored to its former fighting trim. The crew was kept busy as they prepared the great wooden vessel for sea. A fifteen year old warship may not seem old by modern standards, but for the times it was a very old vessel. Wooden warships did not have the lifespan of the steel warships of today. With a lot of hard work and elbow grease from the crew, the installation of the new rigging was finished on the old boat and its walls of oak were soon ready for service.

The captain of the ship was John Burr. He was desirous to win both glory and advancement in his career, yet too wise to rashly encounter danger and risk the loss of his ship. He strode along the deck issuing orders and overseeing the fitting out of the warship. Like all captains he had joined the navy as a young boy. After six years of being trained at sea in setting sail, navigation, astronomy, and trigonometry to find the ships position by using a quadrant, he was made a lieutenant. To achieve this position he was first recommended by a naval officer, and then received a verbal exam by three captains. Unlike the army, the captain received his commission on merit. Captain Burr was an experienced warrior at sea, as his accomplishments, although detrimental to the American cause, will later show. The ship had a complement of 180 men, forty of whom were marines. The marines on board were led by Lieutenant Burn, and the force included a corporal, and a drummer.[24] These marines were more than ready to board and take any Yankee ships they may encounter. The ship had two extra pilots on board also. The extra men on board, along with the pilots, allowed for captured American ships, known as prizes, to be sailed back to a British port separately from the *HMS Milford*.

After it was quickly brought back into sailing condition, the *Milford* was outfitted with nine pound guns and had formidable firepower. Especially when viewed in comparison to the American ships it later challenged.[25] The *Milford* was far superior to any American ship that sailed the coast at that early stage of the war. In addition to men, four large casks of money were loaded on board to pay the Redcoats in Boston.[26] The *HMS Milford* was a class of ship used to protect British supply convoys and to blockade American harbors.

On November 1st and again on December 3rd the Articles of War were "audibly and distinctly read over the Company" in preparation for setting sail.[27] On December 16, 1775, the Lords Commissioner, Admiralty, ordered Captain Burr to proceed, "without loss of time to Spithead, and there wait for further order."[28] Before they left to sail down the Thames River toward Kent on January First it was reported that thirty-two men had run from the ship.[29] Captain Burr reported on the men, "...except something appear in their favour, in my opinion, deserve no Relief."[30] Many of the men on board the warship clearly did not wish to be there. Abraham, as history tells us, had been unable to escape. The press gangs once again had to go on the prowl to capture more men. The ship eventually left and sailed south through the English Channel and on January 5th arrived at Spithead, a common rendezvous point for the navy off the coast.[31] The *HMS Milford*, along with the *HMS Boreas*, later left Chatham, Kent, naval dockyards. This was possibly due to a few more repairs, loading of more supplies, or they had to meet and sail with a convoy. On January 17, 1776, the two ships left to sail together across the Atlantic to support the growing struggle to control the rebellion in North America.[32]

The boatswain's pipe sounded that Captain Burr was coming out on the quarterdeck. The windward side of the ship was cleared of men for him to stand. The *Milford's* captain came out on deck and struck a stoic pose. Captain Burr always spoke first, and the lieutenant on watch would then take off his hat and address him and bring him up to date on position and the conditions aboard ship. Few men had as much power or enjoyed the respect of their men as much as the captain of a British warship. Abraham was cautious not to catch his eye and tempt his anger. Abraham darted behind the mast and falling to his knees busily scrubbed the deck of the ship with his holystone to avoid punishment.

Captain Burr received orders similar to the other captains that left Britain before him. Burr first received the secret signals that allowed communication within the fleet and was then ordered to "seize all ships and vessels belonging to any of the said colonies, or owned by the inhabitants thereof."[33] These vessels or prizes were then to be brought into a British Port outside of the rebelling colonies. On December 19th-23rd 1775, the *London Gazette* printed the King's proclamation from Parliament on the distribution of prizes during the continuance of the Rebellion. The proclamation officially closed all trade and business intercourse in all of the colonies. Any enemy ships they stopped forfeited their cargoes, apparel, and furniture to "his majesty." The rest of the proclamation gave encouragement to the Navy captains and their crews by giving out the percentage of money for the prizes that might be taken.[34] The Proclamation gave the *HMS Milford* and its crew legal permission to be pirates in the service of Britain and the King.

Captain Burr, was a skilled navy man and ran a well organized ship. He had personally overseen the final preparations and made sure the ship was ready for sea. The crew continually drilled to make sure they were ready at a moments notice for any encounter. The guns could never be loaded and fired quickly enough to satisfy the captain. Burr was assigned to follow the orders of Captain Francis Banks, Commodore of the squadron, who sailed on the *HMS Renown*. Commodore was a temporary rank, signifying that he was the senior captain of the squadron. The *Milford*, along with the *HMS Hope* commanded by Captain George Dawson, was assigned to patrol off the coast of Massachusetts, and rendezvous at times in Boston Bay or along Nantasket Roads. This was a busy channel that lies south of the entrance to the outer part of Boston Harbor between George's Island and Point Allerton in Hull, Massachusetts.

The pilot of the *HMS Milford* looked down at his binnacle that held the compass and set his course for North America, three thousand miles away. "Ready ho!" shouted out a stern voice from the quarterdeck. As the ship set a new tack another command was shouted, "Put the helm down!" The great oak ship then shifted about in the wind. "Helm's a'lee!" The wind now struck the sails differently and the men busied themselves with the foresails and square sails in the rigging.[35] The new tack took hold and the sails cracked in the wind and billowed overhead as they filled with air. While Abraham was kept busy manning the pump to clear the vessel of bilge water he tried to learn the various sails names and functions. He had to keep moving to try to stay warm while out to sea in the cold winter wind. Abraham looked for the last time over the stern, past the mizzen and spanker sails, at the shrinking view of Britain and breathed in the fresh salt air. His past was now forever behind him.

Son of the Waves

No record exists to tell of the dangers the *Milford* encountered while it traveled across the ocean in the early winter of 1776. A crew member's journal does exist of the trip across the Atlantic earlier in October 1775, that was taken by the *HMS Orpheus*, one of the first warships to respond to the growing American threat at sea. This offers a window into what the *Milford's* trip may have been like. The *Orpheus* encountered strong gales and extremely high seas during the passage. At many times during their crossing the crew of the ship hoped to return to Britain or go south to save the ship from the horrible weather. Many of the sails and other ship parts had been destroyed by the high winds. The building snow and rolling seas made it difficult to make repairs. The crew was given only a pint of water a day to drink and wash with to preserve their stores. This was later reduced to half a pint. Water was boiled so it could be poured over the frozen sails to melt the ice off so they could be worked and repaired. The crewman recorded this horrifying journey which took the ship and its crew ninety-seven days to accomplish. After it finally arrived in America, the ship required a great deal of repair to be ready to sail again.[1] The *Milford's* trip is not likely to have been much better.

Abraham was unskilled in seamanship, so he worked as a servant to the ship's Officer Joseph Sewell.[2] Sewell was responsible for policing the ship, and he trained men in the use of small arms on board the vessel.[3] It was in this capacity that Abraham may have learned some useful ship boarding skills that could be used later in the conflict. The taking of an enemy vessel often resulted in a man to man battle on deck, and Sewell's men needed to be prepared for it. They had to drill to learn how to fire their muskets from the upper sails as well as how to board a vessel. Abraham busied himself with his role in the service of Sewell while the *HMS Milford* crossed the Atlantic. The young tailor continued to learn how to live and work aboard a British Naval vessel. The hard work and discipline honed him as a young man. After several weeks on that freezing and rough winter voyage at sea, the *HMS Milford* stopped at Halifax, Nova Scotia to let off some caulkers and ship repairman that were needed to repair the fleet in the harbor.[4] Halifax was a major British port during the war, a few days' sail from Boston.

After the mission was accomplished in Halifax, the *HMS Milford* sailed southwest to Boston to deliver pay for the British soldiers stationed there, and to bring military orders to the British leaders now trapped in Boston. When the *Milford* set anchor off Long Wharf after they finally arrived in Boston, Abraham caught his first glimpse of Massachusetts and a city under siege. The British were surrounded in the city by General George Washington and the local militia army that was now heavily entrenched around them. The only way of escape or evacuation for the British was to sail out between the islands of the harbor and then on out to the open ocean. The same route was also their only means of supply. To maintain their position in Boston ships like the *Milford* needed to keep the supply ships safe. The British entrenchments were in place to guard not only against the rebelling colonists, but to keep British Redcoats and Jacktars from deserting over the lines.

On March 17, 1776, Washington put cannon on the top of Dorchester Heights. These cannons had been moved from Fort Ticonderoga in upstate New York, brought down alongside the western shore of Lake Champlain and on into the outskirts of Boston. These large guns placed atop the hill in Dorchester then forced the British in Boston and their fleet in the harbor to evacuate the city. The British had decided to not have troops stationed at this hill; which turned out to be a costly and foolish mistake. That said, most of the British were not upset at all to leave. Low supplies and inadequate barracks had made the service a horrible ordeal for the enlisted man.

The British may have left the mainland, but they continued to dominate the coast off of Massachusetts.

The loyal Tory citizens of Boston and the British soldiers stationed there evacuated and eventually went to Halifax, Nova Scotia. The winter of 1775-1776, had been a harsh one for the Redcoats and Tory's in Boston, who had been confined there with a shortage of food. There was also not enough fuel to warm the barracks. Constant punishments were handed out to the soldiers for their housebreaks and theft in search of money and food.[5] Before the *Milford* and other British vessels had arrived to protect the supply ships, many of the supply vessels had fallen prey to the privateers and the fledgling navy that had been quickly created by Washington to cut off British supplies shortly after his arrival. The American privateer's luck in capturing British supplies such as firewood off the coastline were so successful that it caused the British to tear up the docks in Boston for firewood.[6] In many ways the British leaders and their men were likely relieved to leave the port. The American supply strategy is revealed in a popular song that was sung by American militia troops during the war:

> And what have got now with all your designing, But a town
> without victuals to sit down and dine in; And to look on the
> ground like a parcel of noodles, And sing, how the Yankees have
> beaten the Doodles. I'm sure if you're wise you'll make peace for
> a dinner, For fighting and fasting will soon make ye thinner.[7]

The American strategy was very effective in keeping the British military occupied with gathering food. This effort gave the Americans an opportunity to attack them in small group skirmishes all around Boston and the islands surrounding it. When the British dared leave the safety of the city to try to gather some much needed supplies, the Americans came out to meet them in small groups to try to stop them.

Ships like the *Milford* continued to prowl outside Boston Harbor and set up base on the outer harbor islands. Blockade duty for them meant chasing and stopping every suspected enemy ship as it left the many harbors along the coastline of Massachusetts. The British needed to keep supply lines open. But there was also opportunity for profit. There was money to be made aboard every rebel American ship that Captain Burr and his crew captured. Abraham looked out over the rails of the ship, beside the ratlines that supported the mast, at the coastline of New

England, whenever he was allowed to get some fresh air on deck. He sometimes watched the rolling green sea as it split before the bow and passed the hull. The below deck areas of the ships were dark and the air ripe with the stench of unwashed men, pitch, slaughtered animals, and bilge water. The occasional natural light and fresh air he was allowed to enjoy were most welcome when he managed to escape to the sunlit yet freezing deck. The ship experienced and weathered the northeaster which came tearing through Boston in March, along with other late winter storms that shook the ship as well. He may have been happy at those times to be below, and not holding on for dear life on the slick frozen deck as the great wooden vessel rolled in the heavy North Atlantic seas. Neither part of the ship, above or below decks, was an ideal place to serve.

The *HMS Milford* began to follow the orders from the Admiralty to patrol the coast and Captain Burr and his crew set out to capture American merchant and rebel privateer vessels. These armed privateer vessels may have preyed on unarmed British transports but they were no match for the *Milford*. Captain Burr and his crew did not have to wait long. On April 3, 1776, the British frigate came upon two American rebel ships off Cape Ann, the *Warren* and *Franklin*. The two ships split up and went in separate directions, and Captain Burr chose to chase the *Franklin*. The *Milford* chased the ship while its bow chasers kept up a constant fire. The American ship took flight and was saved by a sudden squall that made pursuit difficult for the *Milford*, the British vessel, only managed to chase the *Franklin* right into the safety of Gloucester Harbor.[8] Having only six cannon on board, the *Franklin* did not stand a chance against the *Milford*.[9] Later in May, the *Franklin* captured a British supply vessel named *Hope*, that was loaded with gunpowder and supplies that Washington desperately needed for his army.[10] This was one of the first great boosts to the American war effort. On the other hand, when the *Franklin* turned sail and ran that day; it merely boosted the confidence and morale of the *Milford* and her crew.

The following day the *Milford* chased and fired upon a ship known as the *Crawford*. The ship must not have been seen as an enemy ship, or was not captured, because there is no record of it being made a prize.[11] Weeks later, Abraham and the rest of the crew on the *Milford* encountered more enemy ships that were recorded in Captain Burr's journal. Abraham continued in his role as a servant on board the *HMS Milford* throughout the spring of 1776, and the young tailor learned the ways of the ship as best as he could to avoid the discipline of the officers.

At eight in the morning on April 19, 1776, the *Milford* sighted sail near Thacher Island off Cape Ann, which lies north of Boston Harbor. Although the *Milford* gave chase to the ship for many hours, the British crew was unable to catch their elusive prey. The following morning rose with clear skies; and from high overhead above the deck a ship was spotted in the distance by a sharp-eyed crew member. Captain Burr came up on deck and ordered the crew to chase the vessel. After firing four shots they captured the sloop *Britannia;* loaded with firewood. This firewood probably came in handy warming the British Redcoats in Boston before they were evacuated. There is no record of where it was sent; it may have also warmed the British barracks in Halifax.

The *Britannia* was sent off to a British port after putting a prize crew of two petty officers and four other men on board to sail her. The *Milford's* crew then saw more sail in the distance and the vessel quickly pursued after them.[12] While chasing the new prey, the *HMS Milford* was joined by two other Royal Navy ships the *HMS Lively* and *Hope*. They chased their prize and fired ten cannons before the rebel craft surrendered. The American schooner *Lydia*, which sailed out of Salem, Massachusetts, was loaded with barrel staves and fish, and was headed for the West Indies. The captain surrendered his ship and his crew was taken prisoner. The prize was sent to Halifax, Nova Scotia to be sold.

On May 9, 1776, the *HMS Milford* gave chase to a sail on the horizon and after firing four of the cannon at the vessel they convinced the sloop to surrender to them. The ship sailed out of Belfast, Ireland, and was on its way to Nantucket, Massachusetts. The smaller ship was no match for the *Milford*, and the disappointed captain reluctantly turned over his vessel. Some men were again sent on board to take the prize to port.[13] On May 11, 1776, the captain and officers of the *HMS Milford* signed a letter to announce they had hired an attorney, Alexander Brymer, to represent their prize interests in Halifax.[14] Hiring an attorney was a sure sign of the success they were having at sea. Others on board the ship, such as Abraham, should have also received a share of the prize money, though far less than the percentage the officers enjoyed.

On May 14, 1776, the *HMS Milford* preyed upon the harbors of Cape Ann giving chase and firing her three and nine pound guns at any privateer vessels that dared to come outside the safety of the harbors to sea.[15] No American ship on the coast was a match for the *Milford* and her crew. Captain Burr stood stoically on the back deck of the warship and commanded his crew in their many duties. Abraham and the others scurried to keep the ship in order according to the captain's commands.

On May 25, 1776, the *Milford* captured another privateer ship and after taking the prisoners and tackle aboard they scuttled the vessel.[16] The ship was in poor condition and was not seen as valuable enough to be sailed off to Halifax. As the ship burned brightly and the smoke rose into the sky in the distance, Abraham began to find the adventure he may have hoped for.

As the *HMS Milford* patrolled the New England coast in June the crew once again spotted some sails on the horizon off Thacher Island. The danger of the waters off the island had caused twin 45' light houses to be erected there by the British in 1771,[17] The last ones, as it turned out, that were built by the king in the colonies. There was far more danger that lurked off the Coast of Thacher Island that day for the *HMS Milford* and her crew than their previous prize encounter there had given them.

Postcard from the authors collection.

The date was June 6, 1776, Abraham went up on deck to enjoy some fresh air and to calm his stomach that had not yet become accustomed to the rolling of the ship, in spite of six months at sea.

Growing up in London he had not yet acquired the sea legs that the rest of the crew had, but everyday his sailing skills improved. It was a beautiful early summer morning in the Atlantic. Abraham and the crew anxiously awaited some action. Abraham noticed the excitement of the crew as they pointed out sails in the distance, "sail ho" the men from the mainmast cried. Although they were not yet aware of the identity of the ship, they prepared for an encounter just in case it was one of the Yankee rebel boats. Sand was spread across the deck and the match tubs were filled halfway with water and a piece of cork bobbed in the tub with a lit fuse. These were then placed near each of the cannon to re-light the linstock that was used to fire the cannon.

They were headed south down along the coast and carefully watched the large billowing sails of the ship behind them. Captain Burr came up on deck and trained his telescope on the ship, and tried to identify it. After he recognized it as a Yankee ship, the wily Captain cleverly imitated a ponderous merchant vessel to try to lure the ship upon them while the gunners waited patiently at their cannon behind the closed gun ports. This Yankee had the "devil to pay and no pitch was hot," the captain may have thought as the *Yankee Hero* squared off against the *Milford*. The men may have disguised themselves or slowed down the ship on purpose to achieve this ruse. The crew in any event managed to pull off this skillful deceptive sailing maneuver. As the lookouts watched the American ship took the bait and began to chase and bear down upon the *HMS Milford*.[18]

Commander James Tracy became increasingly nervous on board the American Privateer *Yankee Hero* as his vessel approached the ship. Having just left Newburyport with a small crew the captain had planned to stop in Boston and fill out his ship with more sailors. When he left Newburyport he had about twenty-five men on board, and just prior to his decision to chase the unknown ship he had picked up another fourteen armed men from a small vessel that was also in pursuit. These vessels were called "Spider Catchers."[19] Small vessels loaded with men who were armed with weapons. They were about the size of a whaleboat, and they brazenly rode out to attack British shipping. These small, nimble boats could surround the larger British merchant ships by easily rowing out and catching them when the wind was calm and the larger ships sailed slowly along. In this case that might have been a foolish mistake; a small whaleboat was no match for the British warship and her marines.

The Immortal Patriot

The *Yankee Hero* discovered the identity of the *HMS Milford* too late and turned sharply to try to escape by going into a nearby port. In his zeal to capture a merchant ship and profit himself and his crew Captain Tracy now found himself in very big trouble. He heard the distant drums on board the *Milford* that called the crew to station. They then began to un-lash the cannon, light the battle lanterns to illuminate the area between the great guns, and to prepare for battle. Tracy looked on in horror as he saw the multiple gun ports begin to open revealing the power of his foe. The evasive maneuver the captain had relied on was to no avail, the wind was in the *HMS Milford's* favor and the ship closed in on the *Yankee Hero* while firing its bow guns.

The *Milford's* cannon were defiantly answered by the small swivel guns of the *Yankee Hero*. The *Yankee Hero* had twelve carriage guns and swivels on board. The shot they had available to them that day was, "round six pounders, double headed, and chaine shot, with a vast number pieces of ragg'd iron as grape (shot)."[20] The men of the *Yankee Hero* fought bravely as the crews exchanged both cannon and musket fire between the two ships. One large broadside exploded and swept into the *Yankee Hero* from the *Milford*. A man lost his arm and fourteen others were wounded as the guns of the *Milford* splintered the deck of the American ship, the sail and rope littered the planking, and left the Yankee Hero decks awash in blood and gore.[21]

Abraham watched as the British gun crew repeatedly stuffed powder, wadding, and then canisters of grape shot into the cannon. These were rammed into the throats of the guns by a gun crew member referred to as the rammer. The gun was then rolled into position. Another man known as a layer was responsible for raising and lowering the muzzle to aim, a difficult task in high seas. After the gun was in position and aimed the powder bag was pricked through the touch hole and then primed with powder. The linstock was then used to light the cannon.

The gun exploded and kicked back with a thunderous roar on the ship. The air became thick with the smoke from the exploding powder charges. The entire ship eventually became clouded up with this "fog of war." The swabber then dipped his swab into a bucket of water and extinguished any remaining sparks. Abraham was ordered to work as a powder monkey, whose battle assignment was to bring up powder from the magazine below. An older experienced member of the gun crew looked at Abraham and said to him through missing teeth and a crooked grin, "Well Abraham, this yank captain is beating a dead horse, we'll have the prize soon!"

The *Milford* crew members fired their muskets repeatedly across the deck of the Yankee ship, giving the American crew one more thing to worry about as musket balls whistled across the deck. The goal was not to destroy the ship, but to capture it and put it into British service to provide more profit for the *Milford's* captain and crew. The *Yankee Hero* hauled in close to the wind, and so the *Milford* was forced to do so to keep pace with this prize they hoped to catch. The *Yankee Hero* was unable to fire its lee guns and the *Milford* backed her bow under the American ships stern and sailed much faster, gaining a great advantage of position to fire from. The ships sailed alongside one another less than a hundred feet apart for an hour and twenty minutes as it blocked the American ship from escaping to a friendly harbor. The *Yankee Hero's* rigging was cut to ribbons, and its yards and principal sails were shot to rags. The injured crew tacked to gain some time but the *Milford* came up and brought the full fury of attack back upon them. The Americans found themselves in need to try to repair the rigging and fire the cannon with hardly any men still healthy enough to be able to do so. The ship had no surgeon on board and was already short of men when they first encountered the British ship. Now they had lost half of those men. The Yankee ship was in dire trouble.

The *Yankee Hero's* deck was littered with groaning injured men and the ships officers counted four dead on board. Captain Tracy received a musket ball in his thigh shot from the rigging of the *Milford*, and feeling faint and losing blood his men worriedly carried him below deck. From his cabin below the injured captain heard the firing of his ships cannon lessen more and more as he faded in and out of consciousness. Just who commanded the ship during this time is unknown. Tracy ordered his men to bring him back up on deck. His men put their courageous captain in a chair and carried him back up to the action.

The lingering smoke from the guns just cleared from the rear of the *Yankee Hero* when the ship received the first of two broadsides that caused the ship to lurch seemingly out of the water. The second one struck minutes later, showing the quality of training the *Milford's* gun crew had undergone. Constant practice had honed their skill as a team. The American ship was unfortunately reaping the full benefit of all their practice. Tracy's crew fired one last desperate cannon stuffed full of metal scraps from the boat and exhausted the vessels remaining powder supply. The captain slumped in his chair behind a chest he was using as a *barricado* to protect himself from the fire of the *Milford*. After seeing the futility of continuing the battle and fearing his ship might be sunk from beneath him, Tracy struck his colors to surrender.

The *Milford* fared much better. The British had only one marine injured by a musket ball shot in the arm.[22] The fact that the *Yankee Hero* survived the battle relatively intact shows that primarily grapeshot and other items were fired at the ship to disable it, but not destroy it. This made the vessel still useful to the British after a quick repair known as a jury-rig. Tars went across to the American ship to help repair it, and render it seaworthy once again. They tried hard not to get sick at the sight of the blood and guts that littered the American deck. They lowered buckets down and filled them with sea water to dump over the deck to rinse off the gore. The bodies of the men were sewn up in canvas and after a few verses from the Bible were sent off to Davy Jones Locker for the sea to swallow and hold their sacrifice to liberty for all eternity.

Captain Burr was said to have later impressed about thirty of the American men to fight for the British Navy. Other prisoners who refused impressment were reported as having perished in the dreaded prison ships in New York Harbor.[23] It is difficult to determine how the captain and crew were really treated because much of the reporting was merely negative propaganda against the enemy. It seems that some were treated well; Captain Tracy survived his wounds which must have been tended to and treated by the surgeon of the *Milford*. In any event, Abraham was witness to great death and destruction that day. It was a profitable victory for the ship and his fellow crew, but it came at the cost of many brave young American lives. Abraham was glad to have been on the *Milford* and not the other ship during the struggle. Burr probably ordered an extra ration of rum for the crew to celebrate their victory and successful capture of the prize. The men shouted and celebrated their success. The *Milford* crew had proven the superiority of their ship through its sailing and fighting ability.

On June 10, 1776, a few days after the encounter, the massive fleet led by General Howe sailed from Halifax for the invasion of New York.[24] From Abraham's view aboard the *Milford* it did not seem like the Rebellion was going to last much longer. He may soon be able to return home to his parents and his former life in London with pockets full of money. The *HMS Milford* had not yet met its match. The British ship continued on as the master of the seas off the New England coastline. The war was far from over, and there was still much in store for the young tailor to experience in the waters off New England.

Below decks, photo by author.

The Battle to End the Blockade

I was eleven in 1975; a year before the United States celebrated its Bicentennial. One of the highlights of the year for me took place when my father anchored us in his small wooden boat off the shoreline of Grape Island in Boston Harbor to watch the battle re-enactment of an event that occurred there 199 years before during the siege of Boston. The British had gone out to the island to gather hay for their horses back in the city, and some local Massachusetts militia went out to stop them. The re-enactment made a great impression on me and the Revolutionary War became my favorite event to study. While researching Abraham's life story I discovered the following event that took place near there, that I only found a slight mention of in a few books and documents. All I found were questions by historians on why the British fleet had left. They had no idea why. The angle on history that genealogy offers can lead to discoveries that might otherwise be overlooked. The following event is one of these....

On May 12, 1776, Abraham sailed off the coast of New England while John Adams wrote from Philadelphia to his wife Abigail that he was "inexpressibly chagrined to find the enemy is fortifying on George's Island."[1] George's Island was, and still is located in the outer harbor of Boston, and offered a good place for the British to control the port of Boston from. The main shipping channel from Boston, then called King's Road, passed through the inner harbor area and out to another shipping channel called Nantasket Road. The Island is clearly visible from many areas along the southern coast near Boston, and the British threat there was greatly feared. To John Adams, the British menace freely skulking around the island was totally unacceptable. His wife Abigail, alone and somewhat vulnerable, was even less happy about the fleets' presence.

John urged Abigail in his letter from Philadelphia to use her influence to get men to fortify themselves against the British threat on the outer islands by "whatever is proper." This shows the considerable trust that John Adams placed in his astute wife to influence political and military operations in New England while he worked in Philadelphia with the Continental Congress. If she was caught with these letters it would be an act of treason, and she would have been severely punished or even hung by the British. This worry did not stop the fearless woman. Adams words to his wife to fortify the coast proved prophetic in only a month's time. Adams and his wife were not the only citizens in the area who were alarmed by the frequent sight of British warships like the *Milford*, that carried Abraham Channell and other British tars off the coastline of New England. This great threat was seen and feared by many other citizens as well.

The legislature of Massachusetts, with Abigail's influence, passed resolves to further fortify the "harbour of Boston" and specified where the redoubts should be placed. The islands are made up of short hills called drumlins that the artillery could be placed upon. Moon Island needed to be fortified in order to keep open communication with Long Island, a large island along the main ocean channel to the city. They planned to place four pieces of cannon, along with the necessary ordnance to support its fire there. They wanted a redoubt on Houghs Neck to keep open communication with Peddocks Island. The cannon there were to be the same in strength as Moon Island. Four independent companies of militia were to be stationed in Dorchester, Braintree (now Quincy), Weymouth, and in Hingham, near the entrenchment locations in order to support the fortifying activity with sufficient troop strength.

The second resolve placed redoubts on the east head of Long Island, another on the east head of Peddocks Island, and another on Nantasket Hill in Hull. On these redoubts it was wished that, "three pieces of cannon of eighteen or twenty four pounders be placed in each of the three fortifications last mentioned."[2] Cannon that large would serve up a nasty surprise for any British ship that foolishly sailed into its range. All the supplies and equipment were to be received from General Artemus Ward, or whoever else was in command. It seems odd that the legislature did not know who was in charge of the military at that critical juncture. Someone had to plan, organize, and execute, this difficult engineering feat.

On June 11, 1776, a Committee of Fortification was appointed in Massachusetts by the leaders in the legislature to carry out the resolves. At the head of this committee list was; Benjamin Lincoln of Hingham, Joseph Palmer of Braintree, Solomon Lovell of Weymouth (all of whom soon become generals), and others. They were given the responsibility of fortifying the coastline against the British ships and their possible return. A lot of responsibility was resting on the shoulders of these men. None of these officers had any prior experience with building fortifications other than possibly helping with the buildup around Boston during the siege, and any earlier service or training they may have received during the earlier French and Indian War. Safeguards were needed to be put into place to stop the return of the enemy. Somewhere along the way the plan escalated to a greater and bolder idea.[3]

Boston Light from the authors antique postcard collection.

Beyond the new fortifications that the committee had planned, several British ships lay at anchor on June 13, 1776, in the outer harbor near Boston Light. Among them, Commodore Francis Banks and his fifty gun ship the Renown, the Hope, and the recently captured and repaired *Yankee Hero*, that was now repaired and refitted as a British vessel. The *HMS Milford* was anchored to the east of the other ships a bit further out to sea. These British ships were anchored along seven other large troop transports. The British had been evacuated from Boston, but they left a fleet within striking range of the city and kept the port effectively closed off to shipping from the outer harbor. Vice Admiral Molyneux Shuldham, had recently been put in charge of all British Naval operations in the area. He ordered Commodore Banks to stay and alert all British supply ships which may be unaware of the evacuation to stop their travel into Boston with supplies for the British troops. This was to help them to avoid being captured by the enemy. Banks was also ordered to "take, sink, burn, or destroy all Rebel Armed Vessels you may meet with."[4]

On board the transport ships lying at anchor with the fleet were around seven hundred Highland soldiers.[5] A fortified British base and sick house was set up at George's Island in the outer harbor of Boston.[6] Abraham longed to go to the island and walk on solid ground again, but he was needed on board the ship. He looked curiously out at the land and the coastline along its edge.

Unknown to the British fleet, Benjamin Lincoln, a member of the fortification committee, had begun his job of gathering local American men from Hingham, Weymouth, and Braintree, Massachusetts militia units. The men began to assemble to take control of Peddocks Island, Long Island, Moon Island, Point Allerton, and other high land areas surrounding the enemy fleet as ordered by the resolves. During the dark night, the Americans left Long Wharf in Boston on boats supplied with cannon, ammunition, provisions and entrenching tools to prepare to entrench the cannon, and then aim and fire at the unsuspecting British vessels on the morning of June 14, 1776.[7] The rebels had planned to catch the enemy fleet in a deadly crossfire from the various islands surrounding them. However, the difficulties encountered in setting up the cannon the night before made this impossible.

The evening was so calm that Colonel Asa Whitcomb, the commanding officer at Long Island in the inner harbor off the coast of present day Quincy, wrote that the men could hear the British talking on deck while the Americans prepared for the next morning's attack.[8] The Americans were aided in setting up the shore battery by skilled

Prussian engineers who built and rose up the defenses in a few short hours.[9] While the tars talked aboard their ships during anchor watch the militia men dug in and hauled supplies up the beaches to the hilltops of the islands and coastal high ground. The faintly lit binnacle light revealed the position of the British to their enemies, who watched them as they worked on the shore.

Abraham and the other men aboard the British ships did not know about the preparations that were going on all around them that dark, still night. As they rested and swung in their hammocks side by side below deck in the forecastle, the Yankees set their trap. There the crew slept among the heavy iron cannon, pulled back from their closed gun-ports. The lanterns hung still in the rows of hammocks in the berth deck, faintly lighting the room. The timbers creaked only slightly with the stillness of the ship. This only amplified the sighs and snoring of the sleeping jack tars as they rested from a hard day at sea. It was hoped that if the wind blew in the colonists favor, escape would be made impossible the next day for the British warships. This might lead to the capture of the vessels by the American militia soldiers. What a bonanza to the American war effort they could achieve if they captured a whole British fleet! It might change the course of the war. The British forces rested at anchor on this quiet, calm evening and were unaware of the enemy busy at work entrenching on the high ground all around them.

Unfortunately the calm, still night air that allowed the militia to hear the British on deck also made it difficult for them to sail the cannon to Peddocks and the other Islands. The fortifications and the American troops in these locations were still not prepared for the attack the following morning. Colonel Whitcomb, on the other hand, had secured the east head of Long Island and prepared two eighteen pound cannon, and one thirteen inch mortar for the morning surprise.[10] Whitcomb commanded 500 men at Long Island; on the adjacent Moon Island there were another 200 men.[11] Stationed at Hough's Neck, located in present day Quincy, were another 200. Colonel Solomon Lovell, a member of the fortification committee and himself a future general, was in charge in Hull on Point Allerton with 200 men under his command. Captain Peter Cushing, under the leadership of Benjamin Lincoln, led a group with cannon from Hingham. Fortunately, one of Cushing's men, Hawkes Fearing, was able to get the cannon into place, but later than the morning plan had called for.[12]

The Immortal Patriot

Major Paul Revere, of midnight ride fame, wrote from Nantasket that problems with the tide and calm weather had caused difficulties in getting the cannon into position. He also wrote that Peddocks Island, under the command of Joseph Palmer, had not been fortified in time. On Peddock's Island there were another five hundred troops preparing against the British. Palmer had tried but failed in his mission to arm the island. In spite of his failure, it was quite an accomplishment of the Americans to get all these men in place without being found out by the enemy on board the ships. The British must have had no fear of attack and had not adequately assigned men to keep a watch out for possible American threats along the coastline.

On Friday Morning, June 14, 1776, the cannon began to sound from Long Island at the sleeping British ships. Abraham awoke startled in his hammock, along with the others on the berth deck of the vessel when the cannon roared. The drums beat the men to their battle stations. Captain Burr ordered the decks to be quickly cleared and sanded for action.[13] After stowing his hammock, Abraham ran up through the companionway and quickly scurried to his position on board the ship to receive orders from the officers. Commodore Banks, began to receive several hits to his ship from the rebel cannon, and ordered a few fruitless shots to be fired in return. Seeing the futility of his position and fearing the loss of not only his ship but his whole command, he signaled for the fleet of British vessels to escape the American bombardment.

His crew quickly began to unfurl the sails from the spars high above the deck. Unfortunately for the commodore, the sails merely hung there limply from the spars due to the still air. The commodore wrote in his report later that he had fired fifty shots in return to redeem himself with his superiors, but this differs from the American account.[14] Revere proudly wrote that the British had fired but one shot before fleeing out to sea.[15] If Revere's account is correct, the British must have felt very threatened and vulnerable from the American attack. Abraham witnessed firsthand the first failure of the British fleet on that morning to occur during his service.

On board all the British ships men simultaneously struggled to turn the capstans and haul up their large, heavy anchors from the sea floor. The rebel cannonball fell close enough to raise plumes of water that splashed over some of the British decks, causing the men to work even faster. The anchor would have ordinarily been fastened to a yardarm tackle and secured to the side of the ship as the calm weather, fortunately for the fleet, changed and the wind finally began to puff out the sails. With the urgent danger of the attack the anchor lines, then known as springs, were simply cut loose. Luck was with the British in the later part of the morning when the ships slowly began to move away from their perilous anchorage. A large mortar fell directly where Banks' ship had been right after he got his flagship out of harms' way. Hawkes Fearing's cannon began to fire from Hull at ten in the morning. They hit the rigging and caused other damage to the British as the fleet finally managed to get out of range after struggling with the wind. The fleet then escaped into the early summer haze.

Later, the sails of five privateers approached on the horizon and headed toward the British.[16] For some reason these privateers were not engaged in battle by the *Milford*. The British captain may have wished for prizes and profits more than the glory of another battle with the privateers. Captain Burr was far too wise a captain to engage the enemy when he was outnumbered. The British fleet abandoned their supplies and sick men at George's Island when they sailed away and left all behind them in such great haste. The Commodore wrote that his fleet left behind only sixteen tons of water casks, but it was probable that he lost far more than that.[17] As they passed by Boston Light, marking the entrance to the outer approach of the harbor, the British lit a timed fuse to two barrels of gunpowder, which caused the destruction of the lighthouse in the wake of their ships at noon. The Americans recovered what metal they could from the light and fashioned them into ladles for their cannon.[18] Two years to the day after the British Parliament had closed the port of Boston, the British had been chased from the port permanently. The lighthouse was rebuilt years later when the war was over, and still serves as a beacon to the entrance of the harbor.

Abraham could not help but respect his enemies for their bold attack on the fleet. He helped the gun crew as they lashed the unused cannon back down on the deck. The surprise attack caused many aboard the *Milford* to believe that their luck had now changed. Sailors are suspicious men by nature and after they saw their entire fleet sail away in fear a great alarm rose in the men. In the following days, unknowing British ships engaged in battles with American privateers at the entrance to the harbor. Three hundred and ten Scottish Highlander troops were taken prisoner after a failed British attack on the battery on Long Island.[19] Boston had a renewed sense of security after the fleet's departure. The cities stores re-opened and life began to return to normal after a year of harsh occupation.[20] General Artemus Ward wrote to General Washington and told him of the successful mission on June 16, 1776.[21] However, ten days after the fleet was driven from Georges Island the *HMS Milford* took another prize laden with pitch tar and flour sailing from Newbury Massachusetts.[22] The battle for control of the seas off Massachusetts was far from over. But for now Boston Harbor was free of Abraham Channell and the powerful British fleet he served.

Postcard from authors collection.

A Modern Day Visit to the Light

In 2009, my wife, daughter and I visited Boston Light. The credit for planning the trip goes to my wife who has an avid interest in lighthouses. We first arrived on George's island, and from there I looked across at the ancient light that has guided mariners to safety for centuries. The light towers over Little Brewster Island, an island that is less than an acre at high tide. After a short, wet ride on a small craft that departed from the dock at George's Island we arrived on the small dock at Little Brewster and climbed ashore.

Our guide led us across the rocky shoreline of the island and up to the ancient lighthouse vestibule entrance as the sun dried the salt spray from my shirt. I looked down at the numerous carvings of names in the rocks on the path to the entrance that marked the service of many lifesavers over the years. While we waited our turn to go up to the lantern room I looked around at the many artifacts on display in the small museum there. My wife and I stood before the huge iron door that was the entry point to the light tower until it opened with a loud creak and it was our turn to enter. The walls at the base of the structure are seven feet thick and thin out to two foot wide at the top of the lighthouse. The walls may very well have been built with some of the rubble left over from the British explosion. Five aluminum bands now wrap around the lighthouse and give added support to the ancient structure. We took great delight in climbing the 76 cast iron spiral staircase steps that led to a ladder spiraling up to the lens room. It was in this room that we were able to see the rare Fresnel lens in the light's beacon.

The 4,000 pound Fresnel lens was installed there in 1859, and has a 1,000 watt bulb that produces 2,000,000 candle power from its lamp. The 336 individual prism lenses are fragile and can never be reproduced or replaced. The method and specifications of construction have been lost. Confederate prisoners once watched the light from

Fresnel Lens in Boston Light, photo by author.

nearby George's Island as they waited out their imprisonment from within the granite walls of Fort Warren, a fort built on the island previous to the Civil War. As I climbed down from the tower I could not believe how fortunate I was to have visited such a historic and seldom visited site, and to not have been visited by the ghosts of the Worthylake's.

The Legend of the tragic lighthouse keepers the Worthylake's was first created in a poem written by 12-year-old Benjamin Franklin. Franklin, like Abraham, was apprenticed as a young boy. In Franklin's case, his apprenticeship was to his brother who was a printer in Boston. The young apprentice wrote and printed the poem as a broadside and then sold them in the streets of Boston. My family was fortunate to visit such a rare historic site, and to safely return to the mainland and avoid the drowning the Worthylake's had suffered as they returned home from church in 1718. The waters off the island are still as dangerous as they are beautiful.

I often read about and had once discussed the ghost legend of the "Lady in Black" at Fort Warren, on nearby George's Island, with the author Edward Rowe Snow when I was a young boy. I followed him around the island during his historic tours of the island. My brother insists he had even once seen the ghost. My father often took us out to the fort to visit after a day of flounder fishing. Rowe and I never discussed the island's history during the Revolution. Although inquisitive, I was still just a boy when I followed along at his heels. The fort has such a dramatic presence on the island it is doubtful that anything survives from the Revolutionary days. I think Snow would have enjoyed my story of the British defeat immensely.

One April afternoon in 2011 my wife and I tried to visit Long Island with a camera to take some pictures and look around for any evidence or artifacts that might remain from the struggle. We were stopped at the guard post before the bridge that crosses to the island. I needed to get more approvals before we would be allowed to cross the old rusting steel bridge to the island. Subsequent phone calls to different government organizations just led me on a wild bureaucratic goose chase tripping on red tape. This is how modern government serves us today. My own freedom to once again visit the island had been violated. I had freely visited all these islands, almost two decades before. George's Island has long been a favorite destination of mine, and I grew up rummaging around the Civil War era fort and prison that was built in 1850. This fort and island can still be visited today thankfully, largely through the efforts of Snow and the popularity of his historic writing.

Later, after being refused by the police to visit Long Island, my wife and I drove to Wollaston beach in Quincy and stopped to get a late lunch while we sat outside and took in the fresh but salty sea air. I looked out at the harbor from my vantage point at the beach and could see all the points that the American militia had fired from; with Boston

Light in the center of my view. The overall locations involved in the scheme were still clearly obvious. It had been a brilliant plan. Only the calm winds and failed leadership had kept the Americans from achieving their goal.

Shortly after World War II my parents had their first date on this same beach. My father, "Fighting Fred" served in the navy through World War II, Korea, and Vietnam. It was here that he and my mother had fallen in love; long before he left the naval service in 1974. Down the road in Wollaston Cemetery were the graves of my grandfather and grandmother Channell, and my great-grandmother on my mother's side. She had followed my grandfather from Scotland to America to find the streets they heard were paved with gold. My grandfather Harry Lee Channell had served in World War I in the army as an ignition specialist working on airplanes. Later he had to raise his two children in an apartment during the Great Depression in this same town. He lost his previous home in nearby Braintree after the financial disaster on Black Tuesday, October 29, 1929. He lost his wife nine years later, leaving my father motherless.

It is interesting how a location can be so important to both military and family history. I wondered if Abraham longed to come ashore from that British frigate and become an American. I wonder if he even had a sense of what being an American was. That sense of patriotism and of belonging which had led my father to join the navy when he was even younger than Abraham may have been. Keeping their memory alive honors their service to both of their respective countries, and shows thankfulness for my own freedom. Freedom should never be taken for granted, and Abraham's impressment shows that freedom has to sometimes be zealously guarded against even one's own country. Nations are not against taking away freedom for what they see as important. I remember well the Vietnam draft of the generation just before I came of age, and the protests of young Americans to guard their own freedom.

Many felt they were being forced into a war they, like Abraham, did not agree with. I have also known many men who fought in Vietnam and the freedom of choice they feel they have allowed others to make with the sacrifice of their own safety they gave with their service. This makes it a difficult moral dilemma to ponder. It appears from Abraham's story that men are far happier to serve when being called on to defend, rather than go on the offensive. I reached for another onion ring and enjoyed the warmth of the sun on my face and my freedom on that Sunday afternoon, after a long harsh winter in New England. I sat there in the salt air feeling fortunate and thankful for my own freedom that so many before me had sacrificed with their own safety to ensure.

Fourth of July 1776

Summer was now upon the *Milford*, as centuries later it warmed me in Quincy. It was a far better time to be out at sea for Abraham than the previous winter. In July the Americans publicly declared their independence on July 4th. It was now no longer a rebellion, but had now become a Revolution. Abraham suddenly heard the excitement of the crew stirring and went up to help out on deck. He had probably not heard of the declaration of the colonists, but it would impact not only his future, but it would impact the whole world's future.

The Declaration of Independence had within it a statement against impressment. "He [King George III] has constrained our fellow Citizens taken Captive on the high Seas to bear Arms against their Country, to become the executioners of their friends and Brethren, or to fall themselves by their Hands." Abraham had experienced this firsthand by being forced to serve on the *Milford*. Impressment of men aboard the privateer and merchant ships at sea, along with those occurring in the streets of London had been on the increase. Declaring independence and winning it are two different things. If the revolt failed, it might just be a treasonous act that would be severely punished. Afterward, it might have just become a forgotten footnote to history. The new country had its work cut out for it. Abraham and the crew still their own work to do, and no time for political ideology.

The response to the Declaration of Independence back in England was not a positive one as might be expected. The declaration was nothing short of treasonable. It was seen as an, "Insult offered to every one who bears the name of Briton."[23] After all the, "King is their common father-nation their Brethren."[24] No group of citizens in a nation had ever tried to establish their own separate laws simply because they wanted to. The southern states were certainly not allowed to do this by Abraham Lincoln at the outbreak of the Civil War. The self evident truths dignified by natural laws in the audacious paper was seen as nonsense created by a few simple title-less individuals to coerce other misguided Americans. It was felt that most citizens would otherwise be loyal subjects of the king. Those guilty of this traitorous act were even foolish enough to sign their names at the bottom. The signatures were preceded by a long list of accusations against their sovereign.

Thomas Hutchinson, the estranged Royal Governor from Massachusetts, did choose to answer the radical document. He agreed that these were "common people" who "have misguided the people and provoked them to rebellion."[25] In the eyes of Hutchinson the rebels had not given any evidence within the document that could label King George as a tyrant. Hutchinson asked if the king had ever "departed from known established laws, and substituted his own will as the rule of his actions?" A tyrant, in his definition, had to have "exceeded the just powers of the Crown as limited by the English Constitution."[26] In his words the declaration, "either grossly misrepresented [oppressions], or [were] so trivial and insignificant as to have been of no general notoriety in the time of them, or mere contests between Governors and Assemblies, so light and transient, as to have been presently forgotten."[27] Citizens in America concealed their sentiments because "in America, no man may, by writing or speaking, contradict any part of this Declaration, without being deemed an enemy to his country, and exposed to the rage and fury of the populace."[28] Of course Hutchinson was absolutely correct with his statement: loyalty to the crown was not tolerated and led to tarring and feathering.

Hutchinson took offense with the statement that "all men were created equal" and that they had "unalienable rights." The ex-governor may have been the first to point out the contradiction of this statement. He stated:

> I could wish to ask the Delegates of Maryland, Virginia, and the Carolinas, how their Constituents justify the depriving more than an hundred thousand Africans of their rights to liberty, and the pursuit of happiness, and in some degree to their lives, if these rights are so absolutely unalienable.[29]

Hutchinson seems to have shared the anti-slavery sentiment of his former home state that led Massachusetts to free their slaves in the years that followed the Revolution. Slavery was left to later generations to deal with on a national level. In spite of his long life, Abraham did not live to see the slaves in the south ever gain their freedom. It took the action of an Illinois lawyer also named Abraham to achieve this.

Finally, on October 31, 1776, the king responded to the colonists declaration in a speech. He was proud to tell everyone that Canada had been recovered. It is forgotten today that Canada and the United States had once had common rule. The king was able to hold onto this major part of his empire. The king took responsibility for keeping the vast territory in his own declaration. The king further stated, "We must, at all Events, prepare for another Campaign."[30] The king stated his objective: "My Desire is to restore to them the Blessings of Law and Liberty, equally enjoyed by every British Subject, which they have fatally and desperately exchanged for all the Calamities of War, and the arbitrary Tyranny of their Chiefs."[31]

On July 25, 1776, the *HMS Milford* still searched for enemies off the coast when they once again spied some sails in the horizon off Cape Ann, Massachusetts. Ahead of the *Milford* there rode at sea the *Princess Royal*, a British ship, loaded with fish and lumber that had been taken off the coast of Bermuda by an American privateer named *Sturdy Beggar*.[32] The *Sturdy Beggar* had six cannon and some swivel guns on board. This unfortunate ship met up with the *HMS Milford* outside the entrance to Boston Harbor. With a crew of only twelve men, led by one officer, they wisely, although not heroically, abandoned the schooner and their prize and fled to the safety of the city of Boston.[33] Whether they jumped off and swam to shore or escaped on a small boat is unknown. In either case they did not want to tempt capture and imprisonment by the much more powerful *Milford*.

After he recaptured the ship, Captain Burr brought it to Halifax, Nova Scotia on August 2, 1776. Later in Halifax, the Admiralty Court judge awarded only a one-eighth award to the *Milford* because the ownership of its cargo originated in Britain. War had brought with it great opportunity for profits, but these had to be won in the courts as well as on the sea. There were still many prizes to be captured off the coastline. There was still much money to be made. The captain and crew pushed out once again to seek their fortune at sea.

Commodore Marriot Arbuthnot wrote the following letter on June 30, 1776, to Vice Admiral Richard Howe, the brother of General William Howe. General Howe was the British General that defeated Washington's army and caused them to flee New York. He wrote to tell him that the *HMS Milford* was in port at Halifax. The Commodore informed Howe:

> The Milford, Captain [John] Burr arrived here yesterday to victual and water, which I have compleated to four Months, and ordered her Commander to Sea immediately: as at present not one Ship of War is on this Coast, and many small privateers are hovering near Boston, and I am very apprehensive will soon find their Way to our Neighborhood: so soon as they learn the State of the Coast.[34]

The British leader was evidently worried that an invasion could come to Halifax that they could not defend against. This is reasonable considering the previous unsuccessful attack on Quebec that had been led by General Richard Montgomery and Benedict Arnold on December 31, 1775. General Montgomery was killed in the attack and Arnold, the future traitor of West Point, was wounded. Most of the inhabitants of Halifax had come from New England during the previous twenty years, and many of them had sympathies toward the enemy Yankees.

Halifax was seriously overcrowded, it was full of sick people and refugee Loyalists from the long siege of Boston. Commodore Marriot Arbuthnot had the difficult task of trying to deal with this, in addition to supporting the British actions in New York.[35] The Commodore knew that he needed ships like the *Milford* to patrol the waters between Halifax and New York and that the lack of British muscle at sea further encouraged Privateers to attack his supply ships attempting to service the army in New York. This lack of sea power would eventually prove fateful to Abraham Channell.

The *HMS Milford* was soon back at sea and off the coast of Cape Ann Massachusetts when Captain Burr saw some sail in the distance and gave chase to them. It was an American prize ship called the *Isaac,* that was taken by an American privateer as it sailed from Tortola in the British Virgin Islands to London. It was said to have on board:

> [T]hree hundred and fifty tons burden, commanded by Captain Ashburn, laden with five hundred hogsheads of sugar, forty-four puncheons of rum, one hundred and fifty bags of cotton, a considerable quantity of old copper, and a number of turtle. She was taken by the privateer sloop Warren, commanded by Captain Phillips.[36]

As the *Milford* chased the prize into the harbor, Captain Burr miscalculated and steered too close to the shore. A rebel fort at Marblehead opened fire and struck the *Milford* on its hull with its cannon fire. The deck lurched as the shot hit the *Milford* like it had been struck by a large hammer. The *Milford* gave up its pursuit and the lost prize arrived safely in Marblehead Harbor.[37] Abraham helped the others as they tried to repair the splintering the blow had caused to the timbers and seal up the gash from the sea. Captain Burr was not pleased with the loss of the prize, but he did not want to lose his ship either.

Although Captain Burr may have been frustrated with that loss; his luck changed the next day. The *Milford* and crew captured a large prize brigantine from Jamaica loaded with rum off the rocks of Cape Ann. The privateers that had captured the prize safely escaped in their small boats back to the shore. The *Milford* captured another sloop later that same day. These captures had originally been made off the coast of Bermuda, and had they not run into the *Milford*, might have been brought safely back home to Cape Ann.[38]

Abraham and the rest of the crew must have enjoyed some of that rum in celebration of their luck. Within days the sloop was re-taken by the Americans, but the *Milford* was already on its way to Halifax with the brigantine, a schooner, and another sloop. The *Milford* left other ships burning within the sight of Gloucester Harbor.[39] Abraham watched the burning ships light up the sky as they sailed back to their base at Halifax. He ate his meal of lobscouse, dried potato slices and soaked salt beef, as he watched the smoke rise off the sea.[40] The captain and crew were having a successful sail as the summer of 1776, slowly came to an end.

On August 26th the *Milford* was bringing several more prizes to Halifax in tow when Captain Burr's crew sighted sails moving south towards them. Coming their way in hot pursuit of the American Continental warship *Warren* was the *HMS Liverpool*. When Captain Burke of the *Warren* found himself trapped between the two enemy ships he struck his colors and quickly surrendered. The ship was a great prize. The vessel was the first one commissioned by General Washington, and was the last of "Washington's Navy" ships to be captured. The capture set off another struggle when the captain of the *Liverpool* quickly dispatched men in a row boat to beat the *Milford* to the

Warren and claim the ship for themselves as a prize. It was later ordered in court that the prize was to be equally shared between the two royal ships.[41] In the American press the *Milford* got the credit for the capture:

> Monday and Tuesday last the British Tyrant Frigate Milford was seen in our Bay, and to have two Schooners and a Sloop as prizes. She has taken the Continental Privateer Warren, Capt. Burk, and is continually cruizing between Cape-Cod and Cape-Ann, that we apprehend she will intercept all our Trade. 'Tis hoped that some of our American Frigates will come this Way and rid our coast of this inhuman Plunderer.[42]

The "Tyrant frigate" *Milford* angered the press and politicians of New England and became the primary target for them to attack. The ship was a symbol of British Naval power and was deeply hated by everyone on shore. The politicians began to take steps to rid their shore of the "inhuman plunderer."

One of the earliest committees in the Continental Congress was "the committee for fitting out armed vessels." It later became known as the Marine Committee, and the group was fully aware of the *HMS Milford* and its success along the northern shores.[43] On September 13, 1776, a letter was sent to Congress from the Massachusetts General Assembly that read:

> SIR: The General Assembly of this State beg leave to inform the honourable Congress that the Milford, frigate of twenty-eight guns, and another ship-of-war, have been for some time cruising on this coast, and have taken several merchantmen and valuable prizes coming into port. We have applied to the Hon. Thomas Cushing and John Langdon, Esq., agents for building the Continental ships, at Newburyport and Portsmouth, requesting that one or more of those ships might be sent out to protect our coast; but are informed by those gentlemen that they have no guns, and if they had, they have no orders to send the ships to sea. Upon this information, the General Assembly of this State resolved to furnish the agent for building the Continental ships at Newburyport, with a sufficient number of guns for one of them, and afford him every other assistance in their power in fitting out and manning said ship, provided leave can be obtained from the honourable Congress for said vessel to cruise on this coast, for the protection of the trade thereof — the agent

engaging to reimburse all the expenses this State shall incur in fitting out and manning said ship, and return said guns whenever said ship shall be otherwise employed. We would further inform the honourable Congress that the guns proposed for the above purpose are twenty-four nine-pounders, which we apprehend are suitable for the ship under the command of Hector McNeill, Esq., and which is in the greatest forwardness for sailing. As said ship will be inferiour to the enemy in force, this State beg leave to suggest to the honourable Congress the great advantage of having the ship under the care of John Langdon, Esq., fitted out immediately to act in concert with her. The readiness of the State of New-Hampshire to give all possible assistance to Mr. Langdon for the above purpose, will appear by a resolve of that State herewith enclosed.
Signed by the President.
To the Hon. John Hancock, Esq.[44]

The letter shows the problem in outfitting vessels with cannon. The Massachusetts Assembly knew that the *Milford* was a powerful foe and that they needed two heavily armed ships to even hope to defeat it. Twenty-four nine pounders would make them almost equal in power to the *Milford*, but whether or not they could defeat the wily Captain Burr had to be proven at sea.

In response to this the Continental Congress sent a letter on September 21, 1776, to Thomas Cushing of Boston, a major local political figure, and ordered him to oversee the building of a new frigate warship called *Boston*. Congress wanted the ship to be fitted out and sailed by the above mentioned Captain Hector McNeill. Captain McNeill was one of the few captains who had experience from serving in the Royal Navy.[45] The Congress Committee also ordered Captain Thomas Thompson of Portsmouth N.H. in the *Raleigh* to assist Captain McNeill in bringing down and stopping the *HMS Milford*.[46] But this encounter between the ships was destined to never occur.

The last encounter the *Milford* had with Abraham Channel still aboard occurred on September 20th off the sandy shoreline of the Isle of Sable; far off the coast of Nova Scotia. Sable Island is one of two places off the North American coast called the graveyard of the Atlantic. Many ships have perished off its coast. The *Milford* chased the American ship *Providence*; that had stopped to fish there off the island.

The captain of the *Providence* was planning on raiding whale and fishing ports along the Nova Scotia coastline.[47] The two ships had a running fire fight that lasted from ten in the morning until sundown that afternoon. The American ship was piloted by a newly commissioned naval officer named Captain John Paul Jones.

Jones was among the fortunate few who were able to escape from Captain Burr. Jones original name was John Paul, and had later added the alias of "Jones" after he killed a mutinous member of the crew and fled to America while he was being tried for the crew members murder. Abraham and Captain Jones seem to have both used the same technique of adding a surname to run from their past. Abraham did not likely know he had an encounter with the captain who later become an American naval legend. Abraham might not have thought much of the legend anyway as Jones fled away from Abraham and the *Milford* as fast as his ship would sail. The marines high up in the rigging fired at the *Providence*, but were unable to stop the ship.

The bow chasers were also out of range. Jones wrote that he tried to "tempt him to throw away powder and shot." The *Milford* proved to be quicker than Jones thought and he sailed hard to avoid capture. Jones wrote that the ship chased him "til night with her sable curtain put an end to this famous exploit of English knight errantry."[48] Jones later had another encounter with the *Milford* and he once again ran away from it after Abraham left the ship. This event took place during a harsh winter storm that may have led to Captain Burr's later sickness and ultimate demise. Burr may have grown sick after he commanded from the quarterdeck of the *Milford* through a cold winter hail storm following the *Providence*.[49]

During the fall of 1776, after his second winter encounter with Jones, Captain Burr began to become increasingly ill with an unknown illness. This brought the *HMS Milford* back to port earlier than Commodore Marriot Arbuthnot had expected when he outfitted the ship. The Milford had been at sea for less than a year since it first left port, but had seen a great deal of service to Britain. Burr and his crew had been successful in taking many prizes and had not been defeated by any enemy privateers. They had become a scourge to the Continental Congress in Philadelphia. The *HMS Milford* escaped capture at Boston Light and so far the British ship and crew had defeated the Yankees at almost every turn. The war was not to last much longer for Captain Burr, whose illness continued to worsen as the days grew shorter at the year's end.

On October 24, 1776, Abraham Channell was discharged from the ship in Halifax at his request, along with seven other servants. Abraham must have gained the respect of his officers to be allowed leave. No reason for his request was given other than for a possible injury he may have suffered while he fought on deck. If he sought medical assistance with the Royal Navy doctors in Halifax it would almost certainly have involved blood letting. It was best to avoid these doctors altogether. In all forty-two men were discharged and at least nine ran from the *HMS Milford* while it was at port. This was a considerable amount of men to have to replace. Some men transferred over to the *HMS Rainbow* and the fate of others remains unknown. Joseph Sewell, the officer whom Abraham served, became ill and was discharged the following year on March 7, 1777.[50] There was a lot of disease on board the ship, which may not have been unusual with such close confines and crampt, wet, living quarters in the berth decks.

Captain Burr lay seriously ill and dying in his room in Halifax during the fall and early winter of 1776, while other captains pressed the leadership for his command. They sought a chance to prove themselves and advance their own careers. On New Year's Day, 1777, an agent came on board the *HMS Milford*, while it was moored in the harbor off Halifax, and he awarded the crew five dollars prize money.[51] It is unknown whether Abraham ever received this, or had made other arrangements with the prize money he had earned when he left the ship. On January 15, 1777, Captain Burr, who had skillfully patrolled off the New England Coast for the British throughout the early stages of the Revolutionary War died. Captain Henry Mowatt, then took over command of the ship and prepared to return to sea.

Four days later on January 19, 1777, during Captain Burr's funeral procession, the *HMS Milford's* crew fired a fifty-two gun salute in honor of their captain.[52] Captain Burr had made the officers and crew of the ship rich men. One hour later the firing stopped, and Burr was laid to rest. The captain who was so effective off the coast of Massachusetts and whom Abraham and other members of the crew had fought for was now dead; his story forgotten. The patriots in New England, however, were not yet out of the woods. The *HMS Milford* and its new master Captain Mowatt; went back to sea and gave chase once again to the Captain and later Admiral John Paul Jones. The *Milford* survived the war and returned to England to be sold. She was a good ship. Abraham's time on board the vessel, however, had already come to an end.

After the evacuation of Boston, General Howe, and a fleet of forty-seven transport vessels and three man-of-wars had arrived in Halifax. Rents had doubled in the city when it swelled with 3,000 soldiers and 1,500 Loyalists that had evacuated from Boston. Fighting and problems not unlike those in the colonies had erupted. But the British military presence was overwhelming and this threat was easily controlled. Rebel news from Boston and Rhode Island was printed in the Halifax papers, but this was quickly stopped by the local British government.[53] No further problems were tolerated from the British military leaders in Nova Scotia.

Abraham walked the streets of Halifax in the fall of 1776, glad to be off the *HMS Milford* and free of his duties as a servant. Sailors like Abraham were called jack tars because of their clothing, that was painted with tar to make them waterproof to the sea.[54] Jack tars were a familiar sight in ports such as Halifax and Boston, but not a welcome one in the now overcrowded city of Halifax. He could not stay in this crowded place for long. Abraham was an ambitious man, and like many young men he sought to find his own success in the world. The young jack tar was struck by the ideas of the American prisoners that he had met while he served on board the *HMS Milford*. Their words and thoughts of liberty and freedom were infectious to him, and he found he wanted to learn more.

His own liberties had been seized by the representatives of the crown and he sympathized somewhat with the prisoners that had been captured and dragged on board the *Milford*. Abraham's own loss of freedom differed little from the prisoners aboard the ship. His prospects were dim in the small port town of Halifax. His prize money was running out, and he had no family to turn to and few opportunities existed in the small overcrowded town surrounded by a wild untamed land. He walked along the docks and looked for work loading and off loading the ships as they came to port. He sat and looked out at the busy harbor and pondered what he should do before his money ran out. He did not wish to get back on-board a vessel but the young man saw no alternative.

Halifax was suffering with a large smallpox epidemic and Abraham feared catching the disease as he walked the streets and saw the warning flags outside the houses of the infected.[55] The price of food was another worry, it had skyrocketed to outrageous levels in the town. The inhabitants of the port quartered the British soldiers for only a week at a time, and then the soldiers had to alternate their lodging and stay a week on board the disease ridden and crowded ships.[56] One British Captain wrote, "Of all the miserable places I ever saw Halifax is the worst."[57] Abraham's only escape from the seaport was the way that he had entered in the first place. His path out of this place was the Atlantic.

It remains unknown whether Abraham found a frigate that needed a crew to bring supplies to British lines in Rhode Island or New York, or if he was once again impressed. The practice of impressment increased in Halifax as the war progressed and more men became needed. The pay on board a frigate would have been better than on the *HMS Milford*, and with his experience he had no need to serve as a servant, and may have been able to serve as an ordinary seaman. He had served with the British and with all the success of his time on board he likely felt he had nothing to fear from the American privateers.

Transport vessels that carried supplies were hired by the British Treasury. They were sluggish, heavy, vessels and later in the war became heavily armed and recruited with soldiers. "Every biscuit, man, and bullet" had to be transported across a vast ocean to fight the rebellion.[58] At the time Abraham was at sea they relied on naval warships for protection. When they left the safety of these ships or blew off course they were preyed upon by the American privateers.[59] Before the war was over a political struggle ensued to see who would take over the responsibility for shipping supplies. The Treasury was forced to continue to take the expensive responsibility of paying for it.[60]

The ship Abraham was on very likely carried firewood or hay for the British military's horses. These were key supplies that the British needed that were sent from Halifax. These commodities were the oil and gasoline of the 18th century. The British troops stationed in the urban American areas like New York and Newport, Rhode Island, had great difficulty in procuring these items. These urban areas lacked firewood, and the troops eventually had to burn fences and docks in order to cook their food.[61] British political leaders back home felt that the troops could source these items themselves. Small American raiding parties that came out and skirmished with them made this impossible.

These small raiding parties greatly increased the expense of the war with the costly necessity of shipping supplies from Britain and Halifax.

The name of the vessel that Abraham ended up on has not yet been discovered. The British frigate was taken as a prize by an American Privateer somewhere off the entrance to Boston Harbor sometime in late 1776 or early 1777. The invasion force that now held New York was massive, and the many supplies the force needed meant that shipping had to pass right through the area the *Milford* had previously protected. Abraham knew the shoreline well.

The invasion army that had left Halifax earlier in the year was thought by British officers to be the final stroke in what would be their great victory against the rebels. It was felt that: "the misled deluded people will at last be convinced that they have been drawn into ruin, by a set of mock patriots, whom they find have now left them in the lurch, to save them selves."[62] The winter of 1776-77, however, began to turn the tide for the patriots in the fighting that now occurred to the south of New England; in spite of British sentiments to the contrary.

Encounter with destiny

As the transport vessel passed the coast of Cape Ann and its many American privateer vessels, the crew may have felt relieved. But as it passed the entrance to Boston Harbor, within sight of its outer islands, the crew sighted a rebel privateer approaching at an alarming speed. Abraham looked out in astonishment and after his experience on the *Milford* he realized their chances for escape were slim. The sluggish ship could never outrun them. His suspicion off George's Island of his change of luck had now come true. The merchant vessel was slow and had lost sight of the warships meant to protect it. The ship was a sitting duck and the crew was readied to repel boarders. The deck of the frigate swirled with activity as the gun room was emptied of what few weapons the men had to save themselves with. Muskets and pistols were hastily loaded in preparation.

As the privateer approached its deck swarmed with activity. The Americans swung their cutlasses and boarding pikes and shouted obscenities at the men aboard the merchant vessel. They cocked back their muskets and held them at the ready. Abraham, aboard the merchant ship, swallowed hard and prepared himself for what could well be his final moment on Earth. At first the privateer fired a warning shot over the vessel from its long gun as it approached the merchant ship. Then several warning shots were fired from the muskets and pistols at the merchant ship from the men stationed in the privateers rigging, this caused Abraham and the crew to fall back in safety as musket balls pierced the deck and sent splinters into the air. The privateer vessel shouted demands to surrender through the ships horn. This also helped to persuade them to strike their colors. The captain could not decide if he should surrender or try to have his merchant tars defend the ship.

Most of the British crew were private citizens, not navy sailors or marines, and had no interest in fighting or dying for their majesty. One blast of grapeshot across the vessels deck was enough to convince most of the crew to surrender. Abraham and a handful of others took up pike's to fight off the members of the privateer vessel. After the grappling hooks took hold and pulled the ships together alongside one another, Abraham quickly found he was surrounded and outnumbered, and he wisely chose to put down his pike and raise his arms up in defeat. Abraham then stood at the ready to receive his fate as the Americans surrounded and then shouted profanities at him and celebrated their victory after the capture of their prize. Abraham defiantly stared back at the privateers to avoid showing his fear and apprehension.

Abraham was grabbed and unceremoniously dragged before the officers of the privateer. He waited his turn while they interviewed the other members of the British crew and prepared to bring the prize into port. Like the *Milford* had done, the privateer needed to impress men to help them return the prize to port. The Continental Congress had laid down rules that British prisoners would be treated well and could be saved for prisoner exchange purposes; so Abraham would not be killed.[62] He was, however, in a most difficult position and had no idea what his fate was to be. Abraham was young and strong and after the officers of the privateer witnessed his brave attempt to avoid capture they asked him if he would be interested in joining the privateer crew.

"Well Abraham, will you join with us or continue as a slave to Parliament?" They might have asked, after hearing of his impressment.

"I will not serve as a pirate!" Abraham shouted defiantly in return. The captain was impressed by the young man's spirit and he wanted to add him to his prize crew. He did not have much time to linger there and had to get back to port with the prize. So he continued to explain the situation to the young man.

"We have declared our independence from Britain Abraham. We sail under a legal Letter of Marque aboard this ship." The captain then said. "Would you rather I lock you in the hold in chains or do you wish to remain free to grow wealthy with the rest of us? I will leave you to your choice Abraham; let me know when you have reached a decision."

Abraham faced a difficult choice on the deck of that American privateer. They had just captured the supply ship he served on and a decision had to be made. Should he go off to an American jail for an unknown length of time or join up with the privateer and eventually make his way to America? He would likely never see his family or friends again in Britain. Should he change from what he saw as a winning; to a losing side? The punishment he might receive if he was caught by the British would be severe; he could be hung if his traitorous action and betrayal was discovered. It would be an act of treason to the monarchy.

He had been unhappy with his treatment on board the king's ship and did not feel any sense of fidelity to the British. Abraham had been pressed against his will in London and forced to serve a slave-like existence at sea. He thought of the brave crew of the *Yankee Hero*, and the bold cause of Liberty they had fought and died for. A fateful decision was made on the deck that day while the wind blew across the sails. He looked west toward the land of North America and made up his mind. That land now became the future for Abraham and thousands of his descendants from the choice he made on the deck that day.

Abraham Channell chose to change sides and fight with the American rebel privateer. He became an American and lover of liberty and freedom. How long it took for him to finish this privateer voyage and make it to Cape Ann is unknown. The privateer returned the prize and prisoners to port and then continued on. At this stage of the war most privateers operated near the coast and Abraham's trip may have been brief.

The British prize was more than likely brought to Beverly Harbor as most of the vessels captured in the area were.[64] Having no-one to turn to, Abraham found support, friendship, and a new family in the crew of the privateer. Although Abraham found a new home aboard the ship, He had grown tired of the wooden world, and so after tiring briefly of this life at sea he saw a new opportunity to fight his former country and put some money in his pocket. Abraham's name next appears in a Massachusetts militia unit from Ipswich, Massachusetts fighting against Britain in Rhode Island in the following year of 1777. He had now become a man who most today would consider an American Patriot.

The Rhode Island Expedition

I rang the doorbell of the quaint Cape Cod cottage belonging to Rita and Gordon Channell. After years of corresponding with Rita online I felt like I knew her well, although we had never met. Without the internet I might not have never met her and gotten so far, so quickly, in my research. In spite of being in her eighties, Rita had youthful energy and appeared to be a much younger woman. Her husband Gordon was a retired police officer, and was a tall, strong man who seemed to resemble the spirit and strength of our ancestor far more than I do. Rita and I looked through her records that she had acquired over a lifetime of forty years of research, and I took copies of those that I needed for the project. What drove her in her relentless pursuit of her husband's ancestor I do not know, but obviously we were kindred spirits and partners in the chase of Abraham's legacy.

If I have put flesh on Abraham's life, Rita was responsible for the bones from her years of research and the information that she had painstakingly gathered. She acted not only as a valuable source of information but also as someone to share my madness with. She became an audience I could divulge my discoveries to; as opposed to the blank stares I received from my uncaring family. Eventually the subject of Abraham's service at the Battle of Sullivan Island came up. This historic, although little known event, had been linked to him in his obituary. The battle occurred in South Carolina in 1776, and was outside the *HMS Milford's* patrol area. Although Abraham is mentioned in his obituary as fighting there, there is simply no evidence that he was at this battle. His service was on board the *HMS Milford* during the concurrent time period of the battle. It is possible he was transferred off to another ship and then found himself back on board the *HMS Milford* again. This is, however, rather unlikely.

I told Rita of my theory; that Abraham's son had misunderstood his father when he told his son he served with the militia at the battle of Aquidneck Island, which is associated with General John Sullivan. This was then recorded incorrectly in his obituary one hundred and fifty years ago. Sometimes oral history can be misunderstood. It is possible that Sullivan and Island had been confused in this way. His obituary and death were recorded far after the event had occurred. Rita agreed that I was probably right given the evidence, I greatly respected her opinion so that was good enough for me. But as it turned out, it was only partly right. There is no evidence that Abraham was in Rhode Island during American General Sullivan's leadership. It is possible he re-enlisted and the muster record was lost. Abraham was in Rhode Island, but the evidence on his muster roll at the Massachusetts Archives showed he was there before General Sullivan was put in charge. This is in itself an interesting story....

Early spring, 1777

Abraham was trying to find his way in the small village of Chebacco (now called Essex), that was then part of the town of Ipswich, Massachusetts. Chebacco was a decidedly anti-British community as proven by the towns many soldiers and sailors that took up arms against their former king. Not to mention the spinning events the women took part in to make cloth to avoid purchasing from the British. Being alien to the town and coming from Britain he may not have been readily accepted into the small New England community, especially with the current conflict. Without any family, and with just a few friends from his time on the privateer, life was a struggle for Abraham in New England during the war. He did odd jobs to survive in the rebellion ravaged village, but money was difficult to come by. He could only rely on the charity of others for so long. A push for more militia men was made for a march to Rhode Island. All able bodied men between the ages of sixteen and sixty were ordinarily members of the militia. Although Abraham was British he was still, at that time, allowed to serve. The service may have even helped Abraham to be accepted into his adopted New England community. The British had taken Aquidneck Island in Rhode Island and the military leaders wanted to use Newport as a base for their naval operations in support of their New York campaign.[1] The American leaders wanted them out.

The money to sign up was irresistible, and Abraham volunteered for service under Captain Robert Dodge of Ipswich with twenty other men from Chebacco parish. On April 25, 1777, Abraham and the other militia units marched south towards Rhode Island, and joined with the other soldiers that served under Colonel Titcomb's 2nd regiment of Essex County, Massachusetts.[2] While he marched south the young militia soldier was struck by the beauty and size of the rural American landscape. On his back he carried a knapsack that held his spare clothing, and a blanket donated by the town. At his side hung a leather cartridge pack, full of bullet cartridges he had rolled up in preparation of hostilities. Under the cartridges he stored an extra supply of flints to fire his weapon. In his hands he carried an old fowling gun that he had been given to use in the village. On his feet he wore a pair of leather shoes with a large buckle. There was no right or left footwear. They were switched daily so that they wore evenly.

There were many clear spring nights that Abraham had to sleep with his back to a tree for support. The common tents he found to be too crowded. He had suffered through crowded sleeping quarters on board the *Milford* and the open skies offered a welcome alternative. The rural countryside was in deep contrast to the busy streets of London. The American men talked late into the night by the campfire. Abraham's stories of the debauchery of London were always a popular topic. Abraham could spin a great tale. He carefully kept the story of the *Milford's* success to himself. Abraham and his other five mess mates prepared their skimpy meal over a wood fire and kettle. One of their worst meals was firecake. A mixture of flour and water flattened out on a rock and placed near the fire until cooked. In spite of the conditions on the march, Abraham liked his new home; surely there was room and land enough for him to carve out his own future here.

In the morning the drums beat out the reveille to wake up the troops. Then the general beat to alert the men to strike the tents and prepare to march. The drums then beat out the assemble signal, to gather at the colors. After the troops gathered they beat the march to move out. The bugle was only used by the cavalry during the Revolution. In 1776, Washington recommended that "hunting shirts" be worn by his troops. This was an easily made piece of clothing that could be used in summer or winter by layering clothing beneath it. If Abraham had such a garment he might have put this on and then slung all his other supplies on over it. In addition he may have carried a knife, tomahawk, wooden canteen, a fire starting kit, and dice or other entertainment.[3]

As Abraham passed through the small towns along the way he saw large "liberty poles." These were erected with banners at the top that fluttered in the wind with patriotic slogans written upon them. Along the way likenesses of "Good King George" had been torn down and replaced by other new symbols of liberty. As he marched to the drum and fife, he joined in with the song to keep pace with the other men marching and singing: "Yankee Doodle, keep it up, Yankee Doodle, dandy, mind the music and the step, And with the girls be handy." The young tailor found he was becoming increasing swept up in the great excitement of the time.

Abraham and the other militia men from Essex County arrived in Rhode Island several days later on May 6, 1777, after they completed their long ninety mile march. The British had landed in Newport, Rhode Island, on Aquidneck Island the prior December, and most of the Island's inhabitants had fled to the mainland for safety. Since Abraham signed the surviving muster roll in Warren R.I., he may have been stationed there, although, Tiverton, Massachusetts, just across the water from the island, was the main concentration of troops. Every scrap of space of the muster roll had been used to record the militia names, and it took a lot of microfilm searching to discover Abraham's signature on it at the Massachusetts Archives. The American General in overall charge of the army was sixty-three year old General Joseph Spencer of Connecticut. General Spencer was given the responsibility of attacking the British and forcing their evacuation from the island.

When he entered the camp Abraham heard the loud booming voice of a man standing on a stump speaking to a large crowd of fellow militia soldiers:

> These are the times that try men's souls. The summer soldier
> and the sunshine patriot will, in this crisis, shrink from the
> service of their country; but he that stands it now, deserves the
> love and thanks of man and woman. Tyranny, like Hell, is not

easily conquered; yet we have this consolation with us, that the harder the conflict, the more glorious the triumph.[4]

Abraham, like the others who stood in the crowd, loudly encouraged the man's words that were being recited from a copy of Thomas Paine's writing *The American Crisis*. Abraham wondered to himself if he could now call this his country? At least for now, it was.

Abraham and the other men struck their tents and began to build entrenchments in case of British attack. The process began by clearing the area with a bill hook; a large broad blade that resembles a machete that army's still use today. The men then stuck a circle of sticks in the ground and wove in other sapling branches between them to make a hollow tube called a gabion. When the trench was dug the dirt was shoveled into the gabions. After this was high enough, other long sticks were piled into bundles called fascines, and laid diagonally across the gabions. This was then held in place by long stakes that were driven into the gabions. These fascines were felt to be able to absorb and stop a cannon ball. Then, sod was laid across this breastwork, and after a lot of sweat and toil the job was done.[5] Abraham and the other men could now relax and enjoy their daily ration of rum.

On March 2, 1777, General Spencer wrote to General Washington from Rhode Island and told him that he only lacked men in the mounting plan to attack the British on Aquidneck Island. On March 15 the two month enlistments of most of the American soldiers ended. Spencer had contacted the governments of Connecticut and Massachusetts and asked for more troops to be sent, and Abraham was one of the men sent for this reason. Spencer was preparing hundreds of boats to carry 8,000 men and artillery in the short trip across the narrow waterway to the island.[6] In spite of getting the men he needed; Spencer did not attack the British. It is still unknown what had happened that caused this failure to attack. General Joseph Palmer, active earlier in trying to capture the British fleet in Boston Harbor, was blamed by some military leaders for not arriving in position on time. The weather may have also played a role in Spencer's reluctance to attack and his failure to take control of the island from the enemy.

The only bright spot in the conflict of the summer of 1777, was the capture of British General Richard Prescott from his bed on Aquidneck Island by forty men who secretly crossed the water and slipped by the

British sentries. These men were led in their successful clandestine mission by Colonel William Barton on July 10, 1777. Spencer happily reported this successful capture to Washington in a letter. Spencer also reported to Washington in the letter that there were 3,500 British troops protecting Aquidneck Island.[7] Washington was pleased at the capture of the British General and arranged for Prescott to be used in a prisoner exchange for the captured American General Charles Lee.[8] Lee was later court-martialed after a battlefield argument with Washington, and an insulting letter Lee later sent to the commanding officer. Washington would have been better off if he did not choose to make the prisoner trade for the ineffective and bothersome general.

By the fall of 1777, the attack was deteriorating, and poor preparation and bad weather was blamed for the failure of the American forces that served under Spencer. Washington's frustration at the failure to take the island must have been great, but there is no record of his thoughts. Washington had other problems to consider with the British forces he and his other generals were facing. The men serving under Spencer had lost respect for him and began to call him "General granny." Other historians have referred to him as "elderly and lethargic."[9] This was not the kind of leadership needed to win a war against Britain. In spite of his superior force, General Spencer failed to attack.

Although a morale booster, the taking of the British General was not enough to save the career of Major General Joseph Spencer and Spencer's scapegoat in the failure; General Joseph Palmer of Braintree, Massachusetts. This is the same General Palmer who had failed to get the cannon set up at Peddocks Island. In spite of his multiple failures, Palmer placed himself in constant political danger before and during the war. He had signed a document on January 23, 1776, that would easily have been seen as traitorous by the British, and which boldly foreshadowed the words of the Declaration of Independence.[10] His son had even been among those "Indians" that had thrown tea into the harbor in Boston.[11] Palmer first came to America from Britain in 1745.[12] He served in the Provincial Congress before the war and also in the Committee of Safety.[13] The luckless general lost his fortune after giving 5,000 pounds to the war effort; and another 1,340 to the town to help with military recruitment. This money, so vital to the early effort in raising troops and supplying them, was never returned to Palmer.

The failure of the Rhode Island Expedition caused Palmer to lose his reputation in the pursuit of the American cause. Having given all his money to purchase military supplies, his business, once located in an area known as Germantown in Braintree (now Quincy), Massachusetts, failed with his absence and his preoccupation with the war effort. He lived out the remainder of his life in small quarters owned by John Adams. A forgotten patriot who gave all but received no benefit from his great sacrifice. Palmer had truly given all but his life for his country. Unfortunately, his lack of military leadership ability darkens his commitment to freedom.

Joseph Palmer was first chosen as a Colonel, 5th Suffolk Co. Regiment of Massachusetts on February 2, 1776. This was made official five days later on February 7. With a quick rise he was chosen and commissioned a Brigadier General on May 9, 1776. On August 21, 1777, he was sent to Bennington (Vermont), then called the Grants, to: "obtain the most authentic Intellegience of the Cercumstan[ces] of the American Forces."[14] On September 17, 1777, he was chosen Brigadier General to command at the secret expedition to Rhode Island under Spencer. Again, two days later on September 19, this promotion was passed by the council. By November 12, 1777, a year later, he was being called in to discuss the failure of the mission to oust the British forces from Aquidneck Island.

When the author and historian Edward Rowe Snow discussed General Palmer in *Mysterious Tales of the New England Coast* he wrote: "Seldom in history has there been a man whose accomplishments in making our country a nation became so universally ignored…"[15] Unfortunately Palmer's failure dampened his memory as a man of action in the early years of the pursuit of American independence. Few historians have written anything about him other than Snow. The failure of the expedition also led to the obscurity of his commanding officer Spencer. The faulty mission likely caused the memory of it to fade in Abraham's eyes as well. It is never good to be part of a failure, and this might be why the struggle never finds itself discussed in American textbooks. The struggle on Aquidneck Island has almost been completely forgotten. The failure contradicts the American exceptional-ism we all expect from our revolutionary leaders. We forget some of them were human.

In defense of himself, General Spencer wrote a lengthy letter to

Congress which primarily consisted of explanations for the economic problems he encountered supplying and paying troops. If the letter is right it may reveal that the real failure at Aquidneck Island was unpaid and poorly fed militia. The letter is supported with evidence from the failure of the early commissariat system to supply the troops with flour, and the difficulties of keeping their supplies from being seized by the British.[16] It is also likely that Spencer was making excuses and not taking responsibility for his inability to attack. He seemed to consider his role mostly a defensive one. In the final part of his letter to General Washington and the Continental Congress he wrote: "...that a pay Master should be appointed to reside Constantly here: there would be a full Employ for one; and that he should be supply'd by your Honors Orders with sufficient Quantities of Cash, for the support and pay of the Army." There were obviously other problems in General Spencer's leadership to overcome besides defeating the British.

In his resignation letter Spencer spelled out his shortcomings after he told the story of what he considered to be the cause of the failure of the mission to Rhode Island:

> Permit me after Making the above Repres'entation to
> Acknowledge that the Difficulties attending the Command of
> this department, Requires a Commander of greater Abilities,
> and in the Bloom and Vigour of life: and that I Earnestly
> entreat your Honors that such a person may be Ordered to
> Relieve me, and that I may have the Opportunity to settle my
> Accounts Relative to my Command: and have your Honors
> leave to resign my Office.[17]

So in the end Spencer blamed his age for his failure. Yet older men than he fought and died in their countries service. His story proves wealth, status, and age, do not guarantee great military leadership.

The British, on the other hand, did not stand by harmlessly while Abraham and the Americans faltered and failed to attack. On May 24, 1777, they made an assault on Bristol and Warren Rhode Island. They burned several homes and stole clothing and supplies from citizens in Warren. In Bristol eighteen houses were burnt and women were robbed of their jewelry. This invasion was repulsed by Colonel Barton and his men, but not until after a town church was burned to the ground.[18] If Abraham was in Warren, he may have helped in this fight to repel the British as they raided the area.

General Nathanael Greene was considered as a possible replacement to take over for Spencer after his resignation. Greene was a man of action, chosen for his talent and not just his status in the community like Spencer was. Greene was reluctant to take command and got his wish when General John Sullivan of New Hampshire took the command in 1778 instead.[38] Greene then served in a subordinate role to General Sullivan, and along with the young French General Lafayette went on to command troops when Sullivan attacked the British inconclusively on August 29, 1778. The battle was claimed to have been won by both British and Americans, with fierce fighting and heavy British losses. It was not enough of a victory though to free the island of the Enemy.

Previous to the battle a bad storm had kicked up, damaged, and scattered, the French fleet commanded by Admiral Count Charles Henri d'Estaing. The fleet was then sent to Boston to be repaired. Admiral d'Estaing's fleet consisted of twelve battleships and four frigates, and when they prowled about prior to the battle they caused the British to destroy many of their own ships to avoid capture. If the French and American forces had worked decisively together at the battle of Rhode Island, the island may have been won and the army captured. Fortunately, years later at Yorktown, the countries came together and their combined effort proved to be far more successful.

Abraham suffered through his service with inadequate supplies of clothing and food. He and the others prepared to march back in frustration from the military failure to Chebacco. Leaving the British army and fleet he once served behind him off the coast of Rhode Island. The event seems to have indeed tried Abraham's soul and he was likely glad to leave the failed mission. There were other problems as well. The French naval abandonment of the attack at Newport almost resulted in a horrible rift between the two allies. The hot tempered General Sullivan was not hesitant to place blame on the French. Washington had to step in to keep the peace between General Sullivan and the French General Lafayette. Abraham took one last look at the entrenchments in Tiverton that he had called home for the past several months. He then turned and began the long march back to his new found home in Essex County.

Today, present day Fort Barton is preserved as a park and pleasant hiking trails are all that marks the American encampment. The battle has been largely forgotten to history. Researching the Battle of Rhode Island gave me a sense of déjà vu. Ten years before I began researching Abraham I had been in Tiverton, Rhode Island, on business and I had walked around what remained of the entrenchments. I walked alone through the faint ruins in a welcome moment of solitude. My young children kept me very busy those days. It was a pleasure to have a quiet moment at the old battle entrenchment. The gabion and fascines that held the entrenchments together were long since decayed into long round ridges in the soil. In reflection I wonder what had caused me to take the time out to examine the fort. Maybe it was just my love of history. Maybe I was again heeding some irresistible echo of the past.

The British forces outside Rhode Island did not fare as well as those in Rhode Island, and began to have trouble during the campaign of 1777. The year began with a successful surprise attack when Washington crossed the Delaware and captured the Hessians at Trenton. British losses later continued with General Burgoyne's defeat as he tried to take Albany, New York, when he invaded from Canada. The British Generals acted largely on their own initiative and their lack of planning cost them the victory that many members of the British government had expected that year. The frontier militia of Northern New York and what later become Vermont cut Burgoyne's forces to ribbons on his march south. At sea the British Navy was being humiliated by their inability to defeat the rebel cruisers that not only patrolled the coastline of North America but were then brazenly striking at the coast of Britain itself. The sight of American privateers in the harbors of France only further encouraged the French, old enemies of the British, to enter the war on the American side. This stretched the British fleet even further with the sudden need to protect their own coast.

A year later politicians in Massachusetts made a decision that affected Abraham's future in the militia service. A resolution was put forward on May 22, 1778, during the first session that "...all persons who have deserted, or may hereafter desert from the British army or navy be, and they hereby are exempted from doing any militia duty whatever in this State during the present war."[39] This resolve stopped Abraham from being able to sign up for any militia duty for the duration of the war in Massachusetts. Although he had now broken his ties with Britain and could be hung as a traitor, the American military and government had turned their back on him. "The summer soldier and the sunshine patriot will, in this crisis, shrink from the service of their country; but he that stands it now, deserves the love and thanks of man and woman," had proven to be hollow words to Abraham as his newly adopted country turned its back on him; instead of offering him its thanks.

The resolve likely kept him from applying for or receiving a pension as well, with no sign in the document of men who have already served being grandfathered in. No pension application for Abraham has ever been found. The resolve goes on to say, "...all contracts and engagements made and entered into, or that may be made and entered into with any such prisoner or deserter........hereby are rendered null and void."[40] This act was passed by the legislature on June 12, 1778. It was okay to be a patriot, as long as you had been born in the colonies or were considered a man of means.

The great British writer Samuel Johnson wrote, "Patriotism is the last refuge of a scoundrel."[41] These political leaders were certainly scoundrels for passing this judgment on Abraham. Abraham must have been deeply angered by the decision forbidding him from supporting the American cause. Whether or not he felt that the leaders in the Massachusetts Legislature were "scoundrels" or not is unclear. Their decision, however, to exclude Abraham and others that had recently sought to help in the cause did make them scoundrels to those who had risked as much as they and were not to be rewarded.

Johnson defined the term patriot in his dictionary as "One whose ruling passion is the love of his country." But Johnson does not define what a country is within his explanation. Does a country point to those men and women who live within it? Did he mean the country that you had been born in? Or does it refer to the government that rules it? In a later addition he added, "It is sometimes used for a factious disturber of the government."[42] Bringing up the additional question of who the real patriot is, the man who supports his government or the one who questions it and challenges its leadership when they disagree? In a time such as the one Abraham lived in there was no time for these questions. To be a patriot was to support the war against the British. To not do so labeled you as a Tory or Loyalist. To not support men who wanted in their hearts to be patriots; surely was the act of scoundrels.

The Immortal Patriot

If Abraham truly wished to help out further in the American cause of liberty, he had to find another capacity besides the militia or Continental Army. He had to find some new service to perform if he wished to make a living during the remainder of the war. With the only option being a day worker on the farms in Chebacco he really had little choice. Once again it seems Abraham had to turn to the sea for employment, and to help America in its quest for independence.

Postcard from authors collection.

Now fitting for a Privateer

During their return march home to Chebacco, Abraham and the other militia soldiers stopped in Beverly briefly to hear the latest news of the war. While he glanced at an advertisement posted on a nearby wall Abraham stepped away from the crowd and began to read of the plan to fit out a privateer and about all the money that could be made by those willing to take the risk.[1] He was taken to this country by a privateer and made a little money on the return voyage. Abraham thought it was time to get back on board one. On board the privateer Abraham had a sense of belonging and democracy that he had been denied in the militia. Making a fortune in a few months sounded quite reasonable to Abraham, with dull prospects that lay in front of him otherwise.

Abraham learned how to sail on board the *HMS Milford* and knew enough to be valuable on board a sailing ship. It was a little different, however, aboard the privateer. These men were more alert and willing to fight due to the money that they could earn. It was a risky venture that brought a different kind of man to the forefront. After his many months marching on land Abraham felt he was again ready to spend some time at sea. Instead of the British Captains and other officers on board the ship receiving the major benefit of the prize, Abraham might get a fair percentage from serving on a privateer. He could look forward to a great fortune if successful, it was a chance worth risking. But just how big was the risk? Sure they had paperwork promoting the legality of their operation and action at sea against their enemy. This paper, however, was

68

from a rebellious government that was not recognized by its enemy or most of the civilized world. Abraham's risk was larger than the traitorous action of anyone else aboard because he left the British service. Only the promise of a piece of paper from a fledgling nation would protect him from being branded a pirate at sea.

Abraham entered Salem Village, a port north of Boston, and went down to the dock to look for a privateer fitting out for a voyage. Salem put an estimated one hundred and fifty-eight ships to sea during the Revolution. Vessels from the town were responsible for half of the captures of prizes made during the war by the Americans.[2] One of the greatest of the merchants putting these privateers to sea was Richard Derby Jr., and his sons Elias Hasket, and John. Abraham sought to sign up with one of the ships that belonged to the Derby family that left their dock on Derby Wharf. The dock bristled with activity as men prepared the ships for sailing making sails and preparing cordage for the vessels in the many sheds that lined the dock. With luck they could occupy themselves stripping British ships of their supplies after capture on the same wharf when the prizes returned to port.

Derby was one of the wealthiest men in Massachusetts and controlled half the privateers in Salem. He maintained a financial stake in most of the others. He was already a successful merchant at the beginning of the war, and through the necessity to protect his ships he had begun arming his vessels after several of his boats were taken as prizes by the British early on in the conflict. After the actions of Lexington and Concord, Derby instructed his son John to sail a ship to Britain with news of the battle to ensure the American version of the struggle was the first to be heard in the British press. Derby's swift ship easily overtook the British vessel that had left four days before with the official military report.[3]

Richard Derby Jr. was later appointed to the Committee to build armed vessels for the government and worked on the Massachusetts ship *Tyrannicide*, turning it into a brigantine from a sloop.[4] Tyrannicide is the act of killing a tyrant and destroying their power. Exactly what the ship set out to achieve. The Derbys, in many ways, had their own private navy, far more powerful than that being created by the Continental Congress. They would do a lot of damage and cause economic chaos to Royal Navy shipping with their privateer vessels and strike at the British leaders they thought of as tyrants.

In the years following the Revolution Derby's son Elias Hasket Derby became America's first new millionaire. Richard Derby's son Elias was the family member most responsible for the privateering efforts taken up by the family. Elias never went to the sea himself, like his father Richard and his brother John had done. Due to the British actions affecting their business ventures prior to the war, the Derby's were one of the first to be willing to strike against them. Elias Hasket Derby's skill also lay in his ability to change boat designs to make them faster and more formidable against the British. Derby also oversaw the shipyards capable of producing them. After the Revolution he turned these well built ships toward China, and was the first to open this port to American trade. His privateer ship *Grand Turk*, captured over twenty-five prizes and was one of the most successful and famous privateers of the Revolutionary War.[5]

Abraham did not have to wait long to find a ship to sign up on. Down the street he heard the approach of fifes and drums and a representative from the privateer vessel loudly shouted out and described the money that could be made and the adventure they would enjoy to influence their decision to sign on. This event often occurred in front of a tavern where drinks were passed out and paid for by the privateer representative. As the bowls of punch and grog emptied the courage of the young men grew.[6] Great wealth could be made, but at the risk of death and imprisonment in British prison camps such as Mill Prison in Britain or the prison in Halifax. They were held in prison with the charge of high treason.

Arming these privateer vessels was costly, and it took several weeks to finish the changeover from merchant or fishing ship to privateer. The bulwark or side of the ship had to be cut to place the cannon through. The magazine to store the powder had to be built and outfitted to make it as fireproof as possible. Shot lockers were built to place the cannonball and other assorted shot that was to be fired at the enemy ships near the cannon. Floors were reinforced to carry the force of the cannon's fire and weight.[7]

These well made fast sailing vessels were a menace to British vessels transporting supplies. The prizes began to pile up from the earliest time of the war, and even more so when they converted over more ships. To keep them sailing fast, the ships were stuffed with as much sail as possible. If the canvas was torn down by chain shot fired from the enemy cannon, it could tear down the sail and stop the vessel dead in the water. The boats were not constructed to be bulky and carry large cargoes but were built sleek and fast to serve smuggling and illegal trading activities under the nose of the previous British trade acts. This allowed them to easily catch sluggish British supply and merchant vessels when they hugged the American coast.

After being given a Letter of Marque,[8] these privateer ships set sail to capture British vessels and bring them back to port. These letters of marque, given by the state, Continental Congress, or both, made it lawful in American eyes to capture enemy ships. Without these papers the captain and crew were considered pirates by any nation. Regardless of this, Britain threatened to treat these captured men as pirates and hang them. There is no record, however, of this ever occurring.[9] The owners risked a five thousand dollar bond and more for bonding larger vessels, thus ensuring that they followed the rules of the Letter of Marque precisely. Many ship owners, including Derby, were willing to take the risk and pay the bond to receive the Letters of Marque.[10]

Many prizes captured from British shipping were brought back to Derby Wharf in Salem and were stored in a then unfinished home, Hawkes House, which still stands today at the end of the dock.[11] Abraham's service on these Salem ships is known only through his obituary, and the details of which ship(s) he served on are not. It was rare for British tars (sailors) to be found on board these ships, Abraham, as stated, would have been hung by the British if he was captured.[12] Few privateers risked more than Abraham by going off to sea. Many of the ships were also smaller than what he was used to. In some cases the crew had to sleep out in the open on board the decks. At least Abraham could expect a great payday if he was successful during the cruise.

After Abraham signed the Articles of Agreement of the privateer vessel, he had money in his pocket and a share of the cargo that he could also sell off in part before his departure. While out to sea economic conditions on land could quickly change and a man had to be careful with his money, it would have been wiser to buy property or start a business with the money than to buy goods with it.[13] This prize money may have given Abraham his start in his new life with property or buying cloth to set up shop as a tailor. His service during this time not only stopped the British supply ships and thereby weakened land forces, but also brought pressure to the King and Parliament to end the struggle because of rising insurance costs to merchant vessels that could fall victim to American privateers.[14] One Member of Parliament wrote: "to exhaust still further the finest country in the world in this prosecution of a war from whence no reasonable man entertains any hope of success. It is better to be humbled than ruined."[15] The value of Abraham's service and others like him cannot be over stated, it was a major factor in the British defeat.

The insurance cost of shipping a merchant vessel was priced at two percent of the value of the cargo prior to the war. Due to the early success of the privateers insurance shot up to thirty percent for ships protected in a convoy, and fifty percent for those not sailing safely in a convoy. In early 1778 it was reported to Parliament that seven hundred and thirty three ships had been lost or destroyed to American Privateers.[16] Not all merchants in Britain lost money. Others who supplied uniforms and other goods made great fortunes from the war. These men might have influenced Parliament to keep the war going. It was not until the losses overwhelmed the profits that overall public sentiment influenced the government to end the conflict.

The knowledge of Abraham's participation on a privateer comes from the evidence of his wounds that were recorded by his sons Charles and Leon in their application into the Sons of the American Revolution. The Sons of the American Revolution is a fraternal organization for the descendants of Revolutionary War veterans which still exists today. In the application it said that Abraham received a wound from a boarding pike to his knee and had the scars of two cutlass wounds on his head. His son Leon attested to witnessing these scars himself on May 15, 1896, in front of a notary public. His brother Charles Stewart Channell also signed a statement on his behalf that all this was true in Stanstead, Canada. In later years Abraham must have begun to show his wounds to people to validate the incredible stories of his adventures at sea. Whether these wounds had been received in the service of the British or privateers is unknown. It may have depended which side of the border he was as to which story he told.

A boarding pike was a highly effective weapon and one that was always reliable, unlike flintlock weapons that may not fire on-board a wet vessel. These spear like weapons were about eight feet long and stored against the masts of the ship to be quickly accessible if needed.[17] The long wooden shaft was tipped with a long eight inch razor sharp blade fastened strongly to the handle. The weapon could be slid through the hand to shorten it or lengthen it as needed. The cutlass that was used aboard the ships during the war was slightly curved and was roughly three feet long.

Boarding a ship was an ugly affair that consisted of rough hand to hand fighting at close range. The men first fired the pistols, and then threw them at their opponents. This would be followed by the thrusting of pikes and the hiss of swinging cutlasses. The shouting and fierce cries of the initial attack led to the groans of those dying and injured on board the prizes decks that were slippery and covered in blood. Abraham's wounds disclose not only his bravery but his greed. In the surviving articles of agreement of the Salem Privateer Ship *Rover* article six clearly shows that the first man on board a prize would receive an additional one thousand dollars and the best firelock found on board.[18] An ambitious man like Abraham would have wanted that money for his own pocket.

The fascinating stories of this service are unfortunately not known as well as the history of his service on the *HMS Milford*. As the stones of history are overturned, this information may someday be discovered. It is likely, however, that his name will never be found on a list. Lists were quickly discarded after the quick trips were made on the small schooners that sailed out of Salem. The danger of being captured by the British might have kept Abraham from signing with his real name. Once again situations and reasons kept him from using his real identity to hide from his past and try to secure his future.

Derby Wharf

I strolled down Derby Wharf and looked out in the harbor as I waited for the schooner *Fame* to come into port. The view from the wharf of the Customs House and other buildings brings to mind the events of the age of sail, not only of the Revolution, but the War of 1812, and the China Trade. For over half a century goods came into this port from all around the world and the sounds and smells of the busy port were now a distant memory. Local fascination with witches from an earlier time during the colonial period puts the history of the sea at a distant second in interest.

Frederick Channell

Most people who come to Salem do not realize the importance of the privateers who struck at the British and caused their supply lines to be cut. This resulted in more British warships needing to be sent to sea to protect them. As I boarded the *Fame* and helped raise the sail of the re-created 1812 privateer I tried in my own way to understand what Abraham had gone through. I grabbed the rope and with the rest of the crew helped pull the sail up into position. The wind filled the canvas and covered part of the deck in cooling shade as I shifted to get some of the afternoon summer rays. With the refreshing sea breeze and warm sun that now warmed my back it is hard to imagine that Abraham's time at sea was all bad. With the optimism of every new privateer endeavor stood the promise of great wealth and adventure for the young tailor and the crew; a promise of excitement that is hard to come by now in the 21th century.

Derby Wharf Today, photo by author.

To My First True Love

In 1937, Nina Fletcher Little, and her husband Bertram, purchased an old farmhouse situated in a beautiful rural setting in Essex, Massachusetts, to house their growing collection of American folk art. This amazing woman with remarkable foresight bought and saved American history at a time when it had little appeal to the majority of art enthusiasts. In the midst of the great depression colonial art held minimal interest or value for most Americans. The Cogswell Grant, as the farmhouse is now called, was lovingly restored by the Littles and after Nina's death the farmhouse was given to a historic preservation organization, along with much of her collection of folk artwork. Fortunately, during a visit to Connecticut, Nina Fletcher purchased two pieces of Channell family history. These consisted of old water colors of a family tree and an illustrated remembrance of Abigail Channell; Abraham's first wife. I discovered these artifacts during a Google search I made, and after a lot of phone calls and luck I was ultimately able to track the water colors back to the Cogswell Grant, and see this evidence of my past ancestry firsthand.

Although the way they met is unknown; the love they shared during Abigail's tragically short life is revealed through their many children. The life of this woman is remembered with the water colors that can still be seen today in Essex; hanging on the wall in Cogswell Grant. As I looked at the paintings, I wondered if the farm in the illustration may not offer a glimpse of their home at the end of the 18th century. The discovery of their home once being in Essex in itself took time. I saw references made to Chebacco, but it took a while to discover it later became Essex. My first visits to the area were brief. As I continued my research, however, I increasingly found the need to return to the area and look around for crumbs of information that may have still resided there.

To most people today the water color mourning piece painted to remember my ancestor would be viewed as a reminder of death and not have a place or be welcome within the modern dwelling. These were once very common in both needlepoint and paintings decorating the home. People may have a photograph of their parents or grandparents to remember them by, but this was not an option in the years following the Revolution. Death and mortality are hidden from sight today in cemeteries and funeral parlors far away from the eyes of the living. Memorial Day, once known as Decoration Day, was a day to honor the dead and decorate their graves after the Civil War. Today, it is all too often used as a three day weekend; or to promote car sales. Few people find beauty in the carvings of colonial gravestones as genealogists do. Every winter season rain and melting snow water is trapped between the slate, freezing and damaging the markers and chipping away at the ancient stone. The ground heaves and pushes them out. Branches fall and knock them over. Landscaper's weed-whacking equipment erases Bible text off the bottom sections of the old slate markers. Few people take up the protection of this historic and vulnerable evidence of our past.

Once, death was an everyday part of life. The corpses of family members were laid out and prepared in the home before the funeral plans were made. Family members had to choose the departed family members final clothing and dress the body and place it in its coffin. They often had elaborate funeral plans and spend a large amount of money in the burial, grave marker, and the party that followed. In some ways this has been supplanted by the modern wedding. The focus is now on the young and their future lives, not on the aging or deceased. States once had to pass laws to limit the expense of funeral spending; when many citizens were bankrupted by it.

The family tree that hangs on the wall in Cogswell Grant may still find a place in the home of a genealogist; those who study their own rich family history. The use of a tree to symbolize a family is a fitting image. Branches reach out and apart from one another, and the roots spread out much the same. We are all a part of one another, our ancestors were once enemies of one another. Through love we are all brought back together. Everyone is of the same blood. What is it that makes us enemies? Is it political ambition, racism, greed, or something else? Can patriotism be blamed for driving nations against one another? The study of genealogy helps one to realize the vast stretches and spider web of humanity.

It was an incredible find to discover and view this ancient family tree, a relic from my family's early American past. A sailor from London and a woman from the colonies, at that time enemies, but through love brought together. This marriage proves that love is stronger than politics and war, and that love not hate will eventually win. The paintings had somehow traveled 220 years through time; down to Connecticut and back to within a mile of where they had first been hung on a wall. The paintings are now once again, just a mile or two from where the love of Abraham and Abigail had begun. Their love created a family that helped build not just one new country, but two.

One day in Chebacco

Abigail walked toward the well carrying a bucket to fill with water for the kitchen garden beside their small farmhouse. Her mother Elizabeth was in the house preparing a meal, and her nineteen year old brother Nehemiah was out tending to animals in the field, or had run off with friends. Nehemiah, seeking his own adventure, later signed up to serve in Maine, still a part of Massachusetts, during the Revolution. The chores at the farmhouse were numerous, and it seemed they could never keep up with the work. Abigail's late father, Nehemiah Burnham, was sworn in at Boston on February 12, 1759. His commanding officer was Captain Stephen Whipple, under Colonel Jonathan Bagley. Nehemiah was first promoted to Sargent on April 3, 1759, and later to Lieutenant. Nehemiah Burnham died on July 25, 1759, at the Battle of Half Moon, serving in New York along the Hudson River during the French and Indian War.[1] Half Moon was a small fort or fortified garrison house. This was a small skirmish of a battle, possibly an ambush; that has been forgotten to history. Abigail was only four years old when she lost her father. Some members of the Burnham family lived in Hopkinton, New Hampshire.

With land values so expensive in Chebacco; this was likely a better place for a young family to settle. The families that settled there did so in spite of the dangers in the area with raids from the Native allies of the French in Canada. If Abigail and her family had settled in Hopkinton, they needed to return to Chebacco after Nehemiah's death.

The role of Abigail's mother, like all colonial farm women, was to be "obedient, faithful, frugal, fertile and industrious,"[2] It is unknown if she had ever remarried. A widow of Nehemiah Burnham appears on the 1782 householders list in the 9th district, known as Thompson's Island, which was possibly Abigail's mother.[3] The exact details of their home remain a mystery. The widow and her children may have lived with relatives. For a family in Chebacco, a farm of forty acres was enough land to live comfortably on. This land may have not been all continuous as some was needed for growing crops and orchards. Other land was necessary for grazing animals and a woodlot was a necessity for cutting up firewood for cooking and heating the home. Parcels of land may have been separated from one another within the town. If men practiced a trade or were a fisherman, they may have gotten by with less land.[4] While walking down the road in present day Essex, still a quaint New England town, I let my imagination and mind continue to wander with the story of how the couple may have first met.

…..Abigail approached the well in her homespun clothes, a sign of her support of the boycott of British goods. These homespun clothes became a politically recognized symbol of liberty and colonial resistance for the women of Massachusetts prior to the Revolution. The women's boycott of British made goods and tea was a powerful and effective tool, causing British merchants to put political pressure on Parliament to change laws in their favor.[5] Abigail was a strong willed young woman of twenty four, and like many women of the time was well read and politically knowledgeable, in spite of her place as a woman in society. Talk of revolution prompted women to think of their own independence. Abigail's long hair was tied up in a knot to keep it out of her dark intelligent eyes. Not only intelligence but kindness could be sensed within her. The loss of her father as a young girl made her more independent than other young women in the village. She approached the well and dropped the wooden bucket down open faced so as not to disturb the bottom and add silt to the water. She brought the water about halfway up the deep well and began to struggle with the weight. The crank was broken and needed repair like many other things on the farm.

As he traveled down the dusty dirt road Abraham saw a young woman about his age struggling with a rope at the edge of a well. He was desperately looking for work in the small village, his money had run out and he hoped that by doing a little farm work he might earn a meal. By the young woman's shaking arms he could see she was having difficulty pulling the rope up to bring the bucket of water out of the well. Jumping over the low fence he walked up behind her with the morning sun at his back. As Abigail struggled with the bucket she first saw a tall shadow loom behind her and suddenly became aware of two hands that reached down the well beside her, and he quickly helped lift up the rope and heavy bucket.

Turning to her side she looked up into the eyes and kind face of a man dressed in well worn yet well made fashionable clothing. Abigail said, "Thank you for your help but I am more than capable of handling the chore." To this Abraham replied in his thick London accent, "I was simply passing by and thought I could be of assistance." He tried to turn while he looked into the loveliest dark eyes he had ever seen and stumbled over a log of firewood and landed abruptly on his back. Abigail giggled as she watched Abraham rise from the ground and dust off his clothes. Abraham began to laugh as well. They stood there staring into one another's eyes, not knowing what to say.

The couple were married December 9, 1779, in Chebacco, Massachusetts. Abigail was two months pregnant with their first child, which was not uncommon for colonial marriages of the time.[6] Often premature marital relations were blamed on an interesting Yankee custom known as bundling. This custom allowed young unmarried couples who were in serious relationships to spend the night together in the same bed, in various states of dress depending on which account of it you read.[7] There was supposed to be an understanding that the line of "innocent endearments" was not to be crossed.[8] It made sense to many people at the time that bundling under the sheets meant not as much firewood was needed to be burned to heat the room. Bundling in any case only happened between "special lovers" and probably only after much urging from an amorous Abraham.

Abigail gave birth to their first son, who they named Abraham, after the boy's father, on June 1, 1780.[9] Abraham junior was the first Channell to be born in the new nation. As a married woman, Abigail became by law a *feme cover*, otherwise known as a woman covered. This meant all that she owned including the clothes on her back belonged to her husband.[10] In spite of this, Abraham had Abigail's extended family populating the village all around, so he had to answer to them if he misused his authority. *Feme cover* existed according to the laws in New England during the period, influenced by British Common Law.

The work Abigail performed during the day was based upon the raw materials that were produced on the farm. Milk from the cow was churned into butter. Bread, pies, and other products were also made by hand. Apples from the orchard were dried or turned into cider; clothes also needed to be washed. Family needs were cared for first, with extra production being available for trade or sale. Any profit from this belonged to the husband, according to the existing laws. During the year 1780, Abraham Channell was taxed 17 pounds and 14 shillings in Chebacco to raise money for beef for soldiers in the war. The fighting was then taking place in the distant southern colonies.[11] He also was taxed 38 pounds and 7 shillings on his house and land.[12] The tax may not have seemed completely fair to a man no longer allowed to sign up and fight for his new country. But more importantly the tax shows that in a few short years after arriving in the country with empty pockets and no family or friends he had begun to amass property.

The beef tax showed a weakness within the American wartime government. The states were incapable and powerless politically to raise the money that was being asked for by Congress and they never met the fund amounts desperately needed to wage war. This tax was an appeal for specific quantities of food for the Continental troops instead of money. Even if the struggle was successful, those who offered supplies could only count on a promise for their future repayment. It shows the primitive ability of the young government to tax and the economic difficulty in placing value on food in a world with fluctuating currency. It was easier for the government to ask for food, rather than money. It made it impossible for the states to determine what to pay or for the government to ascertain how much they had received.[13]

Without funds to supply enough food, food and supplies were often "impressed," as Abraham had been impressed. The next worst thing to being taken captive without permission is having your food stolen. People were given certificates for future payment, but that would be a long time coming. After the war re-payment of the promissory notes varied tremendously, due to a poor organization system. The payment also depended on the urgency of the need.[14] In 1790, Alexander Hamilton estimated $16,708,000 in debt was still outstanding, a great deal of money in the late eighteenth century.[15] Victory had not come cheap. The cost of the Revolution to the former colonies had now begun to really pile up.

The money owed to Americans was only part of the picture. During the war money had first been borrowed from France, then Spain, and later from Holland.[16] Initially money from France was secured with the promise of tobacco and other products. These products also had to pass the patrolling British ships that were still off the coast. Without Captain Burr or Abraham Channell, the *Milford* and other ships still, nevertheless, continued to hunt for American ships. The government had the power to get into debt, but did not have the power to raise money to pay it.[17] Taxation after the war may have been an influence on Abraham's later decision to leave. If one thing came out of all the financial woes of the period, it was the fact that it brought forth a need, viewed by some, for a new Constitution.

In 1782, Abraham appeared on the householders list living in the 10th district in the eastern part of Chebacco. Families like the Channells were closely tied with their land. A large amount of sheep were raised in the 1770 period; sheep husbandry was not labor intensive, and this allowed for inhabitants to practice a side trade such as tailoring. Land was useful in three ways; as woodlot for firewood, pasture for animals, and an area where the orchard, garden, and outbuildings could be found. In Chebacco, there were broad marshes that could be used as feed for sheep. It was not used for cows because it led to sour tasting milk.[18] The hay could also be cut and sold to neighboring communities. Since many townspeople left the area because of the expense of acquiring land there, Abraham may have sourced the money to purchase the home and land from his success as a privateer. It certainly did not come from his family in Britain. It may have come from his in-laws the Burnham and Choate families, through his wife Abigail.

A year after the birth of his first son Abraham on June 1, 1780, a second son William was added to the family on December 27, 1781. The birth of William occurred a few months after Washington and his French allies won at Yorktown. British General Cornwallis feigned illness to avoid handing his sword over to Washington, and sent out a subordinate to surrender. Aware of the slight, Washington sent out General Benjamin Lincoln, who had chased the British fleet and *Milford* from the outer islands of Boston Harbor to accept the sword. The French Navy and American Army, after their initial failure in Rhode Island, had finally learned to work together. Abraham's son William later answered the call of the sea and was eventually married in Cape May, New Jersey. He became a farmer in Port Elizabeth, New Jersey.

A year later in 1782, a daughter was born whom the couple named Abigail, after her mother. Frances, who they called Fanny, was the next daughter born in 1784. Between the births of these two girls the Treaty of Paris was signed and ratified, ending the American Revolution. The freedom that Abraham had fought for was finally theirs. These children were followed by: Robert in 1785, Betsy in 1787, and Sally in 1793, a twin sister to Sally was born who did not survive. Abigail was kept very busy nursing and caring for all these children.

While Abraham raised his young family, a seed was planted for a new government to replace the Articles of Confederation. The Articles had been in force since 1777, and had served as a Constitution for the fledgling American government. The document accomplished a great deal during its time. The Articles had carried the nation through a long difficult war and through the economic hardships that followed. The young nation began to quickly grow and expand under the document. George Washington had felt comfortable enough with the government under the articles to retire back to Mount Vernon after the war. The seed of the Constitution was watered, however, by the blood of a new revolution in western Massachusetts, prior to its conception in Philadelphia and later adoption in Massachusetts.

The new federal Constitution ratified in Massachusetts in 1788, was not readily accepted by all. Delegates from Essex overwhelmingly voted for the new Constitution, thirty-eight votes for and only six votes against.[19] Overall the voting in Massachusetts stood at 187 for to 168 against, and this edge occurred only after some last minute political maneuvering.[20] Essex County in Massachusetts, where Abraham lived, was a Federalist stronghold. The further away from the coast a man traveled, however, the more the support for the document dropped. It was here in the western hills of Massachusetts that farmers began to stand up against the state government and its new aristocracy. These "Anti-Federalists," often lumped in with the Shaysites, were scattered throughout the state. Taxation was again at the center of unrest, only this time from within.

In 1785, John Hancock retired from his office as Governor of Massachusetts. At this time there was an initial postwar economic boom throughout the young nation. James Bowdoin, his successor as governor, sought to support the mercantile and creditor class. He raised taxes sharply in Massachusetts in order to pay off the war debt, over a fifteen-year period of time.[21] This sharp rise in taxes, in combination with a decrease in farm prices, may have been a trigger for Abraham leaving and moving to New Hampshire. It caused the beginning of what is now called the Shays Rebellion in Massachusetts. It was led by Daniel Shays and other farmers in the western part of the state. Shays had many sympathizers in the region, but not as many supporters as he needed for his movement to succeed and help his fellow farmers.

Along with tax issues, the group had several other problems with the relatively new 1780 Massachusetts Constitution.[22] The center of government was far away in Boston for one thing. It was not centrally located within the state, and required a long expensive trip on horseback or wagon to get to any meetings. This made it difficult for their voices to be heard. Could they have seen this as another form of taxation without representation? Abraham's later departure from Massachusetts may show him to have been a sympathizer of the rebellion against the new mercantile aristocrats. Was he among the men and women who supported the rebellion in order to cope in a new nation after the revolution had failed them? In Vermont Ethan Allen wrote of and waged a similar struggle described as "poor honest men of the land and the princes of privilege." Did Abraham also dislike these new "princes of privilege?" Some farmers felt they paid an unfair share of taxes when compared with this new business and political elite. Some things never change.

Daniel Shays was an unlikely rebel. He had enthusiastically joined and served in the Revolution from its earliest days. He fought at Bunker Hill and throughout the rest of the war. He rose in rank to the level of captain through his own talent and initiative. Shays was honored with a sword that was presented to him by the French General Lafayette. Times were so hard after the war that in order to make ends meet and survive he was forced to sell the sword. He also was forced to sell off half his acreage to meet his debts. Later, he and others, after petitioning the state for debt relief to no avail, began to march on the courts to try to shut them down.[23] In many ways Shays was merely continuing his struggle against the new tyrants now in power.

The movement was later stopped by an armed confrontation with General Benjamin Lincoln, who led a private army organized by Governor Bowdoin. Although never mentioned in textbooks as anything other than government troops, the force was in all respects a mercenary force hired by wealthy private citizens with much to gain from the courts staying open. The rebellion is usually given as a reason for the federal Constitution being needed. The question is whether the Constitution was created to establish a system of laws and governance to avoid future rebellions like that of Shays, or to provide the creation of a wealthy class and the opportunity for great fortunes to be created for the new national elite.

Exactly how Abraham felt about the now venerated federal Constitution is unknown; he did, however, move increasingly north and west into the rural farming areas where the document was disliked, and into an area the Shaysites were known to have fled to. His religious view is unknown, however, the lack of religious requirements in the document could have worried him and been a factor in his decision. What if Godless men won an office in the new government? There were many allegations that delegates had been bought off with money from New York in order to vote for the document and that may have angered Abraham as well.

Many members of the wealthy elite held securities and paper that had become incredibly valuable when the Constitution passed and the new federal government assumed responsibility of payment. Ex-Governor Bowdoin owned a large amount of this paper himself. Not surprisingly, after losing his office as governor he was a strong proponent of the new federal Constitution.[24] Many farmers and war veterans were forced to sell off the worthless paper and promissory notes paid out during the Revolution for pennies on the dollar afterward. They had no insider information that this paper would rise dramatically in value after the debt was absorbed. The new aristocracy had little sympathy for men like Shays or Abraham who had risked their lives to win them their economic opportunity.

The federal Constitution also offered the elite a measure of protection against the far less wealthy majority which included tailors and farmers such as Abraham. As we now know the members of this group had both frightened and threatened the wealthy citizens when Daniel Shays and the other men rebelled against the tyranny of the courts that sought to take away their homes in the bad economy that followed the initial boom after the revolution. James Madison wrote that the elite class he represented also wanted to protect themselves from "an overbearing majority which will make its "rights" paramount, and sacrifice the "rights" of the minority." He continued with this thought when he wrote of protecting, "private rights against the danger of such a faction and at the same time preserve the spirit and the form of popular government is then the great object to which our inquiries are directed." The Constitution created both wealth for those who had not risked their lives aboard privateers, and protected the rich from men who had sacrificed and fought for everyone's freedom. They had risked their lives to later see their homes and property foreclosed on by those wealthy citizens who had risked nothing.

Not all of the elite members of society supported the Constitution. Elbridge Gerry served in the Continental Congress throughout the war. He was among those called to amend the Articles of Confederation. When the meeting turned from amending the document to creating an entirely new one, he went along with them, but had reservations with the final document. He felt that, "people lacked adequate means to control their representatives," and that Congress had, "too many ambiguous and dangerous powers," with "too much power in the hands of a few."[25] Elbridge Gerry was not alone with his thoughts. Those who have never heard of him may be surprised to hear he later became the fifth Vice President of the United States.

Another elite member of society who had reservations with the document was Rufus King. King first served as an officer in the Revolution under General Sullivan, and later as a member of the Congress after the war came to a close. King was an early opponent of slavery and had issues with the Constitution, although he was a Federalist and politically supported the passing of it. He knew that those who opposed it had, "apprehension that the liberties of the people are in danger..." and that they felt the document created the, "establishment of two Orders in the Society, one comprehending the Opulent and Great, the other the poor and illiterate." Passing the document would not be an easy task. King lost his election for the United States Presidency in 1816 to James Monroe.

The man who wrote "give me liberty or give me death" did not want to be given a new Constitution. Patrick Henry chose to defend the Revolution by refusing to attend the convention because he "smelled a rat." He recognized all the accomplishments that had been made under the Articles of Confederation and did not wish to see it cast aside. When they argued the document in Virginia he stated:

> ...shall a government which has been thus strong and vigorous be accused of imbecility, and abandoned for want of energy? Consider what you are about to do, before you part with this government.[26]

Henry clearly believed the government was performing well and may have thought there was an agenda behind abandoning it. He did not seem to share the opinion that the Articles of Confederation had failed. He went on to point out that in the past history of the world there had been "instances of the people losing their liberty by their own carelessness and the ambition of a few."[27] He may have feared the Constitution had the power to do just that. Any document creating government is likely to take away the freedom of some. Today people can stand in judgment of the document and decide whether men like Shays, Gerry, and Henry were right.

Many revolutionary thinkers in the 18th century had read Locke and his viewpoint that in nature there existed a state of perfect equality in which no man enjoyed any kind of right or authority or dignity beyond another. Yet this romantic notion was swept aside as the greed of human nature reared its ugly head after the cause of liberty was won.[28] Benjamin Franklin, compared the new nation to Europe in 1782, and stated that, "it is rather a general happy Mediocrity that prevails."[29] The divide between the wealthy and common man in the new United States was not as great as it was in Britain right after the war. Critics of the Constitution may have seen the seed within the document of this divide being created. It was not long after the document was created that the first millionaires in the new nation came into existence. In reality, money is only one form of wealth. In the post revolution world of Abraham, the wealth that he created and the seed he planted was one of a new American family. With his British family gone, this must have meant a lot to him.

The world that Abraham now lived in was a world of opportunity, in spite of politics. Franklin again stated the necessary attitude and perseverance it took to succeed in the new nation:

> If they are poor, they begin first as Servants or Journeymen; and
> if they are sober, industrious, and frugal, they soon become
> Masters, establish themselves in Business, marry, raise Families,
> and become respectable Citizens.

Franklin had begun his life much like Abraham, serving first as a printer apprentice to his brother. Abraham achieved all of these things Franklin mentioned in the years during and following the American Revolution. There was a growing elite and new aristocracy in the young nation, but Abraham enjoyed more opportunity than he had in London. However, as the years went on he either saw a lack of opportunity or saw others doing far better in a land where there was more opportunity for some than others.

Having a large family was an economic necessity on a farm, and women were respected for their fertility and ability to produce large numbers of healthy children. Abigail did well in this department, filling Abraham's life and home with several young children. Abraham added to the family wealth when he purchased seven acres of land March 31, 1788, from John Langsford, yeoman (farmer), for 34 pounds, 4 shillings, and 4d.[30] Viewed today as a large parcel of land, it may have been marshland to supply food for livestock, or a woodlot for firewood. Either way it did add to Abraham's estate. The family seemed to grow and prosper during the late war and following years. Abraham kept busy with tailoring and he learned how to farm from his in-laws in the small village of Chebacco.

The Channell children needed to be taught how to read and write. They also needed to be taught basic math skills. Enough writing exists from Abraham to know that he was literate. Education often fell to the mother, who may have taught them their letters and words. The first book they read was the Bible. The verses in the Bible were already well known to Abraham's children from their time sitting in the pews of the local church. This served and supported their early literacy. Another famous text they may have encountered in their education was the *New England Primer*. Within the text was the following lesson:

Pray to God. Call no ill names. Love God. Use no ill words.
Fear God. Tell no lies. Serve God. Hate Lies. Take not God's
Speak the Truth. Name in vain. Spend your Time well. Do not
Swear. Love your School. Do not Steal. Mind your Book.
Cheat not in your play. Strive to learn. Play not with bad boys.
Be not a Dunce.[31]

The wisdom in the New England Primer is great advice on how to live, but it is no easier to achieve today than it was then. We always wish for our children to have qualities that we often are unable to display in our own lives.

Sheep husbandry in Chebacco supplied Abraham with the material to support his tailoring business. At this time all manufacturing of wool took place in the home. It was a product that was produced by hand in the farmhouse. Shearing, carding, spinning, and weaving this product may have provided Abraham with some of the material he needed in his tailoring business. When the colonies declared their independence, they created an increase in domestically produced cloth that was in short supply, and a material that Abraham needed to support his trade. This product could not compete with the quality of the British made cloth. All this later changed, and led to a second revolution. This one was a revolution of industry that began in 1790, in Pawtucket, Rhode Island.

The couple lived together for some time as indicated by the birth of their children. Two years between children was typical, marital relations were avoided during nursing in the 18th century.[32] At some time during their relationship Abraham left and went to New Hampshire. He may have been looking for more land, expanding his tailoring business, or been escaping a marriage that had been tested by the death of their twin daughter who passed away after only two days of life. We have seen that taxes were high, and other farms struggled during the time. Also, Abigail was sick with tuberculosis, and Abraham may have been trying to keep his children or himself away from his terribly ill wife.

Watching Abigail waste away and slowly die from the disease known then as consumption must have been horrible for Abraham and the couple's seven children, the oldest of which was only fourteen. The girl with the dark intelligent eyes, and the first love of Abraham's life passed away on June 21, 1794. Her death was recorded in the records of the Chebacco Parish Church. Her headstone speaks through the ages of her love of poetry. Quoting a poem written by Alexander Pope entitled Elegy to the Memory of an Unfortunate lady:

> How loved, how honour'd once,
> Avails thee not,
> A heap of dust alone remains of thee
> Tis all thou art,
> And all the proud shall be!

The Elegy was published by Pope in 1717, and the lines appear near the end of the poem on line 71. The poem was a popular one to put on gravestones and appears on several markers I've seen from that era. The willow tree engraved on the slate weeps for the loss of Abigail who died at the age of forty with several young children and Abraham left behind. The stone still stands in the Old Graveyard that dates back to 1680, in the Town of Essex at 28 Main Street, behind what is today the Essex Shipbuilding Museum. Abraham and his children had to find a way to go on without her. A man with seven young children to care for alone has his hands full, and Abraham needed to try to fill Abigail's shoes as best he could. The memorial to Abigail Channel preserved in Essex at the Cogswell Grant puts forth the following statement:

> Farewell dear friend a short farewell
> Till we shall meet again above:
> In the sweet Groves where pleasures dwell,
> And Trees of Life, bear fruits of love.

The memorial was drawn and painted by William Saville, of Gloucester, who was a schoolmaster and went on to become the town clerk in Rockport for 20 years.[33] The words were part of a hymn written by Isaac Watts. After leaving the Cogswell Grant and the beautiful paintings of my ancestors, I traveled to Salem to read the papers of Abraham's next father-in-law.

I arrived at the Peabody Essex Museum and Library in Salem and after parking my trusty car in a multi-level garage I walked into the Library for the first time. The library is a treasure trove of American maritime history and documents. I searched again for the records on the computer, and brought the results to the librarian behind the counter. I was surprised to find out I was getting the actual documents themselves. After going in the back storage room the librarian returned with a large cardboard box of documents which I immediately carried over to a large wooden table in the research room. I was surprised when the librarian turned and left me alone with the ancient documents. Normally, at other archives I looked at microfilm and not the actual documents. I did not immediately start finding what I was looking for. I took out one aging yellow document after another, taking in the sight and smell of great age. I did not know what I might find hidden away inside those 215 year old papers.

Minutes turned into hours and time seemed to stand still as I sat at the wooden table and flipped through the dry and fragile old papers. The fact that they survived and that I had somehow found them was a huge stroke of luck. Luck comes to those who do not give up the search. I was ravenous in my anticipation of finding some clue of the tragic relationship that had existed between them. The life story of Abraham could not after all just be tall ships and war. When I finally saw the name Channel on one of the documents the letter quickly became a time machine and transported me back to the era as if I was listening in from another room, or staring through a keyhole into the past. It was as if I had become some type of time traveling voyeur who was invading their privacy. The papers told me more than I could have ever expected to learn about their life together.

Abraham's next relationship was short-lived, but he entered the family of one of the most respected men in the village of Chebacco. A man who had known and dined with President George Washington. My hands trembled with the fascinating details of their relationship in the ancient papers I held in my hands on the table in the library that day. This was not the history of war or politics. This was the history of a family; and the more I knew the less I seemed to understand. Understanding relationships obscured by time may be the most difficult of historical challenges. I hoped I was up to the challenge as I painstakingly transcribed the papers.

The Ministers Daughter

Abraham was trying to make a new start in New Hampshire in the towns of Hopkinton and Weare. His children either lived with him or with relatives in Chebacco, while he worked as a traveling tailor and farmer in the New Hampshire region.[1] Abraham often returned to Salem and Boston when he needed supplies and cloth for tailoring that were available at the busy port cities. Earlier in America, before the war, the wealthy ordered their clothes from Britain so they could have the latest fashion. The outbreak of the struggle for independence changed all that, and for a while at least Abraham was one of the only tailors who could be turned to for a fashionably made outfit. For a time tailors were looked down upon in Essex County. The Rev. Nathaniel Ward of Ipswich once wrote in the seventeenth century, "If taylors were men indeed, well furnished but with mere moral principles, they would disdain to be led about like apes...It is a most unworthy thing for men that have bones in them to spend their lives in making fidle-cases for futilous women's phansies."[2] In the eyes of Ward, making clothes was the work of women, and the reverend may have been jealous that the tailor knew as much gossip in town as he did. To some people alive then, any business other than farming was distasteful.

Abraham was a welcome sight when he came to town and brought news to the rural countryside from the big cities of Massachusetts. Isolated in the hill towns of New Hampshire, he brought them up to date on current events and enjoyed a homemade meal while he visited their farms. He often enjoyed the warmth of their barns and an occasional tavern for a place to sleep while he traveled in the area.[3] He may also have sold cloth to the women who lived in the farmhouses, and made coats for the wealthier members of the community such as Colonel Nathaniel Fifield. Whose daughter, Abraham is rumored to have had more than a friendly relationship with.

Abraham had gone to church in Chebacco and prayed for assistance with the deep sorrow he felt for the loss of Abigail, and the loneliness that had become part of his everyday existence, even with the large family his wife had blessed him with. After a failed romance and relationship with Colonel Nathaniel Fifield's daughter in Weare, New Hampshire, he returned to Chebacco, where he began a relationship with Elizabeth Cleaveland. Elizabeth was thirty-seven and was said to have had an illegitimate teenage daughter named Lois in a book written about her father, John Cleaveland. Looking at Cleaveland's will this appears to have been untrue. Most importantly, Elizabeth had a loving father and family who had supported her throughout her unmarried spinster life. Whatever flaws she possessed in her character that kept her unmarried for so long were overlooked by Abraham in his desire to try to replace his deceased wife Abigail. Elizabeth's flaws would later be revealed in their relationship. With such an accomplished father it makes sense that Abraham wanted to join the stable family, but he may have jumped too quickly into the new relationship. In the royal navy Cleaveland would have been known as a devil-dodger, but her father was truly a great man. His words on the documents in Salem revealed to me that he had been a thoughtful caring man of God.

Reverend John Cleaveland was born in Connecticut to a farming family and later became a student at Yale. When Cleaveland broke college rules and attended a sermon preached by his uncle Solomon, a layman not certified to preach in the state, Cleaveland was made an example of to other members of his Yale class and expelled from the institution without the degree that he was about to receive. This punishment stopped him from becoming a legally practicing minister in Connecticut. It was this unfortunate situation that brought him to Massachusetts, and eventually to Chebacco (Essex), Massachusetts, where a degree to minister was not needed.[4] His experience as a New

Light minister who challenged the power of the state to control his ministering is not much unlike his later challenge to the British Crown. Cleaveland was not afraid to confront authority when he disagreed with it.

In 1758, during the French and Indian War, Cleaveland served as a chaplain in the army that gathered to attack the French and their Native allies. He rode out to Albany, New York, and then north to minister to the troops during the disastrous attack led by British General James Abercrombie, on the French Fort Carillion, later known as Ticonderoga, at Lake Champlain. It was here that Cleaveland was first exposed to British troops. He clearly disapproved of them when he wrote, "God would remove wicked-ness from the camp" in response to "gaming, robbery, thief, whoring, bad-company-keeping, etc."[5] Cleaveland was fully supportive of the break with Britain years later. British General Abercrombie was recalled to Britain and left with an intense dislike of America. He had failed in his leadership in America and disliked the colonies thereafter, and blamed them in part for his defeat. He later supported the many coercive acts as a member of Parliament that led to the American Revolution. The future father-in-law of Abraham Channell was again made a chaplain to the military during the early time of the Revolution, at the very outbreak of hostilities.

Postcard of Chebacco Church, authors collection.

While Cleaveland served as a chaplain in Cambridge, Massachusetts, men from his town served and died at the Battle of Bunker Hill. Cleaveland preached in support of the men that marched off to dig in at the hill, and prayed for the souls of many brave men who had died after the battle was fought on June 17, 1775. Reverend Cleaveland first preached all the members of his church into the army, and then served the cause of liberty in any way that he could. In spite of being a man of God, he carried at his side a sword with a buck horn handle, just in case he needed to protect himself. It was either in Cambridge or during his later service ministering troops in New York when he met General Washington; not yet the revered leader he later became.

Following the Revolution, on October 30, 1789, newly elected President George Washington was on a presidential tour of Massachusetts, and Reverend Cleaveland came out to visit him. As Cleaveland walked towards The President he took off his hat and tucked it under his arm out of respect. Washington smiled in recognition of the chaplain and said, "Put your hat back upon your head Parson and I will gladly shake your hand." Cleaveland replied, "That he could not wear his hat in his presence, when he thought of all he had done for his country." "You did as much as I," said Washington. "No, no" said Cleaveland. Washington continued, "Yes, you did what you could, and I've done no more." This moment was recorded 100 years later by the *Salem Gazette* and shows how Cleaveland's patriotic actions were remembered by later generations.[6] Washington invited Cleaveland to dine with him; the invitation is also in the collection of the Peabody Essex Museum in Salem, Massachusetts.[7]

Abigail Channell, Abraham's first wife, had been a member of Cleaveland's Church her whole life. Cleaveland had watched her grow up as a young child and had known her parents and family. Cleaveland likely married her and Abraham, and was probably present at her funeral and burial at the old cemetery in downtown Chebacco (Essex). On November 8, 1794, Cleaveland wrote in response to a letter that he received from his daughter Elizabeth, this was in regards to a marriage proposal that she had received from Abraham:

> My Dear Daughter,
> You wish me to answer yours in writing----I hardly know what to write you---I (know) My children have a right to choose for themselves.--- And I have a right to give them my best advice and counsel.----It is probable you will outlive me, and a lonely life is not desirable.---However, I have by my late will

endeavored to make your single-state as my small estate will admit of, should you remain in a single state till after my decease:--Yes I should rejoice to have you change your state while I am alive; Provided you can better yourself by it.[8]

One way of measuring status in the nineteenth century was through economic wealth; as it remains today. It was then said, "The only way women can rise in the world-by marriage."[9] It seems that Cleaveland felt Abraham was not up to their economic status in the community and she might not rise in stature. Cleaveland had used his professional status as a minister to better himself through marriage. His 45 acre farm in Chebacco was purchased for him by supporters in his wife's family.[10]

Cleaveland did understand loneliness from the loss of his first wife Mary, and may have understood Abraham's desire to have a wife to not only keep him company, but to help in the raising of his large family. Cleaveland continues in the letter:

[A]nd be in a situation to serve God and your generation with Christian reputation.---You will need much wisdom and Grace, tenderly and faithfully, to train up a family of children, not your own, so as to please your husband. Keep peace in the family and a conscience void of offense toward God and men.---as you are a Projector Of faith in Christ. And of repentance toward God,-and have always lived where the social worship of God has been daily performed in the family morning and evening.---It is but reasonable that you should express to him, in some proper way, your expectation as an encouragement of your becoming a joint head with him of his family to train them up in the nature and admonition of the Lord. That he will maintain or perform the social worship of God in his family—to beg daily for the Blessings of God upon the whole family, the heads and members of it.---You see I do not disapprove but leave you to God and your own conscience, and shall while I live, ever pray for you, whether you shall be in a single or married state.
Your affectionate Father,
My daughter Elizabeth Cleaveland
John Cleaveland

Cleaveland had concerns about his daughter being up to the task of raising the children, having been brought up as a "pretty soft creature," and spoiled by her middle class existence. She may have fit the criticism and question, "can they govern a family, or take care of the poor babes whom they bring into the world?"[11] Cleaveland also worried about her bringing the children up as good Christians. He seemed to have concerns about Abraham bringing them up with as good a religious foundation as Cleaveland might expect. The good reverend should have questioned if she was up to the challenge of being a good wife. In spite of his concerns, his daughter Elizabeth chose to marry Abraham.

The Reverend Cleaveland performed the marriage ceremony on New Year's Day, January 1, 1795.[12] Not long after the couple traveled to Weare, New Hampshire where Abraham had previously bought a farm that consisted of 174 acres in the northeast section of the town on Sugar Hill, which bordered the town of Dunbarton. He purchased this farm on December 19, 1793. But could Elizabeth overcome the question whether if, "marriage can eradicate the habitude of life?"[13] Could Elizabeth change and become a hardworking farm mother and wife or remain a grown yet dependent child away from her parents?

Abraham bought the farm and 174 acres of land[14] from James Hogg who had been singled out in February, 1793, for having smallpox in his house. This announcement set off a great fear in the town of Weare. A town meeting was ordered on March 2, 1793, to decide what to do. The decision was for Hogg to remove the two infected persons, his children, out of town immediately. The town leaders apparently did not care if another town was infected, as long as the family was out of their own proximity. Hogg sent a letter to the selectmen telling them he could not comply with their demand. The town went wild when Hogg refused to leave and they put three men in charge of making sure Hogg got out of town.[15] The townspeople apparently did not want to go near the house either. People were terrified of smallpox at this time in history. Abraham was apparently unafraid of the disease, perhaps he had already survived it or been inoculated. Abraham bought the home for five hundred pounds; a steal. How he exactly came up with the money is a mystery, maybe he still had some privateer loot to spend. There were no thirty year mortgages then, you had to have access to the funds quick. Abraham was certainly better off financially than his father-in-law gave him credit for.

Abraham and Elizabeth lived in the farmhouse when their daughter Mary Cleaveland Channell was born November 4, 1796. Weare, New Hampshire was sparsely settled and still very much a frontier town.

This era of farming in New Hampshire has been called, "the age of self sufficiency," due to the distance from cities and towns, and the need for farmers to produce their own food. Given the difficulties of achieving this, great profits from clearing and improving property could be made. The highway running near his house was nothing more than a narrow path that traveled around fallen stumps in the way. To accommodate wagons and stagecoaches and to turn a profit for its investors a turnpike system grew. The road system took tremendous expense and manpower to create. In 1796, the first turnpike charter was approved and the building of the first turnpike to run from nearby Concord to a bridge near Portsmouth was begun.[16] With simple hand tools and the strength of beasts such as oxen to aid the road-builders, the paths were later expanded much wider and straightened to allow the sun to dry them out and make them passable after the rain or snow fell. As a traveling tailor, Abraham was well aware of, and made use of this new system.

In 1803, a man wrote of the great hazards and challenges that faced men like Abraham as they traveled along the early roads and turnpikes of New Hampshire:

> The forests they could not cut down; the rocks they could not remove; the swamps they could not causey; and over the streams they could not erect bridges. Men, women and children ventured daily through this combination of evils, penetrated the recesses of the wilderness, climbed the hills, wound their way among the rocks, struggled through the mire, and swam on horseback through deep and rapid rivers by which they were sometimes carried away.[17]

The landscape today is not so different than it was then. A powerful snowfall or heavy rains can quickly change the New Hampshire roads from safe to hazardous and return them to the wild nature they were wrought from. It was not safe to travel west of the coastal areas of New Hampshire prior to the end of the French and Indian War. For Abraham the threat of native attack was gone, but all the other hazards of water crossings and trees falling in a strong wind to block the path of travelers still existed.

The indigenous natives originated these paths as they trod back and forth between the lakes and the seacoast to take advantage of the bounty that the different seasons and regions offered. The presence of these native paths are overlooked in the stories of early settlement and of their use in the military struggles that were first fought out between native people, and later between the French and British throughout their efforts to conquer North America. The rivers and paths of these native people extended from the seacoast of New England to Canada, and are therefore an important part of the story of Abraham. Without these paths he could not have traveled far in the dense northern hardwood forests of New England.

Sugar Hill flowed high alongside the Channell farm with a ridge-line extending three miles. It is one of fifteen hills located in the town of Weare, New Hampshire. Planting crops was difficult and hunting and fishing were needed to provide extra food for the family. While hunting in the hills, Abraham had to be on the lookout for catamount, a large northern mountain lion, and for bear, that were often seen on Sugar Hill. Sugar Hill likely got its name from the maple trees that grew all along it. Abraham learned to tap the trees in the spring to catch the sweet sap. Native inhabitants first taught European immigrants how to turn the sap into sugar by pouring the sap onto heated rocks. The resulting product they called "*sinzibukwud*," made Americans in the Northeast self sufficient from European slave sugar production by providing an answer to their sugar needs. At that time the maple sap was boiled down to a sugar that was easier to store and use for cooking than the syrup we are familiar with today. The maple sugar offered Abraham a long lasting food source that provided energy for farm chores. Benjamin Franklin, urged by his friend Benjamin Rush, pushed for the Northeast to produce as much of this sugar as possible; it was one of the most important food crops at that time. The product was even thought to have been able to battle slavery.

The majority of British sugar was harvested by slaves in the Caribbean. Benjamin Rush was a Quaker who was bitterly opposed to slavery. Franklin's friend Rush invited guests such as Alexander Hamilton and other men and ladies of society to tea to promote the use of maple sugar as a sweetener to replace the cane sugar harvested by slaves. Although a slave holder himself, Thomas Jefferson promoted the use of maple sugar, due to his interest in botany and American products.

Jefferson and Monroe visited upstate New York in 1791, and then Bennington, Vermont, both near the shore of Lake Champlain, where they urged citizens to plant orchards of maple trees, as Jefferson later attempted to do at Monticello. Unfortunately, people preferred cane sugar to maple sugar and it never caught on. Other attempts were made at maple whiskey and beer. After a few years this "sugar fever" ended.[18] It is an interesting and curious coincidence that the wave of interest in maple sugar occurred when Abraham took up residence on "Sugar Hill."

After sugar cane production won out over maple, the product later became primarily used for syrup. Early Americans did not seem to be interested in the slave origins of the products they bought. Sugar cane is the sugar source that poisons today's food with its overuse which leads to childhood obesity and diabetes. Maple sugar is expensive today, but well worth the extra money for its extraordinary taste.

Near Abraham's farm there was good fishing in the Piscataquog River. His children ran in the clearing that surrounded his farm and played games such as graces and hoop and roll to keep them occupied when there were no chores to do. They grew strong and tall there in the hill country. Isolation in the woods caused the children to be close and caring to one another. They all worked together as a family to help their father. Abraham rose early and worked hard to make his farm a success. When his sons grew they joined him in the fields. During the winter he could work as a tailor. Although born in one of the great cities of the world, Abraham began to love the hills and mountains of northern New England. They had become his new home.

It is probable that his farm raised cattle, sheep, and/or pigs. Long before cattle were raised in the west and put on railroads for the east, there was still a need and ready market for beef. At that time cattle were raised in New Hampshire and other frontier areas and then driven down to the cities of Salem and Boston by men known as drovers. Farmers drove as many as six hundred sheep and over one hundred cattle to the area. The roads widened to highways as the cattle were driven closer to market and stagecoaches began to offer transportation to the area. The cattle ate the roadside weeds and plants to maintain their weight for market. In the winter, farmers like Abraham transported pork, butter, and cheese with a sled pulled by two horses that averaged forty miles a day.[19] This business brought Abraham back to Chebacco frequently to stay at his home in the town, and visit his friends and family there. The roads back to Essex County quickly improved from the growth of the new road system.

The turnpike system was rapidly expanding in New Hampshire when Abraham began to settle there in the 1790's. The road building in the area had been put on hold during the American Revolution, but was now pursued in earnest.[20] The establishment of states rights in the new Constitution allowed for eminent domain to take over private land to build these roads. Farmers may have been reimbursed for their property, but just how this value was arrived at may have been hotly argued. The exact route of these turnpikes was also disputed. If the turnpike did not go through your town, your property value might be diminished. If the turnpike passed within reach of your property it might gradually increase its value as it did for Abraham.

These turnpikes were planned and constructed by turnpike corporations chartered by the state legislature.[21] The expense of building these roads was great. Lotteries were approved in order to raise money to support the road construction.[22] The roads were sometimes called "artificial" roads due to their being constructed "with a stratum of gravel or pounded stones."[23] The turnpike approved to be built between Concord and Durham, New Hampshire in 1791, allowed for faster travel to Chebacco for Abraham, but took his new wife Elizabeth farther away from her home and community by the sea.[24]

Elizabeth left a community she knew her whole life and she missed the salt air of the ocean and the familiar faces in her old town. She was saddened by her inability to hear her father preach in church on Sunday. She longed to see the boats launched into the river and missed the taste of freshly caught seafood. Her family and friends were all back in Chebacco, and she had taken on the difficult responsibility of raising a family full of young children and her own infant child. The chores involved in caring for children, working the farm, and cooking meals may not have been enjoyable to a woman raised with slaves and servants to do much of the work. She quickly began to feel that she had made a terrible mistake, in spite of the vows that she had taken in front of her father and her community.

One family that Abraham had befriended who lived nearby on Sugar Hill was the Peaslee's. The Peaslee family had continually moved to the fringes of society due to their own religious ideals that differed from traditional views for a hundred years. In the late 18th century they were practicing Quakers, and a small community of Quakers lived among them in Weare.[25] As the daughter of a minister, Elizabeth was probably quite inflexible in her beliefs, and may not have enjoyed the company of this group. The Quakers had no need for a minister like her father to tell them how to worship. They worshiped on their own, and carried on their own conversation with God.

Elizabeth's unhappiness is shown in a letter from her brother John to her father in Chebacco May 14, 1795:

> Today I went to visit sister Channel and found her much
> …..from her late illness I pity the poor woman………Wants to
> have me settle here to relieve her from her melancholy thoughts,
> I endeavor to give her the best advice I am capable of. Her
> husband appears to treat her with great kindness and affection. I
> wish she may have grace to give superior… to all the momentary
> troubles of this transitory life, …with cheerfulness discharge the
> duties incumbent on her.[26]

Her brother asked other members of her family who lived in Chebacco to write to her and help her through her troubles. The letter may show that she also suffered from some type of depression. Unfortunately, after only a few months the marriage was in trouble. The couple's daughter Mary was born in Weare, but on January 18, 1797, Elizabeth left Abraham with their daughter Mary, and returned to Chebacco to her father's house. Abraham put in the papers that she had left "contrary to my desire" and that he would not be responsible for any charges she incurred after January 30, 1797.

Reverend Cleaveland was at this time in the latter stages of his life and surely struggled with the added expense of his daughter and granddaughter's return home. Having two more mouths to feed and a young infant to care for created more work in the Cleaveland household. Elizabeth had abandoned her husband Abraham in New Hampshire, and in order to get a divorce she had to provide reasons such as abuse or adultery and the proof of their occurrence. Just what caused her to leave and how she returned home remains a mystery. It would be 200 years before no-fault divorces came into vogue. There needed to be a clear reason why a divorce was necessary.

Prior to 1786, divorces in Massachusetts were rare and heard before the governor and council. The couple seemed to have practiced "self divorce" by merely separating and parting their own way. The complexity of this was probably as difficult as it is today. In defense of Elizabeth it was a bold move to leave her husband. She was clearly a woman who grew up in the days of liberty and embraced them for herself. Women even today will suffer through and stay in bad marriages, even in cases of physical and mental abuse. Elizabeth claimed her own freedom from a marriage that was not working. She likely left with just her daughter and the clothes on her back.

The conflict between the two resumed when Abraham visited Chebacco and the Cleaveland household on January 3, 1799. Cleaveland wrote about the situation to his son Nehemiah:

> Mr Channel has been in Chebacco and the vicinity a week today. And was at my house last Monday—evening,--we had considerable conversation together. He was high in the [insults] But avoided telling in particular his demands. I told him, I wished to have my two sons here, to see if we could come to some settlement between ourselves; he saw your brother Parker in New Rowley and had considerable conversation with him, who told him he would come to Chebacco.

Abraham came to Chebacco to put the marriage behind him and was unable to discuss the situation without the interference of his estranged wife's family. He may have been upset at his father-in-law allowing her to return home, and then told him so. Abraham was clearly furious at the interference of her family in their relationship. Cleaveland goes on to discuss the situation between Abraham and his daughter:

> But Mr Channel intimated, as the sentiments lay between him and Mrs Channel he did not see there was any need of her brother being present; but we were of a different opinion: Therefore he left my house, he and your sister had formal conversation together in private, the substance of it I understand was; he asked her whether she wished to return to his house? She answered by asking him if he was desirous of her returning? He replied that he left it to her to say whether she desired to return or not.[27]

Abraham and Elizabeth did have a conversation in private and he may have wanted to take care of her and their child Mary; but the relationship needed work. After two years apart Abraham was still willing to take her back. Abraham gave her the freedom to choose if she cared to return to him. It was unusual to allow this, it still being a man's world. Abraham was obviously not going to beg for her return, but left it open to her if she wished to. Elizabeth's father wrote of the hospitality that he offered Abraham as he continued the letter:

> But when he left my house, for he refused to eat, drink or sleep in my house. I asked him if he would not come and see us again? He answered that he did not know if it would be to any avail to come again, or to that effect...[28]

Abraham refused the Reverend's offer and must have felt that the relationship between Elizabeth and he could not be fixed. The next morning he came once again to see and speak to his estranged wife. The conversation was transmitted by Lois to the Reverend:

> Before Ma'am and I left our chamber.---Lois was present during the most of their conversing together: He told her as I understand, he would never live with her again as his wife. "She told him his unkind treatment of her as his wife was the reason of her leaving his house." But told him "That she had always said, and say it now, that she was ready to return to his house to live with him upon an assurance from him, that he would treat her with the kindness of a husband agreeable to the marriage covenant" or to that effect: Upon her uttering this he broke away in a seeming fit bidding her and the family farewell. But when we came to hear this relation Ma'am and I wished as there is no prospect of his treating his wife with the kindness of a husband (unless he has a new heart) that she had made him a proposal of quitting his estate upon certain conditions.[29]

These certain conditions might have been to financially support Elizabeth and his daughter Mary. Elizabeth now had a young daughter to care for and no husband to support them while she lived in what was then a man's world. Abraham was also likely concerned about claims she may have on his estate and property in New Hampshire. Elizabeth had to rely on the charity of her family or the inheritance that her father had promised.

Reverend Cleaveland was now in his final years, and Elizabeth and his granddaughter Mary had become a burden on him. Whatever the marriage covenant meant to Elizabeth it did not mean the same to Abraham. Not abiding by the marriage covenant may have meant he abused her or that he was unfaithful. His relationship to Colonel

Fifefield's daughter may have continued or had been what made her leave. It seems slanderous to ruminate on this without any more evidence. We just do not know what happened. One perspective of relationships at the time may reveal the answer: "Summer is past and gone-When the husband ceases to be a lover-and the time will inevitably come, her desire of pleasing will then grow languid, or become a spring of bitterness; and love, perhaps, the most evanescent of all pasions, gibes place to jealousy and vanity."[30] Anyone who has ever witnessed a divorce in a family knows how hard it is to take sides. It is far simpler and in many cases correct to say they are both to blame, or simply not meant to live together. The mists of time still obscure the failure of the relationship between Abraham and Elizabeth, in spite of so much evidence.

It seems that Elizabeth was not up to the challenge of raising a family and a newborn in the rural New Hampshire hills. Elizabeth's brother seemed to believe she was being treated with kindness in his earlier letter. The letter showed no evidence of abuse by Abraham. Whatever her words were seemed to upset Abraham a great deal because he fled the Cleaveland household. Elizabeth's brother Parker was sent for to come and meet with Abraham the next afternoon. Word was sent to Abraham to also come before he left Chebacco but there is no further evidence that this meeting ever took place. The next time Abraham and Elizabeth met was in court in Salem several months later.

Abraham could not have known when he left the Reverend's home that it would be the last time he might see him. Reverend Cleaveland passed away April 27, 1799, on his 77th birthday.[31] This left Cleaveland's widow Mary, to continue to provide for Abraham's estranged wife and his daughter Mary. She achieved this with the remains of Cleaveland's estate that he had provided them with in his will.[32] Mary Cleaveland definitely felt that Abraham should pay her for providing them with clothing, food, and lodging. Mary Cleaveland clearly sided with her daughter-in-law and she sought to recover funds from Abraham in her own way.

On January 3, 1800, it was requested in a writ for a sheriff or constable to attach the estate or goods of Abraham to the amount of $70 dollars, and to "take the body of the said Channel (if he may be found in your precinct) and him safely keep so that you have him before our justices of our Court of common Pleas, next to be holden at Ipswich…"[33] Following this, Smith, a constable of Ipswich, billed $1.56 for bringing in Abraham and committing him to the common jail in that town.[34] Mary sought payment of $53 dollars for "sufficient meat, drink, washing, lodging and other necessary things." Things that she said Abraham had promised to reimburse widow Mary Cleaveland for. Abraham, it said in the writ, "neglects and refuses to pay the same." She was backed and supported by her step-son's Parker and Nehemiah Cleaveland. Nehemiah had once been a Justice of the Peace and knew how to work the law.

Abraham was taken from Weare to the jail before the case came to court. He was released after agreeing to return for trial and "let out his farm" until his return. He was unable to work or provide any income for his family during this time. His oldest children must have looked after the younger ones, or been helped by the Peaslees. When the date of the case approached, other witnesses were called in to come to court. On April 3, 1800, Daniel Low, yeoman (farmer), Stephen Boardman, cordwainer (shoemaker), and Benjamin Cogswell, laborer, were called in with widow Mary Cleaveland to appear in court, by John Cogswell, the justice of the peace.[35] Widow Cleaveland wanted to be paid by Abraham for 31 weeks of care for Elizabeth, and the couple's infant daughter Mary.

Abraham hired attorney Charles Jackson of Newburyport to represent him against the Cleavelands. When Jackson was a young boy he met the newly-elected President George Washington when Washington dined one night with his family. Later while sitting with the boy at the fireplace by his feet Washington leaned over and began to pat Jackson on the head. The boy looked up at the president and said, "You have to speak the truth in this house." This was likely a reflection of Jackson's later career as an honest, upstanding judge.[36] Abraham had made a good choice with the selection of his lawyer. Among Jackson's school friends was Francis Cabot Lowell. Lowell traveled to Britain in 1811, and memorized the workings of the British power loom. The British businessmen saw him as a potential customer, not a competitor, and answered his questions for hours on end. He returned to the United States and from his photographic memory he was able to rebuild the equipment in his Massachusetts mill. Through his genius, Lowell, eventually made his new pirated equipment superior to the British equipment he had seen. All these achievements helped launch the

Industrial Revolution in America. All Lowell and his contemporaries later needed was a dependable workforce. Abraham is rumored to have known Lowell, but it has never been proven. This relationship between Abraham and Jackson shows a possible connection between the two.

At the trial Abraham's attorney, Charles Jackson, stated that Abraham had "never promised the said Cleaveland in manner and form, as she has declared against him, and therefore puts himself on the county." Responding to this widow Cleaveland's attorney, Joseph Perkins, said that Abraham's Plea was "bad and insufficient in law, and this she is ready to verify. Wherefore she prays judgment for her damages and costs." After everything was heard and seen by the court they stated, "the plea aforesaid of the said Channel is adjudged good." Abraham recovered $7.10 against Cleaveland. The reverend's widow was not done with Abraham and promised to appeal the case to the Supreme Judicial Court. The record shows that there was another case scheduled in 1801, but neither party showed up in court.[37] Whether or not Abraham today might be seen as a "deadbeat" dad, in the eyes of early nineteenth century justice he was not. This was far from Abraham's last time in court unfortunately. However, on September 10, 1804 an "indenture" was made between Abraham, Elizabeth, and her two brothers Parker and Nehemiah to settle the matter. Abraham was then able to move on with his life and sell his property in New Hampshire. Abraham was free again.

On February 27, 1805, Abraham sold four and a quarter acres of his Weare, New Hampshire, property to Obadiah Eaton, for fifteen dollars "lawful money" that was recorded by Aaron Greeley the Justice of the Peace.[38] A month later on March 22 he sold the remaining one hundred and seventy acres and his church pew in the North Meeting House to Jotham T. Tuttle for $2,334 dollars. It was pew ten located along the westerly wall aside the pulpit.[39] The land was recorded as being in the northeast corner of Weare along the Dunbarton, New Hampshire line. It took Tuttle until July 21, 1811, to repay Abraham his six mortgage payments of $300 a year. Abraham had now returned to Chebacco, after returning an excellent profit on his Weare property.

Elizabeth and her daughter Mary went to live in Byfield, Massachusetts, with her brother Dr. Parker Cleaveland after the death of the widow Cleaveland in 1810. Elizabeth Cleaveland Channell died November 23, 1828, of a "lingering and painful malady." Abraham's daughter Mary died September 26, 1830. But Abraham still had a lot of living to do. The mother and daughter were buried in Byfield Cemetery, along with Elizabeth's brother Parker.[40] Elizabeth's obituary described her as an "eminently devoted Christian." This would have pleased her father. The last name Channell appearing on her gravestone indicates that she never married again. Many couples of this era other than the Channells remarried without a legal divorce from a court.[41] Abraham's daughter Mary never married either. It was there on the beautifully carved slate stone of Elizabeth that the surname Channell first appeared with its current spelling. The stone is located at the Byfield Parish Church Burying Ground on Warren Street in Georgetown, Massachusetts.

New Hampshire Farmers Museum, photo by author.

Austin and the Quakers

O my heavenly father, thou hast seen me in the depth of tribulation, in my
many journeyings and travels….it was Thy power which supported me
when no flesh could help, when man could not comprehend the depth of
mine exercise…be Thou only and for ever exalted in, by and through Thy
poor child, and let nothing be able to pluck me out of Thy hand.[1]

Directly following the Revolutionary War, the Royal Governor of
Canada, Frederick Haldimand, was against any settlement in the
area later known as the Eastern Townships. This area is located in the
lands bordering the United States, above Vermont, New Hampshire, and
New York, and south of Montreal and Quebec. The few settlers that
lived in the area were threatened to be burned out of their homes if they
did not move to another region. He urged them to move to the St
Lawrence River Valley west of the city of Montreal. Haldimand stated
that this was to avoid border conflicts, but it was more likely to keep
smuggling and exchanges between the citizens of the two countries to a
minimum.[2] It seems that Haldimand wanted to save the border area
known as the Eastern Townships for future French Canadian
settlement.[3] It was certainly also useful as a buffer against invasion. In
spite of Governor Haldimand's wishes for this many settlers, some
Loyalists and some not; remained in the area.

The land in Lower Canada that was later known as the Eastern

Townships began to be legally settled and surveyed after The Constitutional Act of 1791.[4] The Act allowed for land to be given out in Lower Canada. This strengthened Canada while reducing the population south of the border which was rapidly expanding and creating a threat through its settlers numerical superiority. The passing of this act allowed for the development of land where the associates of Bolton and their later followers, which included Abraham Channell Jr. and his in-laws the Peaslee family, settled and carved out their frontier home. After The Constitutional Act of 1791, "The English system of Free and Common Soccage was used to establish land grants in the Eastern Townships area, contrary to the traditional French seigniorial long lot system."[5] Land in the area began to be organized according to the township system that had been used in the thirteen eastern seaboard colonies during the colonial period.

American immigration was then encouraged after 1790. After 1792, the new Lieutenant-Governor of Lower Canada John Simcoe, put in place the "leader and associates" system. This system gave large grants of land to men who organized and encouraged others to come and settle with them. Unfortunately, many of these settlers never came to the land and just speculated that as others cleared their lands their own land might rise in value. They then planned to quickly turn the land over and sell it for a profit. Although this system was the one that early leaders in the area embraced, for the most part it failed and did not last very long after the apparent success of the settlers in Bolton. It was the failure of many of these people to settle their land that brought Abraham's eldest son and namesake to the region.

One of the first to set his eyes on this land and its opportunity was Nicholas Austin of New Hampshire. Austin was the leader of the associates in Bolton. Nicholas Austin was a Quaker born in Somersworth, New Hampshire, and like Abraham had a wandering spirit and a thirst for new lands and frontiers. Nicholas Austin had climbed many mountains in New Hampshire, including *Agiocochook* in 1774, which was later renamed Mount Washington. *Agiocochook* means the place or home of the great storm spirit. The ancient tradition of the natives is that there was a great flood and that a native couple climbed to the top and then after the flood waters abated they climbed back down and repopulated the Earth. Christians must be careful in disregarding the traditional story that compares so well to the Epic of

Gilgamesh, Noah and his Ark, and the Garden of Eden.

Looking out over the horizon from the treeless and barren peak of 6,288' Mount Washington, Austin likely saw vast opportunities in the huge unbroken forest. Standing atop the great mountain is an otherworldly experience. It is easy to understand why the Natives once felt a great spirit made his home there. Clearly to connect with this spirit a journey must be undertaken from the base. Climbing up to the peak is the type of accomplishment that makes anything seem possible. Surviving the climb to the top and down again was in itself a great accomplishment for Austin. When the clouds and horizon cleared he looked north to see the land he later cleared and made his home. His reason for being there is probably due to the then recent discovery in 1772, of a notch making the route to his future home shorter from the seacoast.[6] The notch is linked in history to a large silver statue stolen from the Saint Francis Indians in a raid by Rogers Rangers. The statue of the Virgin Mary remains undiscovered. Golden candlesticks from the raid were found in 1816, along the east shore of Lake Memphremagog.

Mount Washington postcard, authors collection.

Today climbing the mountain is far easier than it once was. Austin had no tourist maps and marked trails to guide himself by. He may have hired a native guide to show him the route up. The most exciting way to gain the summit today, other than hiking; is to take up the Cog Railway. The Cog Railway trip is a three mile route straight up the great mountain, and provides the modern day tourist a taste of mid-nineteenth century tourism. To fully enjoy an authentic trip you must book it far ahead of time and try to secure the trip powered by coal. Most of the trips are now powered by bio-diesel. To any lover of rail history this is a must do. The only excitement in driving up in your car occurs if your brakes fail. This, would not be a good form of excitement.

Austin also enjoyed a friendship with New Hampshire's Royal Governor John Wentworth (1737-1820).[7] John Wentworth was the third and final generation of Wentworths to govern the New Hampshire Colony for the British after following his uncle into office. Wentworth and Austin shared an interest in the northern forests of New England, and lived near one another at the end of the Governor's Road. Wentworth had to pass Austin's farm on the way to his own lavish estate in Western New Hampshire.

Nicholas Austin and his friend Wentworth had run afoul of the Sons of Liberty in New Hampshire, when Wentworth and Austin schemed to send men they had gathered in western New Hampshire to Boston to build barracks to house Redcoats for the Royal Governor of Massachusetts, and British General Thomas Gage. Housing of British Troops was a hot topic in Boston, and there had been many disputes over the subject. After being caught doing this by the local patriot leaders Austin had to drop to his knees and swear forgiveness to the local Sons of Liberty, and was lucky to escape this encounter with the patriots with his life.

The taking of oaths was not taken lightly by the Quakers. Austin must have felt himself extremely threatened to have sworn forgiveness to the patriots. The Quaker feelings towards oaths are taken from the apostle James:

> Thou shalt not forswear thyself, but shall perform unto the
> Lord thine oaths; but I say unto you, Swear not at all; neither
> by heaven, for it is God's throne; nor by the earth, for it is His
> footstool; neither by Jerusalem; for it is the city of the great
> King; neither shalt thou swear by thine head...[8]

With this passage it should be clear that Austin was in great danger, and swore to the patriots to save his life, as life is also sacred to the Quakers. Swearing oaths sets up a double standard of truth, men should always tell the truth and should not be obligated to swear they are doing so, by doing this they also admit to sometimes being dishonest.

When news later reached Austin that American Patriots were going out to the Wentworth farm to abduct the governor in 1775, Austin rode out on horseback and with a "reverse Revere" warned the British leader to flee. Wentworth and his wife then made their escape and hid out at Austin's home.[9] Governor Wentworth had a group of fifty supporters who might today, or even then, be seen as British spies. It is not at all unreasonable to believe that Austin was one of them. The best spies after all are never caught or found out, the best ones stay unknown. If Austin had stayed on in New Hampshire and sent information to the British before and after the war it might not come as a surprise. It is, however, a fact that cannot be proven due to lack of evidence. Why was he contacted to hire the laborers to build the barracks for Gage? What else did Austin do that has not, or may not ever, be discovered?

In the months following the Battle at Lexington the area eventually grew too hot politically for the royal governor and politician. Governor Wentworth had cannon pointed at his home by the Rebels and he was forced to secretly flee New Hampshire forever, leaving behind all his belongings and property. After the war in 1783, Wentworth returned to North America and became the surveyor general for the British in Canada.[10] Wentworth then later became the Royal Governor of Nova Scotia. In spite of all his family's wealth before the Revolution he found himself again fleeing; this time from Britain in 1812, to escape creditors. Nicholas Austin had been pulled into a dangerous situation, and whether this was due to his loyalties to King George III, his friendship with the governor, or his desire to make a dollar or two is unknown. He certainly overstepped the impartiality professed by the Quakers in the conflict with his action.

He was not alone in his impartiality among the group. Thomas Paine was infuriated by a publication written by the Quakers condemning the Revolution called:

> The ANCIENT TESTIMONY AND PRINCIPLES of the people called QUAKERS renewed, with Respect to the KING and GOVERNMENT, and touching the COMMOTIONS now prevailing in these and other parts of AMERICA, addressed to the PEOPLE IN GENERAL.

Paine wrote a scathing reply to their address. He accused them of, "dabbling in matters, which the professed Quietude of your Principles instruct you not to meddle with."[11] He also felt, "that we do not complain against you because ye are Quakers, but because ye pretend to be and are NOT Quakers." Paine's final comment was, "that the example which ye have unwisely set, of mingling religion with politics, may be disavowed and reprobated by every inhabitant of AMERICA." It seems that Paine felt that men were able to make and decide their own politics, but not to connect them with religion. Ideas such as this one may have led to the separation of church and state in later times. In any event, the Quaker ideals differed from the patriotic mainstream, and certainly many citizens mistrusted them and may have made them feel unwelcome. But even those who stayed out of it were ostracized.

Quakers like Austin and the Peaslees, the future in-laws of Abraham Channell, were often frowned upon during the Revolution for not taking sides by others in their community. You were either on their side or opposed, in the eyes of those Americans who sought to separate from Britain. There was no middle ground in the dispute with the British in their opinion. You were with them or against them. Abraham Channell Jr.'s future in-laws, the Peaslees, had refused to sign a declaration to "Oppose the hostile proceedings of the British fleets and armies against the United American armies." This was not due to being Tories (British sympathizers) but was in support of their non-violent Quaker beliefs.[12] Their failure to put their patriotism on paper likely brought them much trouble and discomfort in their community.

Because British spies used Quaker communities as cover to spy and report American troop movements, the Society of Friends was often seen as disloyal through no fault of their own.[13] Conflict made it difficult for them to worship and live in peace. The Quakers were guilty by their known or unknown association with these British agents. To most patriots, Quakers were seen as worse than the Tories who they could openly identify and deal with. In later years the Quakers did more for freedom in America by openly calling for the emancipation of slaves more than most groups; something the founding fathers had failed to accomplish.

The exact motivation for Nicholas Austin's movement to Lower Canada is unknown. His friend Governor Wentworth had dreamed of developing the state further inland and pushed for development of the road that he had built to Wolfeboro, New Hampshire. The Governor felt the project was important for the future growth of the state and lobbied for local towns to develop their roads along his planned routes.[14] In addition he dreamed of canals and waterways leading from the New Hampshire coastline to the border of Canada.[15] Later the Erie Canal greatly profited the state of New York as it brought goods from the west.

Austin may have helped him survey and plan these canal routes and through this been introduced to the northern and western lands of the region. The Governor had built a great country estate in the town after he had been inspired by those grand country houses he had seen when he visited Britain. After the Seven Years War rents rose in the English cities like London, and with this new income nobles competed to outdo each other with their lavish properties.[16] Wentworth held affairs of state at his country house and local speculators like Austin may have felt the land surrounding it might someday rise in value. This dream not only came to a close with the Revolution, but also with the building of the first New Hampshire Turnpike that bypassed the area and rendered the Governor's Road to a secondary status. This undoubtedly destroyed the value of Austin's land. In 1916, Austin's house was torn down due to being on a route that had been reduced to a simple logging road in an isolated forgotten spot.[17] It once had four hundred acres, two houses and three barns when Austin sold it. The dream of Wentworth's great road never came to fruition. The value of Austin's farm had continued to plummet as the new nation grew.

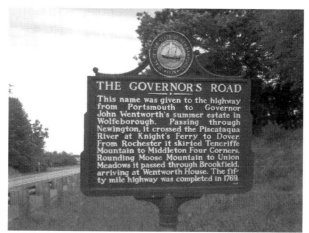

Photo by author.

The Immortal Patriot

Nicholas Austin organized a group of associates that included Silas Peaslee, a relative of the Peaslee family, who also lived on Sugar Hill in Weare, New Hampshire. It seems probable that Abraham met Austin during this time in New Hampshire, while Austin was recruiting associates to join him in Lower Canada. For some reason Abraham did not choose to join Austin in his plan then. Sometime during the last few years of the 18th century Austin and others went north and began to clear and settle the town of Bolton along the western shore of Lake Memphremagog in Lower Canada, over the border from Vermont.

The beautiful lake was formed by glaciers thousands of years ago. It is 27 miles long and sprinkled with twenty remote islands. One of these islands is over one hundred acres in size. The lake served as a means of travel into the wilderness for Austin and the other settlers who followed him north, like the Channells and their in-laws. Austin is said to have purchased a canoe from some natives and pushed off the shore and paddled north along the unsettled beautiful lake. Austin surely traveled to and surveyed the area many times before he made his decision to move there. Austin must have utilized the political clout of his friend Wentworth, or his own British political connections in Montreal to achieve the land grant. In any event he and his associates were the first to get approval out of the many people that were trying for the same.

Many of Austin's associates were not up to the challenge of settling the wilderness along the lake, or simply wished to sell their property for a quick profit. It took families with strong ambition and determination to scratch out a home and life of subsistence from the new land. There were no mills, no stores, and no laws there along the lake shore. Roads needed to be cut, rudimentary cabins built to offer shelter, and all this while trying to find enough food to survive. Abraham Channell Jr. took advantage of these events and moved along with other members of the Quaker community to this wild, untamed, Canadian forest; sometime in the early part of the 19th century.

On May 28, 1800, Abraham Jr. married Sarah Peaslee of Weare, in Dunbarton, New Hampshire. If Sarah was a Quaker she must have broken custom or disobeyed the friends by marrying in a church. The couple were married by the Reverend Walter Harris in the town of Dunbarton, next to where the couple's parents had their farms. Living in sparsely populated areas like the New Hampshire Hill Country

Quakers often had to find suitably partners from outside their faith. Growing up and living there also provided Sarah Channell with the skills to survive in her new home on the frontier. Earlier on May 4, 1800, Abraham Jr.'s sister Abigail had married Moses George in the same town. Abraham's sister Abigail and Moses George settled in Bolton near what is known today as George Pond. They certainly depended on each other for help in clearing the land and at times for their own survival. Land was becoming increasingly scarce and expensive in New Hampshire, and being young and looking to make their own mark in the world Abraham Channell Jr., the George family, and other cousins and Quakers from the area, made their way north to join Nicholas Austin, along the western bank of the beautiful Canadian lake.

The time of their arrival in Lower Canada is usually given far before the records in New Hampshire show. Jonathan Peaslee's name appears in the New Hampshire grantee index as selling his one hundred and twenty-one acre property in New Hampshire on May 7, 1802. He may have traveled there earlier and begun clearing land in the winter for his family. The evidence of the sale does show that he was not fully committed to his Canadian home in Bolton until after this date. His daughter and son in law could not have moved there until after their 1800 marriage.

Abraham Channell Jr. and his wife eventually did move and began to build a life in the northern wilderness settlement of Bolton. Likely visited by his father and namesake from time to time. Their land appears to have been in the area that borders what is now known as Channell Bay on Lake Memphremagog. Abraham Juniors Peaslee in-laws were now free of taxes and criticism for their reluctance to fight in the American Revolution. They found peace for a while, until civilization once again caught up with them as it had always done. As civilization expands, it will always find those that seek to leave it.

Pearl and the Embargo

Historians and genealogists cannot hope to practice their craft without libraries. One of my favorite research places is the Dyer Library in Abington, Massachusetts. The library was created a century ago from the monetary gift of a wealthy female benefactor named Marietta Dyer. The library is a treasure trove of old tomes of local and national history. The collection and assistance you receive from the research assistants there is much different than the typical small town public library. I sometimes walk along the collection of books that extend from floor to ceiling and pull one down that interests me to examine. It was on one of these trips that I pulled down an index for a large collection of family registers for Massachusetts and looked up the name Channell.[1]

I saw several results for the name Channell in the book, most I recognized, but the two that caught my attention were Mary and Susan. They had died over a century ago in Harvard, Massachusetts. This was a town that I had never heard of before, in spite of living my whole life in Massachusetts. I did not have these women recorded in my tree, and so I had an insatiable urge to research them and see how they fit in. A historian might not give them a second glance. Why would they?The discovery of this led me to visit to the Massachusetts Archives on Columbia Point, not far from Dorchester Heights, the place where the cannon had been entrenched to force the British Evacuation, to find out more information. I found the proper reel of microfilm for their death record and weaved it into the machine. Spinning through many pages I beheld small fragments and remnants of many past and forgotten lives. After a time I finally found the page I was looking for. I saw the name of Susan Channell, and moved the record over past the cause of death and her life span recorded by years-months-days. Then her father's name and occupation appeared: Abraham Channell-tailor, born London, England. I had discovered another daughter! Who was she and why did she end up in Harvard, I wondered? This moment led me into a window that glanced into a remarkable and very different world.

On April 27, 1802, and later recorded May 3, 1802, in the Registry of Deeds in Essex County, Abraham Channell Sr. bought land in Ipswich from Joshua Burnham for $84.[2] Abraham continued to travel and work through the area in the early 1800's. Buying and selling land was one method Abraham used to survive along with his tailoring pursuits. He was a remarkable industrious man. He worked throughout New England tailoring clothes and possibly working odd jobs as he reached middle age. His working area must have included Boston, Massachusetts, because on November 19, 1807, Abraham married 43-year-old Mary Smith there. Abraham's third wife. The ceremony was performed by Reverend Clay.

Mary's original maiden name was Dyer, she was a previously married woman with her own older children.[3] An interesting coincidence that I found Mary Dyer in the Dyer library. On November 26, 1807, Abraham's son Robert married Lydia Butler, and he later moved to New Hampshire and began his own farm.[4] Abraham had remained unmarried for a number of years since his failed marriage to Elizabeth. He must have hoped this third marriage would be the charm for him. A rumor persists that Mary had lost her husband at sea, but I have never found anything to substantiate this.

Had loneliness or love led Abraham to once again take the vows of marriage? In any case once Abraham had seen her in the church choir he was enamored. He was willing to give marriage and love another chance. Her angelic voice tempted him to give love another try. Mary's voice had once entertained an American founding father. Abraham brought his new wife Mary back to Chebacco to begin a new life together. She told him proudly of her greatest audience.

Thirteen years earlier on Saturday, October 24, 1789, President

Washington was making a tour through Boston. Washington made a grand entrance when he rode into town atop his white horse. As he entered the city men, women, and children lined the streets to pay their respect to the man who caused the British to evacuate their city less than twenty years before. After the Constitution passed he was unanimously elected president and embarked on this tour. Washington passed under a large arch and canopy with a beautiful eagle atop it and after getting down from his mount he strode into the entrance to the State House. Going upstairs he walked through the hall and exited onto the gallery of the Colonnade overlooking the street below.[5] From his view there he could see the site of the Boston Massacre, one of the triggers of the revolutionary conflict. Washington looked out on the crowd and bowed deeply to his well wishers. The crowd below shouted three cheers to President Washington and then a choral group sang:

> Great Washington the hero's come,
> Each heart exulting hears the found,
> Thousands to their deliverer'r throng,
> And shout him welcome all around![6]

Abraham's future wife Mary was a member of the choral group that sang those words to Washington on that day; years before she met Abraham Channell.[7] Singing to President Washington was one of her proudest moments.

Abraham's recent marriage had unfortunately not mellowed him out at all. In the spring of 1808, Abraham once again found himself in trouble with the law. On May 5, 1808, Abraham was in the company of five other men when they brutally attacked a man named William Pearl, a mariner from Manchester Massachusetts. Manchester is another seaside community near Chebacco, today known as Manchester by the Sea. Abraham, along with John Edwards Jr., teamster, Aramiah Edwards, mariner, Aaron Burnham, yeoman, John Edwards, yeoman, and Daniel Low, blacksmith, all of whom lived in Manchester, were accused of attacking Pearl with "force and arms."[8] Clearly the old privateer Abraham had not lost his taste for a good fight. The case shows Abraham as a man who was willing to help out his friends and one that was prepared to avenge a wrong.

Abraham and the other members of the vigilante group were avenging a beating that William Pearl had given earlier to John Edwards, and an assault Pearl made upon Abigail Edwards, likely a wife or daughter to John Edwards. Pearl later encountered Daniel Low and assaulted him. With this nasty and violent mariner Pearl seemingly out of control, Abraham Channell and his friends found it necessary to come to Manchester and set things right, and give Pearl a beating of his own. A beating that Pearl seems to have deserved to receive from the now middle aged privateer and his friends, for the crime he had committed. Pearl must have been a rather tough individual to survive such an attack.

A jury trial was first given to Pearl, and his peers did find him guilty of the crimes he was accused of. It seems the beating he had received was viewed as ample punishment, and the indictment was not prosecuted any further by John Prince, the Attorney for the Commonwealth. In the case of disturbing the peace brought upon Abraham Channell and the other members of the gang, Edwards and Low were found not guilty. They had a reason to strike back after their own beating. The rest of them, however, including Abraham, were found guilty for their crime. Again no further action or punishment was taken upon Channell or his friends, but they likely had to keep their noses clean for a while and stay out of trouble. By the end of 1808, Abraham was out of court and jail and returned home to his newlywed wife Mary, who certainly chided him for fighting in the public streets.

The street fighting was just one sign of the economic problems and international politics of the period. Why after all was such a rugged mariner wandering around getting into mischief and not out at sea? While Abraham Channell fought for justice in the streets of Massachusetts, Napoleon fought and continued to conquer Europe. Ludwig van Beethoven wrote music and planned some of his final concerts to display his great symphonies as his hearing faded. Francisco Goya viewed and later painted the horrors of the 1808 French occupation in Spain in his Third of May painting of 1814. In the United States the British practice of impressment at sea to fight the French Fleet of Napoleon was becoming an issue once again. The same kind of kidnapping that Abraham had once suffered in London was still being practiced at sea, and brought the United States and Britain once again to the brink of war.

On June, 22 1807, The American ship *Chesapeake* was approached by the *HMS Leopard*, while the *Chesapeake* was still within American waters. The British vessel *Leopard* demanded that they be allowed to search for deserters from the British Navy. The Americans refused and were fired upon by the British. This act resulted in three Americans being killed and others injured. With battle raging in Europe the British Navy had a serious shortage of tars to sail their ships, and did anything they could to get more men. This event enraged Americans and brought new demands for war. If the young country had any sizable military power it may have challenged Britain. Keeping a wise head, President Thomas Jefferson fought with economic pressure instead. This policy unfortunately caused a great detriment to the northern economy and the new home of Abraham Channell.

On December 22, 1807, Jefferson passed the Embargo Act that effectively closed all the ports and shipping in the United States. The leaders in the north began to criticize Jefferson and his policies:

> Our ships all in motion once whitened the ocean,
> They sailed and returned with a cargo;
> Now doomed to decay, they have fallen a prey
> To Jefferson-worms-and embargo.[9]

Jefferson, a wealthy farmer in the South, had little understanding of what kept the economy working in the northern seaports. His policy had a negative effect in the region beyond what he may have first envisioned when he passed it. It shows a lack of understanding in national policy existed between the southern agrarian and the merchant world of the north.

The act led to economic disaster in the north, as ship-owners lost all their income, and mariners like Pearl were trapped in port with no work. All the supporting industries such as sail making, supplies, and cordage (rope) factories came to a standstill. Public sentiment and condemnation rose in the north in the papers:

> Embargo read backward, O-grab-me appears,
> A scary sound ever for big children's ears.
> The syllables transformed, Go bar 'em comes next,
> A mandate to keep ye from harm, says my text.
> Analyze Miss Embargo, her letters, I'll wage,
> If not removed shortly, will make mob-rage.[10]

With these horrible economic conditions, there was not much

opportunity for Abraham to tailor and make money to feed his children with. Trade temporarily skyrocketed with Lower Canada until even this was banned by the Jefferson administration. Many in the border region living near Abraham's son and namesake wondered why land trade was restricted if the embargo was meant to prevent impressment at sea.[11] Why was the government foolishly restricting land trade in the north? It later continued trade secretly through an increase in clandestine smuggling in both Northern Vermont and New Hampshire, with the British citizens of Lower Canada.

The increased trade with Lower Canada may have turned Abraham Channell's eyes north to the townships where his son Abraham Jr. lived. With no local opportunity and an unstable economic disaster occurring in the coastal ports of New England, Abraham began to think of the opportunities to acquire cheap land and a return to stable British rule. He was not alone in his dislike of the American administration. Many unhappy political leaders in the area formed the Essex Junto during the embargo. They were a Federalist group that pushed a plan for Northern States to secede from the Union. In spite of this, Abraham had cause once again to celebrate with the marriage of his daughter Fanny to David Balch on December 11, 1808. The couple went on to farm in the nearby community of Topsfield, Massachusetts. In the case of Abraham, embargo or not, money and opportunity were things he desperately needed as he was once again going to become a father.

On January 1, 1809, Susan Channell was born to Abraham's third wife Mary. Mary was in her mid-forties and it may have come as a surprise for her to have a healthy baby girl. It was indeed a blessing from God. It may have been even more of a surprise because she may have been born after the couple's marriage was nullified. No official explanation for the cause and result of the marriage nullification can be found, but it can be assumed it was because of her later actions. It will later be seen Mary was interested in alternative religions and their groups. She was fully caught up in the Second Great Awakening. Abraham was again a father needing to care for a daughter in the midst of a horrible economic time period, possibly in another unhappy and failing marriage.

Abraham was blessed with a newly born daughter and the United States, received a newly elected president when James Madison (1751-

1836), took office in 1809. When every new president takes office there is a hope that things will get better. It is seldom that simple. Some changes were made to the hated embargo, but trouble with shipping goods here brought on by the struggle in Europe during the Napoleonic Wars continued. Abraham's marriage in Boston may show that he was purchasing his cloth from Francis Cabot Lowell, a wealthy Boston merchant we met earlier in the story. He later developed the first large mills in Waltham after his return from Britain just prior to 1812. Abraham had certainly met Mary Smith there in Boston. The Embargo hurt many merchants, but it caused the textile industry in the United States to thrive, with less cloth and clothing arriving from Europe. This explosion of construction and business is known today as "cotton mill fever," and later on it strongly affected other members of Abraham's family.[12]

At the end of 1809, Abraham's daughter Betsy married Elisha Tucker, a trader and furniture maker in the city of Boston, at the Second Baptist Church in the city.[13] Tucker's amazing cabinet work can still be seen in museums today. His furniture is sometimes sold for hundreds of thousands of dollars. It is unknown what price his furnishings commanded in those days; but it was certainly not inexpensive, he made furniture of very high quality. Abraham borrowed some money from Tucker that year, and he may have already made plans to go to Bolton in Lower Canada to purchase some land. Abraham traveled to Bolton in 1809, and he signed a power of attorney to Abraham Savage to purchase a tract and parcel of land on July 10, 1810, known as lot number twenty-eight in the tenth range from an associate of Nicholas Austin. The power of attorney was witnessed by Ezekiel Lewis and John Porter.

This property contained one hundred and fifty acres of land, more or less, and was owned by Jonathan Weare, who had come from Weare, New Hampshire. His father Peter Weare had previously conveyed the land to him on February 17, 1798. The land was only a part of the original parcel that had been owned by Jonathan Weare's father. The property had been worked and cleared for a number of years, but there is no listing that a dwelling or outbuilding had been built on it.[14] According to one source, Abraham built a dwelling on the property that he used as an inn.[15] In the early 1960's the property was known as the Woodacres House. Unlike today, the land was the real item of value and not the house that rested on it. The land was on the western side of Lake

Memphremagog and rises up from the shore at a spot on the lake known today as Channell Bay. Channell Hill Road, located in the area, also still retains the name of the family.

The land exchanged hands without Abraham's presence on August 18, 1810.[16] The method Abraham used to raise the $600 dollars is not completely known, but it seems that the money was borrowed from his friends and family. The sale was witnessed by John Porter and Sterling King. The Notary was Leon Lalanne. Lalanne was a Notary during this time in Lower Canada and he had greater power than a notary would have today in the United States. He also served the townships as a Justice of the Peace and Magistrate.[17] The transfer of property was made at Lalanne's home in St. Armand in Shefford County, Lower Canada. As will later be shown, Abraham was quite fond of this man Leon Lalanne.

Another important man who traveled to the shores of the lake in 1810, was Richard Holland.[18] Holland also came from the Cape Ann region of Massachusetts like Abraham. Here Holland built a tavern on the eastern shore of the lake in Copp's Ferry, where early settler and Bolton associate Moses Copp built and operated a ferry, across the lake from where Abraham and his son owned land.[19] Moses had come to Canada from Wakefield, New Hampshire and was one of Austins associates.[20] After later selling his tavern, Holland built mills southwest of the lake where the Missiquoi River flows near Lake Champlain in Vermont. Holland seems to have been a talented builder and engineer. These were essential skills in a newly developing area.

When Abraham traveled to Lower Canada he may not have known that war would soon break out and travel between his old and new home might prove difficult. Had he planned for Mary and his new daughter Susan to come there or had he abandoned them? Had she left Abraham? If he did abandon her he may have had a good reason. Mary's interest in a radical new religion may have been the cause of this abandonment. She could have attended camp meetings and been caught up in the religious fervor of the Second Great Awakening that was then sweeping the nation. Essex County was described as a religiously turbulent area at the turn of the century.[21] Missionaries working the camp meeting from the Utopian community may have convinced her to leave the world and join them.

If this is what happened it is clear Abraham wanted no part of it.

The group likely seemed as strange to him as could be imagined. Today the word "cult" might be used to describe it. This group asked more of its members than any other religious group did. Members had to give up their family, their children, remain celibate, and give away their property to be members of a larger non-biological family.[22] It was said of the group in 1811, that they may join, "in consequence of which women have been abandoned by their husbands, robbed of their children, and left destitute of the means of support."[23] Abraham thus began a new life and left his wife Mary to fend for herself and her daughter. But Mary and Susan were alright once they found themselves in the safe confines of this radical new religious movement.

Mary and young Susan left Chebacco and "the world" behind as they fled west to a strange new community. They joined a new radical religious experiment some see as early American communism. Not the same communism that later became the enemy of the United States during the Cold War, but a communism in its most basic form. A group of people united in such a way that they served as a model for Karl Marx. His writing eventually evolved into the economic system of the Soviet Union, hated and fought against by my father throughout his military career. In some ways both Abraham and his wife Mary had abandoned the new United States. Abraham fled across the border, and Mary fled her current way of life, and the still young political system of the United States. She fled democracy and capitalism into the arms of religious utopian socialism.

Copp's Ferry, from *Canadian Scenery* 1841

Shakers of Harvard

Nothing on Earth is more beloved and honored in the world's great heart, than a noble youth, whose aims are high, and whose life is a moral lesson."[1]

Mother Ann Lee came to America in 1774, shortly before the outbreak of hostilities in the American British Colonies. Born in Britain, Lee was attracted to a new religion after trying to cope with the loss of her four children. The religion she embraced had its origins in France, and foresaw the second coming of Christ in a female form. In 1770, Mother Ann was proclaimed, "as the perfect human vessel" for the spirit of Christ to make its second appearance within.[2] Lacking the belief that she was worthy, she entered a period of self discipline for nine years until she felt she had received a testimony from God. This testimony "against the corruption of man, in its root and every branch; which is, properly, the testimony against the flesh,"[3] was in direct confrontation to women being, fruitful and multiplying, as it was within the other more common Christian traditions. Mother Ann now had a message to spread to the world.

Mother Ann held religious services which included dancing, singing, and shouting. These services so infuriated her nearby neighbors, and disturbed the peace, that they broke in and dragged her off to a prison for mental patients known as Bedlam. Mother Ann used her time in prison to both polish her faith and as an opportunity to "withdraw her spirit inward."[4] She had to look to herself and her spirit to survive the terrible ordeal. After she survived two weeks in Bedlam and was found to be sane by the prison authorities, she returned home and continued to infuriate the local citizens and politicians with her meetings. Mother Ann proclaimed a prophecy that the American Colonies would gain their independence. For this treasonous yet prophetic statement her life was said to have been put in peril. Mother Ann and her followers soon fled Britain. Her group then survived a rough trip across the Atlantic by the grace of God, as she was said to have asked her Lord to fix the leaky worm ridden boat once or twice during the journey. After this, the religious group traveled to upstate New York and purchased land.

In Upstate New York they again suffered persecution and imprisonment when they were incorrectly accused of supporting the British. Their strange new ideas and non-violent beliefs brought them much unwanted attention. The fear of the British was great during this time throughout New York State. The British, as previously stated, had led a huge invasion of New York, and launched another attack down the Hudson River Valley from Canada. Although this was repulsed, local citizens were fearful of more action. When another controversial religious group in Harvard, Massachusetts became leaderless, Mother Ann went to the area and eventually absorbed the members of the group that lived there into her group. After Mother Ann and her group arranged the purchase and took possession of the property, fierce Yankee individualist local townspeople who disapproved of their celibacy and communal living experiment, forced Mother Ann to leave the area. Mother Ann and her leaders left temporarily, yet often returned, and each time they did return they received physical beatings, verbal threats, and were tied to stakes and whipped openly in the community. Eventually, after the war with the British ended, the group was grudgingly accepted in the town and left alone. The public had found after a time that the group bought, sold, and traded like everyone else, they just did so in a group form. They were less threatening to the economic system than later communist ideals were in the twentieth century.

The harsh treatment that Mother Ann experienced led to her early death on September 8, 1784. She had, however, planted her religion successfully during her ten years in America. Her followers chose to continue where she had left off and the experiment grew. The new faith and religious movement she brought to the young nation forecast the future struggles of women, with members of the group enjoying truly equal rights between males and females, and shared leadership between the sexes. The group welcomed the orphans and outcasts of society, who were fed and educated and then given the choice of staying with the community, or leaving when they came of age. Women that were widowed or distraught by living in unhappy or abusive relationships now had someplace they could turn to for shelter. Mother Ann created a place where women could find support and safety in a man's world and worship God. It may have been for this reason that Mary Channell sought out the Shakers to help her with whatever desperate time she had found herself in, with Abraham's departure to Lower Canada or with the failure of their relationship.

But there was a price to pay for all that security. When they joined the group they had to enter into a contract to gain membership. When members tried to leave the group these contracts were fully supported by the American court system. They would not be given any severance or property; since the property belonged to the group and no longer to themselves. In the 19th century contracts made between individuals were more iron clad and held no legal loopholes such as they do today. Freedom of choice was a right of the individual but had to be carefully considered before signing a contract. They were binding and enforceable. There was no second choice once Mary decided to join the Shakers.[5]

In addition to the contract, all of a person's wealth was given to the Shakers. Irregardless of how rich they were when they joined and how much their toil and work had helped to profit the group they left all that behind them if they later chose to leave. Their contribution also did not gain them any status in the group. Only in rare cases of being too young and not being sufficiently intelligent to understand the contract were exceptions made. Yet if Mary had no wealth, she may have had nothing to lose. Her economic status is unknown; but Abraham does not seem to have married any women without property previously. She had been married, probably widowed, and likely had some wealth or property.

The contract was based upon the traditional church covenant, and was at odds with the separation of Church and State as defined by the federal government. The covenant hymn was even sung by society members during their service so that the covenant contract would be fully understood by the Shaker members. The covenant was written for, "sin-sick souls," to help them, "cast off their burdens of sin." The covenant was, "strongly guarded from the aggressions of envious, jealous and vituperative backsliders."[6] Although cloaked in religious phrases, the economic section of the contract was fully enforceable in court. The real enforcement of the spiritual part of the covenant could only occur in the court of Christ. The Shaker Covenant does not seem to have been interested in the previous "Marriage Covenant" that existed between Mary and Abraham or its other members.

On August 5, 1816, Mary Channell and Abraham's seven-year-old daughter Susan were admitted to the Shakers in Harvard. It had been a long trip out to Harvard from Chebacco and Mary had come to the decision to join after she looked inward and found she wanted to seek a higher level of spirituality. Her estranged husband had gone to Lower Canada, and with or without her knowledge he remarried there. Oddly enough on June 3, 1816, only months before Mary and her daughter fled to live with the Shakers in Harvard, Abraham and his new wife Wealthy had another daughter born. She was also named Susan. Perhaps in some despondent manner Abraham tried to replace what he had been forced to leave behind. Whether the despair of losing his daughter in his second failed relationship since the loss of his first wife, Abigail, haunted the old privateer or not; the couple both went on with their lives in very different worlds.

Although Susan may have had only one mother before, the kindly Shaker women all treated her as one of their own. She now found herself surrounded by caring women. In the Shaker community relationships were built on love and choice, not upon the duty and obligation that are at the core of marriage, entered into with the marriage vows and promise made to God. Without these vows and promises to honor and obey their husbands, women in Shaker society were empowered. Mother Ann had advised mothers to gently love and nurture their children as gifts of God and to keep them clean, neat, and well fed.[7] Susan had found a new family of faith and physical support among the Shakers. The men of the village were equally kind and good to her. They served a paternal role for the young girl. She was fed and clothed by the good Shaker people as well as any child could hope for in the days that followed the War of 1812.

Many youths left the Shakers after they reached the age of eighteen or older. Susan stayed with the Shakers throughout her life, which may show she had received kindness and nurturing under their supervision. There was fear driven into the younger Shaker members "that a departure from the society or its faith, will be followed by disgrace and ruin."[8] But how is this that different from other Christian traditions? Most religions preach that theirs is the one true way. The legal definition of her acceptance into the group was similar to being indentured. Before Susan reached maturity in the community, she had become a possession of the group. She was likely separated from her mother so their traditional sense of affection did not interfere with her mother's pursuit of her own spiritual progress.

In their eyes, order in Shaker society was more easily carried out without the complications that were a part of more traditional family relationships.[9] One might think that this resulted in some sort of institutional deprivation and an inability to form lasting relationships in life, but this was not the case with Susan. She had many close friendships with other Shaker members. Social roles were altered to benefit the group in Shaker society, but this did not alter her ability to make lasting relationships.

Children rose in some Shaker communities at 4:30 in the morning, and after their prayers they began their daily chores. They cleaned their rooms, fed and watered the farm animals, milked the cows, and in winter brought in the firewood. One of Mother Ann's rules in raising children was: "You must keep them to work; not allow them to be idle; for if you do, they will grow up just like the world's children."[10] This rule kept them busy most of the time. There were good times as well. During the summer the children enjoyed half a day a week to swim in the river, play games or have picnics. The children had no "world's toys" but made their own toys out of everyday objects they found around the farm or in the woods. They were not allowed any commercially made toys. Mother Ann had felt that they should, "let them look at their hands and fingers and see Gods work."[11] They were also denied bows and ribbons on their clothing. In spite of the rules that may have denied them, they made their own toys and enjoyed their childhood. This may have raised their sense of creativity and invention. These were skills the Shakers were known to have an abundance of.

At meals the children were not overfed and were taught to have very good table manners. Discipline was not severe and children over the age of twelve had no fear of being struck with sticks. Only in rare cases of very bad behavior were children physically punished. If children were that big of a behavior problem, they were thrown out of the order and returned to their parents. In the case of Susan this would have been difficult. Of course, the offending children also would have been told of the possibility of their descending to Hell for their bad behavior. Their education was primarily religious, but also consisted of reading, writing and arithmetic. The Bible and other religious texts needed to be accessible to them.

The children of the village received their education in a small schoolhouse located on the property. Their training and education was based upon their natural talents and in what way they could best serve the group. Girls went to school in the summer, and boys went in the winter. Susan learned her lessons well in the school, as can be seen by her years of work in the office and her skillful journal writing. At age fourteen she moved in with the adult members of the society and took on a full work load. Her formal education in the schoolhouse would have then ceased. As Susan grew she helped out at most of the trades in the village, and she worked for years in the office. Later in life she chose to work as a tailoress, like her father, as her primary role in the community.

It is unclear whether Abraham could have been able to come and reclaim his daughter or not if he wished to, after she was taken in by the Shakers. There are cases of parents who left the group and tried to take their children with them. There was also a murder case in which a Civil War veteran came to reclaim his child, and ended up shooting and killing one of the Shaker leaders of the community when this was denied to him. To many parents outside the Shakers they "conceal(ed) their children in hiding places provided by the sect."[12] If Abraham had first become settled in Lower Canada and then tried to reclaim his daughter, it would have been very difficult for him to get her back.

Later, while Susan worked as a tailoress, she struggled with a problem that would not trouble most people living in today's modern society. Susan was dedicated to her job, and carefully cut her cloth and stitched her clothing together with the greatest degree of care and pride. It was within this pride that she found her greatest conflict. You might not want to hire anyone to work for you who does not take pride in their work in the modern day. It is more difficult to find someone who does take pride in their work. This particular kind of pride is fine, but lies close to the sinful pride of feeling you are superior. Susan had to show care to not carry over into this pride, one of the seven deadly sins.

It is written in the Bible in the Gospel of Mark 7:20-23 that: "Thefts, covetousness, wickedness, deceit, lasciviousness, an evil eye, blasphemy, pride, foolishness: All these evil things come from within, and defile the man." Being well versed in the Bible Susan naturally guarded against this sin. Pride was also a topic on Abraham's first wife Abigail's gravestone:

> A heap of dust alone remains of thee,
> 'Tis all thou art, and all the proud shall be![13]

Pride should be more of a matter of concern today. People take too much pride in their material possessions such as their expensive cars and homes. This was not a part of everyday life in the Shaker Village. Susan did not care about riches on Earth, she held more concern for storing wealth in Heaven. Prayers and good deeds alone store this wealth. Susan seems to have conquered her struggle with pride that she may have inherited from her father, and we should all attempt to do the same.

In order to join the Shakers, Mary had to live with them for a minimum trial period of one week. This time could have been and often was much longer. At the end of this time the daily cross was taken up, to regenerate and strive for salvation. The first cross taken up was to confess all of your sins to the elder. Until this was done a person could not hope to find any peace or any pleasure in life. Any sins in the community were witnessed by four angels that were placed there by Mother Ann in various places in the village to watch over her children. These angels could only be seen with the eyes of faith.[14] Some of the Shakers used invisible golden glasses to see the spirit world. After this initial entry Mary entered the novitiate trial period that lasted for at least two years. In Mary's case it seems to have lasted longer. During this time Abraham's estranged ex-wife lived with the "gathering family," who lived in the Harvard community within the South Family dwelling house.

On October 11, 1821, Mary officially followed her daughter Susan into the Shaker community. Susan was quickly accepted into the group because she was a child and she lacked the sin of an adult. Mary was treated for an illness she had on her face that the modern medicine of Doctor Sewall in Chebacco had been unable to cure. On January 10, 1821, they made medicine for her to take to help out with her illness which were recorded in the Shaker diaries. The medicine was likely prepared with herbs and other natural ingredients. If this treatment cured Mary, the Shakers succeeded where the modern medicine of the period had not. There is no further mention of her illness from that point on in the journals. The Shaker medicine and prayer seems to have cured her. At the time of this care she was staying with the East Family of the Shakers, and on September 17, 1822, she moved in to live with the South Family from the East Family. With so few personal possessions, moves occurred quickly.

On May 31, 1823, Mary's daughter Mary Smith came on the stage for a visit from Boston. Although Shakers like Mary had left the world behind and had a new faith family, they stayed in contact and visited with their biological families. Two days later, on June 2, 1823, they had a public meeting on a Sunday and sixty to seventy people came from the world to watch. Mary was among those at the meeting. In a rural world lacking radio and television it seems the Shakers provided an interesting entertainment medium to members of the outside world and local community.

These public meetings were typically held in the spring and summer and the Shakers had a designated service planned. A sermon was given by one of the group's best public speakers to introduce Shaker religious thought to the visitors.[15] The Shakers used dance as a part of their worship. Before the dance the men and women waited in solemn silence wearing special thin shoes while waiting for a small bell to be rung. Once the bell signaled to come in the men and women entered the room and the brothers lined up on the right side and the sisters on the left. The two groups faced one another about five feet apart. The elder entered the space between, gave a short speech, and then the dancing commenced. A few chosen Shakers sang in the middle, and there were no instruments used to accompany either the singing or dancing. It would be surprising, if Mary was not among the chosen singers.

At the end of the dance the Shakers came forward and let the elders know if they had received any gifts. Often these gifts were given to them by angels. The gifts may have included being told of the visits of spirits of dead Indians who sought salvation, or spiritual gifts of invisible fruit that Mother Ann had sent from heaven. Mother Ann and Jesus sat together in heaven as head elders. They lived there as the Shakers did on Earth, but in a more perfect way. From Heaven they sent the Earth bound Shakers their gifts. The entire Shaker community was made up of these spiritual gifts. Clothing designs, furniture designs, and the designs of buildings and their interiors. With the incredible beauty and simplicity of Shaker design it is easy to imagine that these may have been Heaven sent.

If we follow the life of Susan Channell through the Shaker diaries, her story begins to appear prominently in them in the late 1820's. On June 16, 1829, she traveled to the Shaker village in Shirley with the ministry. Traveling with the ministry shows she held an important place in the community.[16] She may have worked as a secretary or recorded information or transactions. Another Shaker was listed in the journal that day leaving the village to go to the Connecticut River to gather broom corn. The Shakers made brooms, an easily learned trade, and were the inventors of the flat broom. This idea may have also come from a divine inspiration or gift. And who can really question where the sources of great ideas come from? They achieved the new broom design by flattening out the traditional round broom in a vise and used thread to flatten it out permanently and improve the sweeping surface.[17] This broom design survives in broom design in the modern day. Brooms were once a huge industry in New England. Outside the Shaker community they made them also, and these brooms served as a cottage industry to make extra income for those with extra time and ambition.

On May 26, 1830, Susan went with some of the Shakers to get sand in Acton, Massachusetts. The diary does not say what the sand was to be used for; sand had many uses on the farm. On August 13, 1830, the following was recorded in the Shaker diary:

> Pleasant, Benjamin Winchester sen. Eliza Babbit, Susan K.
> Myrick Susan Channel, Sarah Winchester, Clarissa Orsment, &
> Abigail Babbit went to Littleton a Whartle berrying, they had a
> span of horses.[18]

Some of the berries were likely consumed by the Shakers, and extra berries were processed into jelly and other goods and sold to "the world." This diary entry and the one before it demonstrate the community spirit that the Shakers approached their work with. Many hands made the work easier and more pleasant to complete with others to carry on conversation with. The news of the world, however, was never discussed if you wished to be a good Shaker, although mention of events outside of their society does appear in the Shaker journals. Private letters were to be shown to the Elders, who decided if this correspondence could or could not be read. Magazines and books were only allowed to be read by the Elders in Harvard.[19]

When other Shakers were ill, Susan Channell helped in their care, such as she did on March 31, 1831, when Sister Betty was said to be feeble.[20] But the Shaker life was not all consumed in work and caring for others. On July 30, 1831, "Simon T.A. Olive Hatch, Selah Winchester & Susan Channel rode around Lyttleton Square."[21] This showed that the Shakers enjoyed a ride to see the sights and sounds of "the world." The Shakers traveled on wagons to local communities to visit and sell their goods. Susan received a visit from some cousins on the Smith side of her family on May 30, 1835.[22] On September 2, 1837, Mary Smith came to see her mother with someone described as an "aged man."[23] A month later Susan received a visit from another aged man, but first a jump forward to the events at the Holy Hill of Zion.

Outside of the village stood a tall hill where the Shakers began having their meetings in the early 1840's. These outdoor areas were known as "feasting grounds," where Shakers feasted on spiritual gifts. The hilltop was ten rods long and eight rods wide and contained a half acre of land that was cleared and flattened with great effort by the Shaker men. A fence was built around it, and a double row of maple trees were planted along the edge. At the center was placed the Lords stone. The Lords Stone was surrounded by a low hexagonal area outlined by a low fence, and on this stone it read:

> For the healing of the nations, who shall here seek my favor.
> And I will pronounce all people who shall come to this
> fountain, not to step within this enclosure, nor place their
> hands upon this stone while they are polluted with sin. I am
> God the Almighty in whose hands are judgment and mercy.
> And I will cause my judgments to fall upon the willful violator
> of my commands in my own time according to wisdom and
> truth, whether in this world, or eternity. For I have created all
> souls, and unto me they are accountable. Fear ye the Lord.

Roben Campbell, a local Shaker researcher, described an event that took place years ago at the location of the stone atop the hill during a private tour she took me on. I had received an e-mail with Roben's contact information after a visit, and many calls and e-mails to the museum. It seems no one at the museum wanted or cared to help me with Shaker Susan's story. I suppose I should have given up, but then I never would have received Roben's help, nor made her friendship. Roben and I climbed Zion Hill one hot early summer day. We were the only souls on the hill that morning; at least the only souls that we were aware of.

On the way up she told me of a tour guide, who gave a lecture years ago atop Zion Hill, and mistakenly lost his balance and stepped on the carved base of stones that once held the Lords stone. The sky immediately turned dark and a tremendous storm swept in with a torrential downpour. Everyone ran down the hill and away from the wrath of the Lord's stone. Neither Roben nor I wanted to test the power of the stone base on that hot summer day. I kept my hands and feet away and just took photos; in the shade of the tall trees that now grow atop the hill. Whether I was being superstitious or just respectful, I did not decide to tempt the power of the stone. The Lords Stone still remains hidden wherever the Shakers have hidden it, waiting to be discovered.

Lord's Stone slot on Zion Hill, photo by author.

The journey to the top of the hill takes a bit of physical exertion and energy and it is not known if the older Shakers made the journey to the top in wagons or if they stayed below in the village. Climbing the hill released what we know today as endorphins, small protein molecules that are naturally released in the body and act with the brain and nervous system. Endorphins are known to; relieve pain, reduce stress, suppress the desire for addictive substances, and to create a natural high and euphoria such as that enjoyed by long distance athletes. Endorphins allow warriors to continue fighting in battle in spite of injury, and for others to accomplish amazing physical achievements of strength. The unknowing pursuit of these endorphins through Shaker dance rituals and climbs up that steep hill made the Shakers healthier and extended their lives by slowing the aging process. The natural endorphins released in the blood are a far more powerful drug than anything that can be obtained over the counter from modern medicine. This exercise may have released an ecstatic feeling on top of the outside ceremony area that was attributed to a religious experience in Shaker journals. Not to say that these experiences should or can be easily explained away by modern medical science or modern understanding of adrenaline.

The sect was visited by all manner of spirits and received many "gifts" on top of the Holy Hill of Zion. Roben Campbell told me "A gift can be a decision made as to a course of action, and a gift can be a message received in ecstasy when the celebrant would need the physical support of others around them."[24] The Shaker diaries put Susan Channell on the hilltop on June 8, 1844, but surely she was there on many other occasions and was a part and witness to the goings on among the Shakers on top of the hill. Susan Channell was one of the oldest among them to receive these "gifts" from the spiritual realm.

One example of Shaker gifts that were received was the appearance of their long dead leader Mother Ann, along with George Washington, who served as her escort. They had their celestial messages read by a Shaker that the spiritual travelers had given their gift of this message to. A couple years later the father of the country again returned, and this time Washington brought a bowl of strength, with an invisible spoon to eat it with. This was passed around and enjoyed by the Shakers. They were often visited by deceased Shakers who had other various gifts to share. Quite often they were visited by dead Native spirits.

The Shakers enjoyed game that their spiritual guests had hunted for them. This spiritual food was placed alongside their common earthly food. The Natives also once brought a gift of a canoe full of love. The Natives had accepted Mother Ann early on in New York and respected her and their spirits seem to have continued a spiritual connection with the Shakers after her death. The social structure of the Native

Americans may have also seemed similar to that of the Shakers. The Harvard group also enjoyed visits by William Penn, the Quaker founder of Pennsylvania, and a visit from some French prophets, the early inspiration for their movement.

The Shakers typically ate the food that they grew and cultivated on the farm. This consisted of a diet of grain and animal proteins. Shakers avoided alcohol use because it was felt to increase sexual drive and lead to a decline in moral and physical health.[25] In later years they experimented with vegetarianism when influenced by other religious and philosophical movements that were taking place in the area. Shakers were open to change. They were always open to new ideas and innovations that made life easier and allowed more time for prayer and were essentially gifts from the Lord.

It might be easy through modern ideology to categorize these events as crazy or insane. One may also question whether they had stumbled on some strange herbs and hallucinated after eating them. These were hard working people who led a Spartan lifestyle and so if they relaxed and let their hair down on that mountaintop, acting out fantasy as spiritual gifts as a temporary escape, then it may make sense. Years ago I did work at a state mental hospital and I recall being led around by a man who I was later told was a patient. I was surprised because he seemed quite sane to me. They told me that once he was taken out of the dormitory, he was like everyone else, but while he was with the other mental patients he seemed quite insane. So perhaps Susan Channell and the others, although sane, were part of some group psychosis. Or just maybe, they were in touch with the spirit world far better than we are today.

Today we focus on material possessions and economic gain in the United States that serve to not only offer us temporary happiness, but stimulate and spur our economy forward. Matters of the spirit that once drove the Puritans to these shores to seek control of their religious worship have fallen by the wayside in the modern world. Science and medicine serve a role as an answer to all of life's problems and it is only after these solutions fail that people often turn to solutions offered in holistic medicine, and things such as meditation to find peace of mind in a busy stressful world. No drug can offer answers as to why your child or loved ones life is tragically cut short. Only a connection to either your internal or an external spirit can offer the strength to deal with the loss and continue living. The few who survive alcoholism, or drug addiction, do so through an understanding that they are powerless against it and need a greater spirit to help them. If you believe in God or an afterlife then you cannot discount that the Shakers, in a higher state of spiritual alertness, may have encountered some of the things they stated without being a hypocrite.

If you believe we enjoy a healthier and longer lifespan today than a century ago you need to take a walk among those at rest in the Shaker cemetery. There are many graves of Shakers who lived to be eighty years old and older. There are some that died from pneumonia and consumption (tuberculosis), such as Abraham's first wife Abigail. But if they were blessed with a resistance to these maladies they could hope to live as long, if not longer, than we live today. Their production of fresh healthy food, low stress levels, and fresh water source, along with exercise from physical work and dancing, proved to have been a good combination for a long life. If anyone does take a walk through the Harvard Shaker Cemetery they will see the work of Susan Channell firsthand.

After the loss of her mentor Caroline King, who she called "mother," Susan was unhappy to see her final resting place and the Shaker cemetery fall into ruin. The Shakers, always looking for a better way, adopted the cast iron markers in 1873, that still mark the Shaker graves. In 1879, after the death of Mother King, Susan began to work diligently on the project, as she noted in her diary. She began this in spite of the Shaker group itself falling into ruin following the Civil War. The new focus on graves and the dead that followed the tragedy of the Civil War may have been an influence on her actions as well. She wrote in January of 1879: "a year ago to day the burying ground was burnt over, this last fall it was grown up and look worst than ever and it was mowed over and brush piled up. What next."[26] Susan was upset at the state of the cemetery and set out with determination to repair and restore it.

Driving in iron stakes and replacing the large slate slabs with cast iron headstones is not usually work for a woman who was then seventy years old, but she was determined to get the job done. She diligently and determinedly continued the project. She received help in the project from Shaker member Brother Elijah Myrick, who was himself fifty-seven and among the few men who still lived in the Shaker group as the male population slowly dwindled and diminished. On December

8, 1879, she wrote "Go to the grave-yard, the last Tablets is set."[27] And she thus succeeded in her mission to repair and restore the cemetery. The following spring Shaker Susan was interred there as well, her work on Earth then over.

In many ways the Shaker cemetery reflects the Shaker beliefs and Shaker Susan Channell's ultimate defeat of pride. Traveling through other cemeteries throughout the world pride can be seen being taken to the grave by people who purchase large monuments to put atop themselves or their leaders. When you walk through the Shaker cemetery all the lollipop markers are the same and are without any prideful statements or adornments. Some members of the community surely gave more than others with the gifts that were given to them from above. But in the Shaker cemetery they all lie beside one another resting as equals.

As stated before, the Shakers, through the act of celibacy and the denial of other earthly pleasures, may have reached some higher plane of spiritual reality. They certainly reached higher levels of design in furniture and have had a lasting effect on architecture also. Their pure simplicity and functionality is striking and beautiful. Their fresh water supply was bottled and offered as a cure for many illnesses. This may well have been true with the long life spans of the members of the sect. Today the spring bubbles out of the ground untapped and unused, while people pay for much lower quality water in plastic bottles that now litter and pollute the Earth. Not just on land but also in the world's oceans. The immortality of plastic is not an attribute to humanity. Mass produced and quickly discarded goods are the rule today, in sharp contrast to the quality of Shaker goods that were made to last.

Susan and her mother Mary lived out their full long lives with the Shakers, and are buried in the cemetery, along with their other Shaker brothers and sisters. Mary Channell died June 24, 1855, at the age of ninety-one, and her daughter Susan died on May 2, 1880. both of them were good Shakers till their last breath. The Shaker membership dwindled and the Harvard Village closed for good in 1918. Celibacy made it impossible for their group to reproduce themselves and replenish their membership. The age of mass industry and cheaply made goods made inexpensive goods very accessible, and their high quality Shaker goods less desirable. Today Shaker furniture is highly prized by collectors and command high prices for their magnificent and often imitated design. Skillfully made goods enjoy a sense of immortality of their own.

Today just a few Shakers remain at the final existing Shaker village in Maine. Perhaps Eldress Marguerite Frost said it best in 1967, when less than twenty Shakers then remained. "Someday, people will know from the light in our faces and our kindness that Christ is in all of us. Someday the world will come around."[28] Let's hope that someday the gift of peace and lack of pride that the Shakers enjoyed for over two hundred years will be heard by leaders around the world. In a world where all people are fed, clothed, and cared for out of a spiritual love for mankind such as the Shakers cared for their own.

Mary Channell's grave, Shaker Cemetery, Harvard, MA. photo by author.

Defiance on the Border in 1812

I arranged to meet my new friend and fifth cousin Lewis Channell on my way back from dropping off my oldest daughter at Lake Ossipee in New Hampshire. My younger daughter sat in the back seat listening in rapt attention to her iPod and was not too surprised to find her father had yet another adventure in store for her. When I arrived at the parking lot of the Lubberland Creek Preserve in New Market, New Hampshire, Lewis and I shook hands as we met for the first time. Lewis was much larger than I am and my small hand was lost within his great firm grip. I also correspond with Lewis's wonderful sister Ruth, who had discovered and sent to me many of the Essex County Court documents that I used to piece together much of Abraham's legal story in Essex.

I followed Lewis as he crashed deep through the brush to show me the foundation of Robert Channell's home, the third born son of Abraham. Lewis and I may have been separated by many generations, but we have a similar sense of humor and like to trample through thickets and battle vicious mosquitoes as big as birds in search of adventure. There by the Great Bay, the insects staked their claim by biting us unmercifully. Over 230 acres of land once owned by the Channell family and their descendants have been safeguarded there. The New Hampshire Channell's cut stone by hand from the land to build many of the mill structures in the nearby community. They carried food to market in

Portsmouth, N.H. and the local mill town by wagon and sold it there in the city. Family members traveled back and forth between Bolton, in Lower Canada, and the New Hampshire sea-coast to visit and help one another with planting, harvests, and construction projects. The women helped one another with the care and childbirth of their children. They were a family without borders.

We first visited the overgrown foundation of the home and the nearby well which supplied Robert Channell with fresh drinking water, water that sustained his health until he almost reached one hundred years of age. The lichen covered slabs of granite were all that remained of the old Channell homestead hidden in the dense shade. Lewis left for a minute to find the foundation of the old barn that he remembered from his youth, before vandals sadly burned it down. The deep well near Robert's home was covered over to prevent anyone accidentally falling into its depth. The home-site was now surrounded by tall trees and brush that had reclaimed what had once been a clearing, where a busy family left and returned from carrying out their farm chores. I made a mental note to someday return with bug spray and search for artifacts that surely lay right below the surface. This could be the perfect site for a bit of archeology.

I was quite engrossed searching for the well cover so I could lift it up and peer down inside. Light shone down here and there through the trees, and I struggled to find the way to clear the leaves so I could pry back the lid. I swatted constantly at mosquitoes and cleared the sweat that dripped steadily from my forehead. Just about then a large shadow loomed over behind me and I froze for an instant. I tentatively looked behind me and was relieved to see Lewis had returned. I breathed a sigh of relief. "Lewis you scared me half to death," I said. "Well who did you think was coming up behind you here in the woods?" He said with a big grin. "If he only knew." I thought to myself. "if he only knew." It felt like the spirits of our family were all around us.

Lewis and I then went to a coffee shop and sat down to talk. My newly discovered cousin then surprised me by taking out a Bible which was over two hundred years old and had once belonged to Robert, my 4th great-uncle. This was a relic of my family's past that had been passed down from father to son through the many intervening years, decades, and centuries. Lewis handed me the Bible to look at while he told me it was as much a part of me as him. This meant a lot to me. His family had cherished their past and mine had abandoned theirs. It was wonderful to feel I had recovered a bit of it. Nothing brings the past alive like holding an artifact like that in your hand. I carefully open the ancient vellum cover and peered at the contents inside. The smell of antiquity and time leaped off the page and assaulted my senses. The vital dates of the family's life offered me more clues in my research, written in the hand of Robert or his wife Lydia. Although separated by centuries, Lewis and I found family and friendship. Through a war, Robert and his older brother Abraham Junior strove to keep their family together, although they lived on opposite sides of the conflict that now threatened to tear their world apart.

The War of 1812, brought great opportunity for profit on the border between Vermont and Lower Canada, for men daring enough to smuggle products across it. The war was unpopular in the Northern States, and the prevailing political sentiment of the dominant political party, the Federalists in the north, did not support the war or President Madison's Republican administration. Supporters of the war were often called a "Jeffersonian jackass" or a "Madison fool." Because of this political divide Abraham would not have been seen as an enemy on the U.S. side of the border. Since he lived just over twenty miles from the border, Abraham might have been in great danger, if there was a serious attack. Abraham and his family remained safe for a time, due to the lack of a concerted effort to mobilize forces, and the opposing local public opinion to fight in the north.

Poor roads in the area made the lake a more desirable method to quickly transport smuggled goods on. Part of the lake shore touches on either nation, and this made it a useful path to move about supplies. Especially those items that needed to be moved quickly and secretly. One of the most famous smugglers of the lake, immortalized in a poem recalled years later by Abraham's grandson, was Uriah Skinner. Skinners infamous hangout was in a cave, twelve feet high and thirty feet deep on an island in the northwest area of the lake. Just north of where the Channell family lived in Bolton.[1] Other beasts are said to lurk in the area which we will get to later. Skinner avoided capture by rowing into the secret cave on the island, and hiding there from the customs officials.

American General George Izard knew that the lucrative smuggling activity supplied the British army with food and ship parts, but he did not have the manpower to deal with it.[2] Beef, lumber, potash and pearlash continued to be smuggled across the border and on to lucrative markets in the great city of Quebec; north of Vermont. These goods sailed right by the ever watchful eye of Abraham Channell when they passed by him on the lake. We cannot tell if Abraham took a part in this. It seems difficult to believe that he would have missed an opportunity at such a profitable activity.

All that was found of Uriah Skinner, according to the legend told in the poem, was his bones in the cave that he called home.[3] But others were ready to pick up where he left off. Pearlash and potash were lucrative products once they were brought to and sold in Canada. The products were created from the ash of burned trees and branches; a side product of clearing farmland. These salts were then turned into a variety of products. The new difficulty in bringing potash into Canada created by the war likely raised the price, which may have resulted in bigger profits when sold by enterprising smugglers like Skinner in Montreal.[4] The fact that the story was later told by a grandson of Abraham may implicate the family knew the smuggler well.

Lake Memphremagog formed a natural bridge between the people of northern Vermont and the large French speaking cities to the north. It was far easier at that time for them to get goods to market in the Canadian cities, than in the cities located in the south such as New York. The demand for beef had grown quickly with the outbreak of war in 1812. Unfortunately, this demand was to feed British troops, who were supposed to be the Americans enemy. This caused a difficult situation for customs officers who were appointed to stop smuggling on the border in Lower Canada. These armed customs officials were no match for the overwhelming smuggling problem that they were empowered to stop, and they were only slightly successful in doing so.

The resistance of the local inhabitants of the Champlain Valley in New York and Vermont to the embargo shows that many members of the population put their own economic interests before those of the federal government. They also had little interest in supporting the war that was being pushed for far away in Washington by the War Hawks. They had very different political ideas from those in Washington. Their resistance to the groups of armed customs officials may have been reminiscent of earlier mistrusts of standing armies, such as those that once occupied Boston at the outbreak of the Revolutionary War.

Freedom to these rugged individualists who lived on the fringe of civilization like Abraham Channell meant not being told who they could or could not do business with. The so called representative government then controlled by the Virginia dynasty of Jefferson and Madison and their War-hawks in Congress clearly did not have the best interests of Abraham and other settlers in northern Vermont and New York at heart when they passed laws that cut into their livelihood.

The war did not discourage travel into Lower Canada from the Northern States, as can be seen in a letter sent on June 27, 1813, to Robert Channell from his brother Abraham in Bolton, Lower Canada:

> Dear Brother; I take this opportunity to wright to you to inform you of our health and likewise the situation of father Channels health in partickelar; being very unwell all this spring back; and now is worse than ever and thinks he shal not live a greate while at the longest; all though he makes out with much adue to come over and see me once in a greate while; and seems to be all the while concerned that he shall not see you no more; and perhaps none of the rest: Unless you come and see him amediately.[5]

The illness that Abraham suffered from is not given in the letter; it must have been of great concern to his son Abraham to have sent the letter to his brother Robert. The illness, whatever it was, had lasted months and likely weakened the man considerably. The letter continues:

> He is desirous; that you should come and see him and take your paper:, that belong to you; as you ought to have them; brother come to the commanding officer of the gard and ask liberty and permishion from him to come and ask for your father and friends no doubt but what he will grant you a permishion and put it in your letter that you could wright to your father or friends to come and see you there in derby the other side of the line where the gard is kept to let him no that you have come in order to see him an els you perhaps you might stay longer than needful it is onely about twenty miles from the gard to your friends: there is no difficulty on this side of the line in a mans coming in and seeing his friends at present and returning in safety as yet and probably will bee father Channel lives on his farm with the family that he let his place two for this season he lost considerable of debts by the turn of times.[6]

The Immortal Patriot

Abraham urged his brother to come to the border guard and call for his family to come and see him there. This part of the letter shows that the war was not causing travel to be stopped between the two areas. Most of the inhabitants, now known as Late Loyalists, had recently immigrated to the area and still had family on the other side of the border. Other than the aging Loyalists from the Revolution, there seemed to be no animosity yet towards the American threat located south of the border. Just how the war had affected Abraham senior's financial situation is unknown. The letter does place him still living on the western side of the lake. Some men prospered with the coming of the war, but it seems to have had a negative effect on Abraham's income.

Abraham Junior continued with his letter discussing a man from the area he grew up in:

> Father Channel was in the town of Stanstead on business and found and new Burnham of Chebacco and seys that he cannot find the man that gave him that note for his fur; he, looks and says that he is destitute of--- property him self and the appearance of him he must be poor indeed he is quite ragged and works out at day; works I saw him myself last week—

From this part of the letter it appears that Abraham senior had begun to trap for fur and had others who lived at the home he had in Bolton. He had sold some fur but not yet been paid for it. This may have been while he lived with the family that he later sold his property to. Abraham junior continued in his letter:

> Brother Robert I have seven children the six is a daughter the next boys; my wife is quite unwell the rest in joy a reasonable have health at present I have had the small pox this spring I kitch the disorder in montreall on the road hom taken sick and detained twenty nine days before I could start: it cost me twenty nine dollars and half: I have twelve in famerly; sister George has a family of boys all well at present; (unknown) has one young Frenchman with my regards to you all gave my respects to all who should in quire for me like wise the rest of the friends wish to be remembered to all who should inquire for them So we remain your friends and brother
> Abraham Channel jun

Going to the city of Montreal greatly increased the possibility of catching disease. Abraham Jr. was likely bringing goods from his farm to Montreal to sell. In a time without healthcare insurance the burden of the expense had to be faced and paid for by the family. The letter also shows the migration of French speaking citizens from the cities to the English areas in the south to help out on farms. Abraham Juniors first wife Sarah may have caught the smallpox from Abraham; she later died, possibly from this disease on April 14, 1814. The younger Abraham, my fourth great grandfather, remarried a woman named Jane Taylor, and had another six children. More offspring than his own father had, in spite of his four marriages.

Up until this point the war had not troubled those who lived in the Eastern Townships. Militia were organized to defend the area in case of attack, and the local Captain who was put in charge of the militia was Moses Copp. Copp lived across the lake from Bolton in a place then called Copp's Ferry. Copp had fought on the American side during the Revolution in the New York and New Jersey campaigns and earned the rank of sergeant.[7]

His commanding officer was Colonel John Nixon; who later earned the rank of Brigadier General. Back in 1776, he had been stationed at Fort Mount Washington on Lake Champlain.[8] Today the site is known as Fort Independence and is one of the best preserved Revolution-era forts. Copp now found himself on the British side in this later conflict and needed to defend himself from the nation he had once served. He may have enlisted on the side of the Americans in the Revolution, but his sympathies could have lay with the British, as we will see from his in-laws. Not enough to incriminate him, but enough to make a person wonder.

His brother-in-law David Merrill is said to be the man who had rowed General Benedict Arnold out to the *HMS Vulture* to escape the wrath of General Washington, after Arnold's traitorous plan to surrender West point to the British had been discovered. Merrill received a large sum of gold for his help in the escape.[9] It remains unknown if Moses Copp had assisted Merrill in Arnold's escape, but Copp did claim to have been there when both Major John Andre was captured and Arnold escaped.[10]

The motivation of Copp and others in the area to join the Lower Canadian Militia was more likely for self preservation and protection of property than political ideology. It also may have raised his reputation in the community and increased his influence. There is no record of the enlisted men in Copp's militia, but the Channell, Peaslee, and George families, who had traveled there from Weare were likely called out to train. Why Abraham Channell senior was not in a leadership role with all his military experience is a mystery. Perhaps he had grown tired of war. He may have strongly sided with the Federalist view opposing Jefferson and the Republicans, but had not been willing to take up arms against the United States.

In the United States, filling out the militia was proving to be difficult. Many citizens in the north did not favor the war and President Madison had trouble filling out and building up his army. The Militia Act of 1792, had added to the Constitution the power to take control of militia troops if the country were invaded, or feared invasion by foreign powers or Native tribes. In cases of insurrection, or if there was a need to execute laws, the militia could also be taken under federal control. There is no mention of using the power for invading foreign nations, and many men refused at various times to cross the border. There is a clear difference between defending your own home; and attacking the home of another.

The search to find men to fill out the army brought about a struggle in the senate. Daniel Webster and others argued against this draft in Washington in 1814:

> That measures of this nature should be debated at all, in the
> councils of a free government, is a cause of dismay. The
> question is nothing less than whether the most essential rights
> of personal liberty shall be surrendered, and despotism
> embraced in its worst form.[11]

Webster knew that many men did not want to invade Canada, he stated, "For the conquest of Canada the people will not enlist." He also argued in Congress against the plans that the War Hawks were trying to implement to force men into military service. Webster continued:

> Is this, Sir, consistent with the character of a free government?
> Is this civil liberty? Is this the real character of our
> constitution? No, Sir, indeed it is not. The Constitution is
> libeled, foully libelled. The people of this country have not
> established for themselves such a fabric of despotism. They

have not purchased at a vast expense of their own treasures and their own blood a Magna Charta to be slaves. Where is it written in the Constitution, in what article or section is it contained that you may take children from their parents and parents from their children and compel them to fight the battles of any war which the folly or the wickedness of government may engage in?[12]

The American government wished to draft and force men to fight; to stop the British from impressing and forcing them to fight. Clearly the American leadership was going to have trouble conquering Canada militarily. The draft found tough opposition once again during the Vietnam War and its public protests a century and a half later.

In Quebec, Lieutenant General Sir George Prevost held power from 1811-1815, and was fluent in both English and French. Prevost began to implement reforms that put some French speaking leaders back in power, which turned the French population successfully back into the government's graces.[13] Prevost had both military triumphs and failures during the War of 1812. The war was caused in part by perceptions that the British were aiding and influencing the Natives in the west to harass American settlements. Native Abenaki in the Memphremagog area were no longer a problem to the settlers who lived in the region as they had been before the French and Indian War. So there was no fear of them attacking the Northern United States as there had previously been. The natives were, however, a threat further west. British impressment is now the usual American textbook definition for the cause of the war.

The U.S. economy was hurt by embargoes of American trade in Europe, and the War Hawks in Washington pushed for the war to advance American prestige. Some of the War Hawks may have also wanted to add Canada to the nation. They had failed to accomplish this during the Revolution and this failure may have been still fresh in the minds of some War Hawk leaders. The Impressment of American seamen was important, but in the northern United States this was seen as being of less importance than totally closing down the ports and the ensuing economic disaster it created. The states of Vermont and upstate New York near Abraham were not concerned with impressment; they were too far from a seaport. Abraham, of course might have had his own strong opinions about it, having once suffered at the hands of his own impressment.

When Prevost began to recruit men for the militia, he knew that the regular troops were the ones he must depend on. The militia would serve a secondary role in support of them. Prevost proved to be a good leader as he faced an overwhelming opponent with a vastly larger population. The Atlantic region around Nova Scotia was vulnerable, but the areas of Upper and Lower Canada were seen as most vulnerable. The men under the command of Moses Copp and the other captains were seen by Prevost as "ill-armed and without discipline." Men like Copp had to do a lot of training and drilling to make their men become good soldiers.[14] Prevost had concerns about arming men like Abraham Channell, who had only recently emigrated from the United States. He felt that in Upper Canada only 4,000 out of 11,000 troops would be loyal.[15] It is not likely they would have crossed the border and attacked their extended families and former communities in the states.

When the war broke out in June 1812, the British still had their hands full in Europe with Napoleon. The complexity of defending a border that then stretched thirteen hundred miles was daunting. The population of the United States was eight million, while all of British North America in the Canada's was only a half million people. The strategy of Prevost included holding Quebec at any cost; to be later used as a port for reinforcements from Britain, if any lost territory needed to be retaken. His orders from Britain were to take a defensive stance in the area, which he dutifully implemented.[16] Montreal and Quebec held the largest centers of population in Canada, and they were clearly important population areas to defend. Prevost knew that any offensive military action taken by him may change public opinion in northern U.S. cities and force retaliation from their current passive position. The defensive strategy taken by Prevost and the many family relationships such as the Channell family which existed between the regions of Lower Canada and the surrounding Northern States effectively stopped a large assault coming from the cities in the United States.

Orders were issued from Montreal on July 9, 1812, for the militia to hold themselves ready and be prepared to march at the shortest notice. Some recent settlers of the Townships now had to choose their loyalties for real. The time for sitting on the fence had come to an end. They may have traveled to Canada to easily acquire inexpensive land but now they had to choose sides. The Channell family chose to stay in

Lower Canada and protect their new home against a potential American invasion. News from home in Massachusetts, however, held no sign of hostility for the moment.

Prevost reveals his belief in not angering the citizens of the northern United States in a letter to British Prime Minister Robert Jenkinson, the Second Earl of Liverpool in 1812. "In the present state of politics in the United States, I consider it prudent to avoid every measure which can have the least tendency to unite the people of America."[17] He knew opinions of northern U.S. citizens differed from the war-hawks in the American government. The north enjoyed and benefited from the business of reciprocal trade with Lower Canada. Nevertheless an American army was brought to the border, and an attack on Montreal and Quebec was imminent.

Charles-Michel de Salaberry was an experienced and capable Canadian leader who led troops at the Battle of Chateauguay. This took place on October 26, 1813.[18] He had raised 380 of his own men and earned himself the military title of lieutenant-colonel.[19] He was also given an attachment of fierce fighting Mohawk Natives to supplement his troops. Men under his command were commissioned captain if they were able to enlist thirty-six men. This may have been how Moses Copp received his rank as captain in the local militia, and why Abraham Channell had not.

Just prior to the attack on Chateauguay, on October 11, 1813, an American attack force entered Missiquoi Bay on Lake Champlain. This area lies just to the southwest of Bolton and not far from the Channell's home. The American force had one sloop, ten bateaux, two scows, and a troop strength consisting of four hundred men. They raided a village, a store, and took a large amount of goods and some militia supplies. The Americans took a great many prisoners after an ineffective defense by the Canadians, and then marched their Canadian prisoners back to Burlington, Vermont by land.[20] Attacks like this continued to raise alarms in the Townships region. But later that month a successful defense was made by the French Canadian militia under Salaberry. The American's luck was about to run out.

Unlike the American Major Generals Wade Hampton and James Wilkinson, Salaberry was a highly experienced officer. Salaberry enlisted in the British infantry at the age of fourteen and served in Europe for fourteen years; and returned in 1810.[21] His experience came in handy at the battle. The American forces meant to cut off supply lines to the west of Montreal with the cities capture, and quickly end the war. It was imperative therefore for Salaberry to repulse the Americans and win this battle. The attack lines were to the west of the area Abraham Channell lived in, but close enough to create apprehension for anyone who lived in the area. To hope to win Canada, however, the Americans first had to get by the clever Salaberry and his *Voltigeurs*.

The Canadians had set up strong defensive positions and blocked the advancing American movement by cutting down trees to slow their path. This was just what had been done to British General John Burgoyne during the American Revolution by the Continentals. Salaberry's Canadians then dug in defensive trenches and prepared for the American attack. Salaberry had received good intelligence and knew the American troop strength and movement. The Canadian Colonel had to win this conflict; he and his *Voltigeurs* were all that stood between the Americans and Montreal and control of the route to the Great Lakes. The future of Canada rested in his leadership. After the American plans to encircle the Canadians failed, the American army misread a small controlled Canadian retreat and charged fully into the main force. They then received huge casualties from heavy musket fire.[22] After this show of poor leadership by the inexperienced American Major General, Wade Hampton, the battle was over.

General Hampton was a wealthy South Carolina planter who owned a large amount of slaves that worked his plantation. At the time of his death he was the wealthiest planter in the United States and held over 3,000 slaves. He had seen some service in the American Revolution, but was ill prepared to lead in his attack on Salaberry and his defensive position in Chateauguay. Hampton survived an investigation into his loss in the attack but later retired from public service after his failure in the battle. William Duane, a secretary to U.S. President Andrew Jackson, shared his own opinion about General Hampton: "I would not trust a corporal's guard nor the defense of a hens roost to him against any equal number of men."[23] The lessons about picking out generals that should have been learned in the revolution had been forgotten by the American military leadership. They were still chosen for all the wrong reasons and not on merit. The northern cities of Montreal and Quebec and the waterway that served as the key to winning Canada remained in British hands.

On the Canadian side, Salaberry became a local legend for his great victory in defending his position against a superior American force. This also cemented French Canadian loyalties in British eyes and was seen as a great victory for them. Beyond this, except for a small British raid in December, 1813, on Derby, Vermont, that resulted in burned storehouses and barracks, the winter remained quiet in the townships near Abraham. However, the war was not over yet.

In March 1814, the American military leader Major General James Wilkinson sought to strike back against the Canadians in order to retrieve some honor from the sting of his own military failures the previous year at Chateauguay. Striking out across the melting snow, Wilkinson and his troops attempted to take the Canadian stronghold located at Isle-aux-Nois over the frozen river ice, but the British defenders had kept the ice broken up just in case of an attack such as this. Five miles before the Isle-aux-Nois they tried to capture Lacolle Mill, a large stone three-story building that was only lightly defended. French Canadian *Voltigeurs* and *Fencibles* came out in defensive support and some British gun boats fired on the Americans as well. The British employed Congreve rockets that were not only capable of setting buildings on fire, but could explode and spread musket balls. This was new technology for war. Some casualties were caused by these rockets; the effectiveness of them may have been mostly psychological.[24] The end result was that the stronghold was held by the British and Canadians.

In 1814, Napoleon was defeated in Paris and a large amount of British veteran regulars, no longer needed in Europe (not knowing Napoleon would later return from Elba), were sent to Governor Prevost. After Prevost received this much more powerful force he changed from the defensive strategy that had worked so well, to an offensive one. The British held naval superiority on Lake Champlain, but the Americans had been building vessels to challenge their dominance. As previously mentioned, citizens in Vermont had been supplying the British with beef and supplies, so Prevost did not wish to attack there. This would have cut off his own supply; that came from those that were supposed to be his enemies. Prevost then settled the attack plans on the town of Plattsburg, on the western New York side of Lake Champlain.

The winter had seen both sides struggle to build up gunboats in order to gain naval superiority on the lake. In addition to this, U.S. military leaders were gathering veteran seamen in New York and Boston. along the seacoast, to send to the lake to pilot the vessels. Spars, masts, and barrels of tar were crossing the border from Vermont, and being sold to the British to help build their gunboats. Sometimes these supplies were captured, and in some cases not. Smuggling of beef and other supplies was proceeding at a furious pace, If not for this the British might have found great difficulty feeding their troops. Prevost wrote to London:

> Vermont having shewn a decided opposition to the War, and very large supplies of specie daily coming in from thence, as well as the whole of the cattle required for the use of the troops, I mean for the present to confine myself in any offensive Operations....to the Western side of Lake Champlain.[25]

Small skirmishes continued back and forth across the border throughout the summer months while Prevost laid his plans and built up his navy. It is unknown how this may have affected Captain Copp and the need to call up his men to defend their homes. their drilling and preparation likely continued. Abraham Channell was fortunate for once to have rural roads that made attack difficult. Prevost was under pressure from London to make his move and take the initiative. He did not want to take the offensive until he knew he had naval superiority. He did not want to lose.

Although Prevost had kept his plan secret, General George Izard, a subordinate officer of the failed American leader General Hampton, began to hear about the buildup of troops across the border in August. Much to his dismay, he was ordered out west with a large group of his men. Izard left knowing the folly of this decision. This left his replacement, General Alexander Macomb, with only 1900 men to defend Plattsburg against an estimated 7,000-14,000 British troops that had been battle hardened in the Napoleonic Wars.

Panic spread throughout the Lake Champlain area in early September. People fled south in droves to escape the powerful British force led by British Generals, Thomas Brisbane and Frederick Philipse Robinson, with Governor Prevost commanding right behind them. These men were very experienced and capable officers and veterans of the European campaigns against Napoleon. The slow advance of the huge British army while they waited for the fleet to get in position, however, allowed valuable time for the Americans to build up their defenses, and get their own fleet into position. All this was to no avail as the town of Plattsburgh fell quickly to the British land troops on the first day. The town was then occupied from September 6, until September 11, the day of the naval engagement. The defensive position was placed south of the town across the Saranac River. It was never to receive an attack from the powerful British force.

This was because of a quick and vicious naval battle that occurred between the British and Americans outside the harbor of Plattsburgh on September 11, 1814. Both sides received heavy fire and casualties, but when the smoke of war had cleared the American ships were victorious. The British fired from some shore batteries they had thrown up, but stopped their fire in the middle of the afternoon. To the disgust of the British officers, Prevost, ordered a retreat the following day. He did not wish to take the heavy casualties he feared they would receive if they attacked the defensive structures on the other side of the river. Two days later in Baltimore, Maryland, the British began bombarding Fort McHenry while Francis Scott Key watched from a British vessel. The next morning when he saw a large American flag raised he began to write a poem. This poem survives today as the American national anthem, the Star Spangled Banner. No famous poems were written about the events at Plattsburgh that day, and the event remains overshadowed by the victory in Baltimore. The tide of the war had changed with these victories, and with their loss in New York the British now needed a scapegoat to hang the blame on.

Prevost's leadership and decision to play a defensive role may have saved Canada from falling to the Americans, but his failure in his offensive attack on Plattsburgh cost him his political role in Canada. He was called back to England in April 1815, shortly after he received news of the Treaty of Ghent; that ended the war. Prevost was supported by the French citizens, but attacked by the British citizenry in Canada; a division that existed between the two political groups was once again amplified. Prevost died January 5, 1816, before the court martial that might have cleared his name. This battle ended the struggles in the War of 1812, in the area just south-west of Bolton and the Channell family. Peace had come again.

Hospitality on the lake

One day I received an e-mail from Serge Wagner, a retired university professor who lived in Montreal, Canada. Although English was his second language, he was very fluent and sent me the following e-mail message: "Sir, I am doing a research on cemeteries in Austin, PQ, and have found an abandoned cemetery with the stone (partly broken) of John A. CHANNEL." John A. Channell was the grandson of Abraham FitzJohn Channell. It was the one grave of all my Channell ancestors that I had not found up until that point. Serge felt fortunate to find the remnants of the markers of John Channell and his wife which were almost lost to time. I felt fortunate to have heard of his discovery. I quickly planned to visit that labor day, my only break between classes at the university as I worked on my history degree. I never would have found this cemetery without Serge's help. Even calling two broken up stones on a hillside a cemetery is a stretch. Serge was working tirelessly on historical projects in Austin, Quebec, for the local cultural committee and paying all the expenses out of his own pocket. His historical pamphlets and research tell the story of Austin and all the early settlers. Hopefully his discoveries of small local family cemeteries on private land will lead to their being better cared for and respected.

Near the forgotten stones on a lonely hillside stands a home whose owner was kind enough to let us wander across his property and visit the fallen headstones. The home was too new to have been built by my ancestors. After a short discussion he told me the new home had been built on an old foundation. There is no way to prove it that I could find, but this was likely the foundation to my ancestor's home. When I asked Serge where he thought my ancestors property was, he merely waved his hands around in front of him and said, "It is all around you, they owned all this." Later, after our many adventures that day visiting mill ruins and other local cemeteries he brought me to his vacation home overlooking a pond. There his wonderful wife prepared a meal for all of us. Some local neighbors came to visit, but I unfortunately could not speak French with them. I have since worked hard on learning the language and have been able to roughly translate French records I have used in the story. The hospitality I received that day from Serge and his wife is a fitting introduction to the hospitality my Ancestor Abraham gave to many weary travelers across the lake in what is today known as Georgeville.

In 1814, the year the war ended, Richard Holland began building an Inn on the shore of Lake Memphremagog in Copp's Ferry. The town was named after the ferry service Captain Moses Copp then operated on the lake. Later the following year, on June 1st, Abraham Channell married for the fourth time. His wife's name was Wealthy Cox, whose family had come to the area from Hanover, New Hampshire. Wealthy was born December 16, 1782, and raised on the New Hampshire frontier. She was up to the challenge of settling and raising a family on Memphremagog. Wealthy was thirty-two, but had not yet been married. Abraham, at sixty-six, was thirty-four years her senior when they married. Her isolation in New Hampshire had kept her from meeting younger eligible bachelors and preserved her as a marriage option for Abraham. The two lived on the edge of civilization where few marriage alternatives were available, and she fell for the charm of the much older Abraham. The marriage was Abraham's longest and lasted for 44 years. Holland did not own his tavern for long before he decided to sell the property. Abraham and Wealthy bought and later made the property and tavern a success together.

Earlier in the year 1815, before his marriage, Abraham traveled back home to Chebacco and Durham, New Hampshire, to borrow large sums of money from members of his family, this was likely so he could buy the tavern. Oddly enough the property the tavern stood on or near was purchased by Abraham from James C. Peasley on June 22, 1815.[1] Holland may not have owned the land the tavern stood on, or he may have traded Abraham for other properties. Abraham paid $154 dollars down, and had to pay another $206 to Charles Goodhue who held a mortgage on the property when Peasley purchased it. Abraham found a way to get the property; he was not a man to be denied what he wished for.

A topic of conversation I have with many people somewhat familiar with the story of Abraham is why he chose to leave the United States for Lower Canada? There is no trail of documents or letters that definitively answer the question. With property in Massachusetts and the property that he later sold in New Hampshire, he seemed to be doing fine financially. We have seen hints of possible answers to the question. The loss of his first wife may have led to unpleasant memories of Chebacco and an unwillingness to stay there. Legal problems in both criminal and civil cases are a strong possibility. The severe economic downturn that was caused by President Jefferson's embargo in the years leading up to the War of 1812, is just another reason.

His marriage to Mary Smith had ended in failure. He had lost a daughter and wife to a strange new religion that he likely disliked and felt was odd and possibly blasphemous. He may have felt buried in medical debts for the care of his estranged wife and daughter and this may have troubled him. His daughter needed a place to live in Chebacco and he could have felt it best to let her take over the home. Overwhelmed with heartbreak, he may have sought a fresh start.

Political problems at home also escalated. This began with the collapse of the Federalist Party and the decrease of New England's political influence that had first triggered the American Revolution. A radical wing of the Federalist Party was then centered in Essex County called the "Essex Junto." Although they were a radical offshoot of the Federalist Party, they opposed John Adams, the Federalist candidate for re-election as president in the election of 1800.[2] Some members of the group planned a succession and wanted to form a new "Northern Confederacy" with Canada. Abraham may very well have thought the area he moved to might eventually become part of some new nation after he moved there. Through Abraham's move from England to America, his move from Massachusetts to New Hampshire, and later move to Lower Canada, can be seen a path that moved toward the frontier and its opportunity away from civilization. Although he once lived in one of the largest cities of the world, Abraham rode on the outer wave of civilization as it flowed out to the wild unclaimed lands of the frontier. He was born, and had grown up in an urban life, yet he was drawn to an opposing existence. He now rejected city life for the wilderness.

There on the frontier a man could re-invent himself and through his own hard labor create a new world for himself. Out on the frontier land was cheap and with an ax and ambition a farm could be won and wrestled from the wilderness. Land, not money, was the real measure of a man in Abraham's day. Thomas Jefferson, George Washington, and John Adams all had farms and vast amounts of land. It was everyone's dream, and what they were judged by. So Abraham sought his own great expanse of land there in the frontier of Lower Canada. He yearned for his own bit of country. Along the lake shore and the ancient forest behind it lay a savage land that could be civilized and become more valuable with a lot of sweat equity. Abraham could create his own world anew.

There on the lake the formerly civilized citizen of London became more savage. He trapped and fished in the dense forest and along the shores of the mountain lake as he had learned in New Hampshire. He swung his broadaxe and felled and split trees. He kept a rifle at his side to protect his property and livestock from the beasts that prowled the forest. Beasts that are now extinct and mythical such as the catamount and wolf still prowled the woods in Abraham's day. In modern times sightings of them are scoffed at. Abraham's well made shoes were replaced by moccasins and thick fur boots in the winter. He adopted the warm hats of the french fur traders and trappers. His breeches, stockings, waistcoat, and jacket were set aside for more durable clothing made from fur and leather. He walked the forest in snowshoes atop waist deep snow. He became responsible for his own failure and success. In the forest that cradled Lake Memphremagog Abraham became a self made man. He found true freedom, a freedom that was not given by a political system; but earned by courage and commitment.

The first group of men, led by Nicholas Austin, came along in a canoe and picked out a good spot to begin to cut out and build their rudimentary shelters. With a few animals and tools they could create a new home and beginning. The next wave of settlers planted orchards, built better homes and bigger barns and then began to cut better roads and bridges. Abraham was in this second wave of men. It was the next wave of men that Abraham Channell did not seem to care for.

The group that followed the first two waves of men that flowed into the frontier included men of laws, capital, and industry. They build churches, schools and raise the taxes to pay for it all. Luxury items, fancy clothing, and beautiful homes began to pop up where wolves had once prowled. In their desire to escape civilization men like Abraham had created the opportunity for it to follow them. By the time civilization found Abraham again, he was too old to flee from it anymore. Pioneers are young men, and Abraham was no longer among that group. Rousseau had his own views on society:

> Such was, or may well have been, the origin of society and law,
> which bound new fetters on the poor, and gave new powers to
> the rich; which irretrievably destroyed natural liberty, eternally
> fixed the law of property and inequality, converted clever
> usurpation into unalterable right, and, for the advantage of a few
> ambitious individuals, subjected all mankind to perpetual labour,
> slavery and wretchedness.[3]

This destruction of natural liberty may have been what Abraham had fled the United States to escape. Abraham had in mind a liberty that is captured by the man, and not given to the man by society. He sought a true and natural freedom. The laws of nature create equality. The laws of men on the other hand, promote inequality and self promotion.

Turner stated: "the frontier is productive of individualism. Complex society is precipitated by the wilderness into a kind of primitive organization based on the family. The tendency is anti-social."[4] Abraham still carried within his heart the spirit of the American Revolution. Not the spirit of democracy so much but the spirit of the search for individual liberty. Abraham sought his own liberty and freedom, not liberty or freedom for any state or country. Abraham was his own sovereign, not a subject of a king or congress, until the sprawl of civilization once again caught up with him.

The frontier line that Abraham followed toward the Saint Lawrence River was one of the first frontier lines to be attempted in the colonies. The power and danger of the French allies the Wabanaki people made earlier frontier settlement impossible. The "people of the dawn" were a more potent adversary than any other native people ever faced by the English Colonists. It was their land and they had every right to defend it.

It was not until after they were destroyed by the English that anyone dared to settle on their land. The rivers and trails that Abraham followed north were the same trails that the Wabanaki and French had traveled down to raid the frontier towns of Massachusetts and New Hampshire during the colonial wars.

The dense forest of what became the Eastern Townships then served as a buffer against invasion and retribution. All that changed when Rogers Rangers attacked the Native village of Odanak and afterwards escaped south along the shore of Memphremagog. It had taken a hundred years of fighting to open the frontier of Memphremagog up to Abraham and the other settlers. The blood of conquest then gave way to the sweat of the early settlers. Yet some of the spirit of adventure of the Natives and knowledge of the forests were needed in order to survive.

All that blood was spilled for land. Land is perhaps the only thing more valuable than gold. It is often overlooked today as an item of great value, until a person tries to acquire some. Even today the farther from urban centers you search the more likely you will be able to acquire some inexpensively. A small carry over from the frontier days. Unfortunately, licentious lawyers, exorbitant taxes, and eminent domain threaten the ability to maintain ownership. An entire lifetime can be spent working toward ownership to potentially lose your property to a frivolous lawsuit, or an overburden of taxes.

In Canada it was said that the land was almost free for the taking. There were vast amounts of land and few settlers. In the United States, half of a man's profits were given away in taxes. There in Canada, Abraham had hardly a trifle of taxes to give and everything was cheap to purchase and there was almost no duty.[5] There were also negative sentiments towards the U.S. Constitution in Canada during Abraham's time. One settler of Canada stated:

> The Constitution is I think for my part, copied from that of England, with a great many foolish absurdities along with it. Ragamuffins vote as well as men of property; and to make the best of it, they are governed by slaves and negroes: for the people to the southward, have votes according to the number of their slaves.[6]

The man went on and continued his thoughts:

One cannot but wonder though, that they should hold out so long, where continual janglings, factions and parties, are carried on by a set of interested penniless men: first one up, and then another, and knocking down all that was done by the former: the house that is divided against itself cannot stand: they will soon separate: they will have their kings soon, I am sure.[7]

It is clear from this that some of the early settlers of Canada believed that the U.S. Constitution would not survive too far into the future. While the United States has avoided ever having had a king, it does have and has had kings of banking and industry who wield entirely too much power. It is also interesting that the writer perceived that some citizens in Lower Canada were Canadian, mostly the French, while others were British. In Abraham's time there was a clear division of nationality in Lower Canada.[8] This division survived far after his death and into the next century. The man's prophecy of a "house divided," often quoted in the Bible, was proven all too true in 1861, with the beginning of the American Civil War. Abraham Lincoln warned of that house being divided. Abraham Channell may have also enjoyed laws that were more favorable to him in Lower Canada. There were no game or excise laws whatsoever.[9]

It was also pointed out at the time that "morality and good order are much more conspicuous amongst the Canadians of every description, than the people of the States; drunkenness is undoubtedly much less common amongst them, as is gambling, and also quarrels.[10] These words were written by an Irishman who had come to visit and traveled through both the United States and Canada in the late 1700's. It is worth noting this fact because he was not overly biased to either country. The visitor felt that men like Abraham, who were born in Britain, felt most at home in Canada. This is one belief that Abraham may have also shared. The Irishman also said that the Canadian people, "are in the possession of as much happiness and liberty as those of the neighbouring country."[11]

People today purchase houses not land. Bigger houses and smaller lots are the rule. As long as your home is surrounded by a postage stamp frame of grass the average person today is satisfied. Along with this property, most people become slaves to their lender for thirty years. They then become slaves to their employers in order to pay their lenders. They stay in unsatisfying jobs, to pay for a dream of home ownership many never reach. All this while struggling to buy things to impress other people. This is in direct contrast to Abraham Channell, who never bought property he could not pay for out of his pocket, even if it was with money borrowed from family and friends. No banks existed in the surrounding frontier near Georgeville. No financial institutions fettered men like today. In spite of enslaving people in mortgages for decades, the greed and corruption of banks has caused them to collapse today in the present recession of the early twenty first century. Abraham never shackled himself to banks, lenders, or their capitalist ideals and entanglements.

Land is a finite commodity that can never be increased. Every day new children are born who will someday wish to own a home. That home must rest on land. As the population grows the value of land grows along with it. As more homes are built, there is less land to build on. Economic downturns and government policy can affect the value of land in the short term, but its value is always on the rise. Land was scarce and expensive in Britain when Abraham was impressed. Only the nobles and royalty owned vast amounts of it. This may have held some special meaning to Abraham in his pursuit of his own property. To a man like Abraham, land meant the ability to gain a level of status that may have eluded him in London. By embracing the settlement of land and not the more common pursuit of trade as businessmen in Britain did, Abraham showed that he had now embraced the American ideal of land ownership, as part of his new Canadian dream.

Photo by author.

Grave Robbing and Lake Monsters

There are more things in heaven and earth, Horatio,
Than are dreamt of in your philosophy
-William Shakespeare

The years following the war of 1812, are usually referred to as the "Era of Good Feelings." This was due to the lack of political party opposition to the re-election of President Monroe, the evidence of which hints at a satisfaction with his government. These years did not hold such good feelings for the Channell family. On January 10, 1815, Abraham wrote promissory notes to Elisha Tucker, his skilled furniture making son-in-law and husband of his daughter Betsy. He first borrowed $100 dollars, and then $87.33 on the next note from him.[1] This was a large sum of money to borrow from his family, but this was not all the money that he borrowed. After going home to Lower Canada and discovering he needed more cash he went to visit his son Robert and borrowed $79.00 dollars from him on October 10, 1815.[2] The following day he borrowed $18.00 from his unmarried daughter Sally who lived in Chebacco.[3] What Abraham needed such large sums of money for can only be guessed at, but it seems probable he used the money to pay off the tavern owned by Holland and the land owned by Peasley.

On June 3, 1816, his wife Wealthy gave birth to a girl the couple named Susan. Abraham was now 67 years old. It has already been stated that he gave this daughter the same name as the child born to Mary, his estranged Shaker wife. Perhaps Wealthy named the child while he was away and she did not know about Mary and her child. No simple explanation exists for giving two daughters the same name. Two months later on August 5, 1816, seven-year-old Susan was admitted to the Shakers in Harvard, Massachusetts. Mary either left her daughter or lived in the village while she awaited membership. It must have been a strange year for Abraham in Lower Canada. The odd events of the summer of 1816, caused it to be known as the "year without a summer."

On June 6, 1816, the temperature dropped and suddenly the entire northeast was struck with a hard frost that killed crops and food supplies. This was followed by heavy snows; a strange sight for the early summer. It should have been a time of blooming new plant life. Snow accumulation reports in the area varied from an inch or two to a foot. This unusual event continued for the entire year. The winter weather was caused by the largest eruption known to human history that occurred in Indonesia at Mount Tambora.[4] The resulting ash blocked out the sun and cooled the air temperatures considerably. No greater blow could be struck at an agricultural area like the farms around Memphremagog and across the rest of Northern New England. Abraham and Wealthy's new marriage was surely tested.

The hay crop across the region was a total failure. This crop was needed to feed farm animals such as sheep and cattle and as a result these poor creatures perished in large numbers. Everything was eaten that could be eaten. This led others to recall the period as "the famine year." Nettles were boiled, wild turnips, hedgehogs; all these were consumed as the prices for grain skyrocketed. Fortunately for the Channells, the lake fish could be caught and eaten. The community gathered together for days of fasting and prayer for an answer to their problems.[5] It has to be assumed they did not know of the eruption or the cause of the bizarre weather. In the southern part of the United States hurricanes pounded the coast and destroyed all their crops.[6] It must have been a difficult year in the Townships all around the lake. Food shortages grew and prices soared after the cataclysmic event that continued to spread havoc across the continent. The year of "eighteen hundred and froze to death" was one that would be remembered for many years to come in the area.

The bizarre weather was not the only strange event that year for Abraham. One day while fishing along the shore on Lake

Memphremagog to help his family survive, he had an amazing experience. Abraham, Ralph Merry, and men named Wadleigh and Rider, looked out onto the lake and saw a large serpent's hump slicing through the still water. It amazed Merry so much that he wrote about the strange experience of witnessing this phantasm in his diary. The diary was found years later hidden in his home and donated to the Stanstead Historical Society in Stanstead, Quebec. Abraham was at sea for years in both the British Navy, and as an American privateer, and he had spent a lot of time staring out over the horizon. Sailors do tell their yarns about the beasts that lurk in the sea and Abraham had certainly heard a few while he served aboard the *Milford*, but just what did he see out on the lake that day?

From *Uriah Jewett and the Sea Serpent of Memphremagog* 1917

One tale that Abraham may have heard on board ship was of a creature known as the kraken. The creature was considered a foolish myth by many until evidence of it was later found.[7] In 1880, a giant squid was found washed up on a beach in New Zealand, and that monster's tentacles were over 65 feet long. It is believed they exist in the deep ocean at even larger sizes.[8] This beast resembled the monster described for centuries in folklore. It seems once myths are discovered they then become part of science. Before this occurs they are scoffed at. Latin names are attached to the beasts which are studied by men who are not ridiculed, while the men that seek the undiscovered beasts put up with the smirks of skeptics. What else may be in the deep cold waters of the world waiting to be discovered?

Ralph Merry, Abraham's friend and fellow witness to the creature along the lake shore had many other visions besides the serpent. In 1809, while he lay ill in a cabin he suddenly had a life changing vision. He saw, "the appearance of a man in the sky with blood streaming from him, and it seemed as though I saw him with my natural sight, but probably it was only a verry strong mental view presented through the medium of powerful faith."[9] Whatever powerful event happened to Merry that day, it resulted in a very strong religious conversion.[10] And whatever he thought he saw lurking in the water in the lake, probably represented evil to him. Whatever it was; was not natural. We only know of the monster's appearance and subsequent sighting through Merry and one of the other men that were with them. There is no evidence Abraham ever spoke of it, or even if he just went along with the story for some other reason like attracting visitors to his tavern. With the odd weather and thin dwindling food supplies it is likely Merry looked for some sign of evil in the world to explain the odd weather phenomenon. Could the weather, the serpent, and the economy, have been a punishment from God?

Historians ordinarily resist the temptation of researching and writing about lake monsters, it is generally not a subject that is taken seriously by scholars. But if surviving sources of the belief of them if not actual evidence of their existence exists, it may help to understand past people by being aware of their beliefs and fears. Dragons are a part of both western and Asian culture, but why? History should not have any subjects it is afraid to tackle. History, be it family or society, has no small questions. The more minute the details, however, the more difficult they become to examine. They become as complex as the present as the shroud of time is removed. the black and white of the past becomes more difficult to examine as more is revealed. Everything from the past though should be available for scrutiny. This includes the myths and legends of creatures in the deep. You may not believe in them, but it is interesting to wonder why others did and it gives a look into their society.

Lake Memphremagog is located along a path of lakes around the world that occur on a line described by some as the "monster latitudes."[11] This term refers to the many reports of monsters seen in deep water lakes across the continents at this latitude. Loch Ness is at this latitude. Lake Champlain and many other lakes across Scandinavia and Siberia all share this latitude and similar reports of creatures. These lakes are often found existing in coniferous boreal forests.[12] They share deep water and similar temperatures. Memphremagog shares all of these characteristics.

Strange too is the resemblance that most of these mythical animals share. Scottish legend, recited long before the fame of their current favorite lake monster "Nessie," tell us of encounters at the edge of the loch centuries ago. These lake beasts were known as water kelpies, mythical creatures that were rumored to live in the lochs of Scotland and said to have horse-like heads. Another characteristic also attributed to the serpent said to be in Lake Memphremagog. It was not until the 1930's, however, that Nessie grew in fame to become the most famous of all the lake monsters. And of course every lake monster, if they truly exist, will need a mate to reproduce.[13]

The male of the mythical species is larger and said to have a flowing mane of hair and whiskers on its horse shaped head. The size of this creature is said to vary from 40 to 100 feet according to its age. The female of the species is said to have smooth skin, a longer neck, but a body that varies from 30-70 feet.[14] Of course all this is speculation, as no remains have ever been discovered. However, as we know from the kraken, this may just be a matter of time. Given the odd drop in temperature it seems likely that the beast could have been stirred out of its lair, or that men were spending sufficient time fishing for their survival to have seen it. The clearing and settlement along the lake would make the animal more visible to settlers who made their home along the winding rocky shore. In earlier times, according to legend, the beast had not only been seen by the Natives who traveled across the shore, but had been born from their very blood.

According to the legend the beast lives in a deep underwater lair far below the summit of Owl's Head Mountain. The large brute was then known as Anaconda. The beast was born from the blood of a young, adulterous, Abenaki wife. The chief took his consort to the banks of the Lake for revenge, and once his wife realized her fate, she began to run away in horror. But she was no match for her fleet footed vengeful husband, and she fell on the bank in full knowledge of what her failure to escape would bring. By the light that glinted off his knife she saw death coming. She cringed as vengeance plummeted when the sting of cold steel death entered her. As she lay weakly on the shore her dying blood ran into the water of the lake. A passing snake tasted the wife's blood and stopped to enjoy more of this rare human delicacy. Blood spiced with revenge appealed to the little serpent. The reptile cried out for an ever greater quantity of blood and the chief threw the body of his wife into the lake to appease the hideous creature.

The snake feasted on the flesh of the unfaithful wife and every day thereafter the snake grew larger. In a month's time Anaconda had become a giant fearsome beast. He grew ever hungry for more human flesh. The serpent then went to his lair deep at the bottom of the lake and waited. Many months later the chief pushed his canoe out onto the lake and paddled out far away from shore. Unknown to the native, far beneath the chief's boat, followed a large ominous shadow. The evil creature slowly rose to the surface, and its humps caused a large wake to form as the demon swiftly gained on the hastily paddled craft. Seeing the beast lurch from the lake behind him the chief dug his paddle deeply into the water as he tried to evade his looming death. He could feel the hot breath of the creature whose head resembled that of a horse with red piercing eyes. All too quickly he felt the sting as fangs dug deeply into his back when he was lifted from the boat and pulled beneath the waves to his watery tomb.[15]

The beast must have been satisfied with this final taste of blood. Although he has been sighted many times since, he has never been caught killing anyone else. Yet there is at least one unexplained disappearance. The mayor of Newport, Vermont went missing in the lake in 1915, and this led some to think the beast still feeds when opportunity arises.[16] With the presence today of many lakeside cabins and frolicking children there are many other tempting meals that might serve as easy prey to him. Proving the old adage that revenge is never satisfied until two graves have been dug; the saurian seems satisfied with devouring the native couple. As for the Abenaki, they were so fearful of the serpent in the lake they refused to bath or swim near it.[17] Other people who grew up near the lake were told much the same thing. This leads some citizens to feel it is the most dangerous of all the mythical creatures that may lurk in the dense mountain forests of the area.[18]

The story of the demon basilisk was a favorite of those who traveled on the lake on-board the steamships of Abraham's later years. It did, however, paint a picture of the Abenaki as being morally corrupt, and somehow the story caused the creation of this unknown and seldom seen lake attraction. The captain of the steamship, Uriah Jewett, told a tale that he had left sheep heads as bait at the shore to try to catch the monster. When he returned the next day the bait was gone, but no monster was ever apprehended. He had seen a reptilian creature crawl out of the lake once, but had never been able to capture it.[19] This may have been a younger version of the monster. This offspring of the initial beast; is hopefully less malevolent than its parent. Uriah Jewett thought so much of the monster that he wrote a book about him.

The story survives into the present day and the beast is now known by the disgustingly cute title of Memphre. Why every lake monster gets stuck with such a foolish moniker boggles the mind. The serpent has most recently been seen by Dr. Curtis Classen in 1935; and by others in 1972 and 1976. It continues to be a story to tell tourists who visit the lake. Abraham may have told the tale himself on the porch of his tavern to pass a summer afternoon and entertain his guests. One can only wonder how four grown men, who all lived in and were used to their natural surroundings could say they saw a serpent on the lake. Henry Wadleigh, one of the men with Abraham, was also vocal in telling of his encounter with the beast in his later years. In the January 21, 1847, *Stanstead Journal* it was reported he said "I am not aware whether it is generally known that a strange animal something of a sea serpent....exists in lake Memphremagog. Near the same time in August of 1850, David Beebe, saw a giant snake while he fished off Magoon Point. Then as now, ridicule naturally falls upon the person who admits to having seen the great serpent. Yet some are so convinced of what they saw that they are still willing to share it.

Abraham did not need to travel to the northern lake to see a monster lurking in the deep. He could have seen one just as easily back in his earlier home in Essex County, Massachusetts. After a few brief sighting in 1815 and 1816, the Gloucester sea serpent stepped into the limelight and made itself known. In August 1817, it was reportedly seen by over one hundred people.[20] In a very short length of time, the Gloucester sea serpent became the most viewed mythic creature of all time. The phenomenon remains a question today of exactly what so many people saw that year in the Atlantic?

On the other hand who wishes to live in a world without mystery? I hope someday to catch a glimpse of Anaconda myself. Perhaps the beast could reveal himself to a descendant of one of the first non-native men to see him in 1816. Abraham and his friends are in fact the first to witness or report a lake monster in North America as far as I can tell. The beast has been sighted many times since, and continues to be as elusive as its cousin Nessie in Scotland, and its cousin (or mate) nicknamed Champ in Lake Champlain. During my infrequent visits I have gazed out upon both lakes with a watchful eye and my camera at the ready, but so far without any luck. Monsters aside, the following year the area surrounding Abraham became a far safer place militarily with the inauguration of a new American president.

In 1817, James Monroe (1817–1825), took over the presidency of the United States. He had no real party opposition in his election. This was in spite of the fact that his predecessor James Madison had the White House burned by the British while he was in office. Yet after the war the people seemed happy with how the conflict was handled. In 1817, Abraham appointed attorney William Scott to petition the crown for the lease of lot 27 Range 10 in Bolton, across the lake. Abraham's thirst for land could not be quenched. The lot was called the Coolidge Place.[21] The following year on April 16, 1818, the Rush-Bagot Treaty was ratified between Britain and the United States. This treaty largely demilitarized the border in Upper and Lower Canada and has led to what is today called the largest undefended border in the world. Later treaties that year set the border at the 49th parallel and made the fishing and other rights clear between the nations. Many situations over the years have threatened this treaty. The American Civil War, World War II, and September 11, 2001, to name a few. Yet the treaty has survived.

Elisha Tucker wrote to his sister-in-law Sally Channel in Chebacco on July 19, 1817, about their family and her father. He was planning a visit to see his father-in-law Abraham in Lower Canada and may have wanted to discuss it with her. He had also received a letter from Abraham June 1, 1817, complaining about business. "Sir writes that money is very scarce there and business very dull in the taverns."[22] It seems he wanted Robert to come up and collect some interest from him. This may be why Tucker was headed there. Money was not as safely transported as it is today.

Frederick Channell

On September 9, 1818, Dudley Choate wrote to his brother in law Robert in Durham, New Hampshire, The following letter:

> Dear Friends, For such we shall call you till time shall be no more. I would inform you that we enjoy a good state of health, for which we are very thankful and do hope that you and yours enjoy the same blessing. I have nothing new to write only that we received a letter from Sir Channel and he wants me to buy the house and if you and I can trade for what he owes you at his decease and pay what he owes you now, I will buy it. If you will come down next week, for if I buy the house I want it now for I want to be to work and my year is most out where we now live. I should like to have you fetch down your notes, then I could tell what the house would cost. Come soon. Give our love to Mr. And Mrs. Balch.
> N.B. Your money in Gloucester Bank ought to be taking out if you have not got it for they will cheat you out of it if they can. I would also tell you that David Choate is very sick and has been ten weeks and Mrs. Sewall too.
> Your affectionate friend,
> Dudley Choate[23]

The letter serves as an introduction to looming economic problems on the horizon. The Panic of 1819, heralded in a severe economic time when banks were not to be trusted. Property values fell across the country, and tensions over slavery began to rise in politics. Abraham wanted to sell his house and cut his ties with his property in New England. Abraham had found happiness in his new home in Lower Canada.

Back in Chebacco, Abraham's son-in-law Dudley Choate drafted an alarming letter to his brother-in-law Robert in Durham, New Hampshire on November 21, 1818. Doctor Sewall, a local physician, had threatened to take Dudley Choate to court for $100 that his father-in-law Abraham owed the doctor for the medical care of his ex-wife Mary and their child Susan. Dudley and Sally had married on September 28, 1817, and the old family home in Chebacco they apparently now lived in was threatened by the doctor's lawsuit. The letter as it reads:

> Dear Brother,
> Doct[or] Sewell has got a bill against sir Channel and he says he shall take the house and sell it to get his pay. He don't tell how

much his Bill is but as much as I can learn tis near one hundred dollars if he should take the house and sell it he will spend about all. The most of his bill is for Mrs Smith child after sir went to Canady whether he can gett the whole or not I cannot tell. But if he should go through the law he will spend about all the house will fetch if he should gett his case. we are all well at present and hope that you and yours enjoy the same remember us to all who may ask after us.

Yours Dudley Choate[24]

Doctor Thomas Sewall was a well respected physician and graduate of Harvard College. However, some of his modern scientific methods soon proved shocking to the community of Chebacco.

In addition to Doctor Sewall's medical practice he also trained students in medicine and had a need for fresh bodies to provide "anatomical studies" to them. At the time there was no way to procure bodies for instructing medical students in human anatomy. Bodies cannot be stolen because they are not property. Doctors like Sewall preferred the term "resurrection" to body snatching or grave robbing. It was a resurrection just a few months later, the largest on record; that may have saved the Channell home in Chebacco from the litigious doctor.

It was a cold snowy night in January 1818, when lights were seen flickering about in the old graveyard. This aroused the suspicion of some members of the town. Unfortunately, the snowfall covered the phantoms tracks when they were investigated early the next day. The snow slowly melted as the sun rose in the sky. Later that afternoon a hair ornament was found that had belonged to a recently deceased girl named Sally Andrews. A hair ornament she had taken into the grave with her. This led to a full investigation of the events that occurred the previous night in the cemetery. At least eight bodies were removed from the graveyard that Abraham's first wife Abigail was buried. Eight empty coffins are said to be buried under the present structure that stores the town's ancient horse drawn hearse. The coffins of eight men, women, and boys were put on display as a reminder of the crime, and a $500 reward was offered to find the perpetrator.

In order for Sewall's men to have robbed the graves, a three foot square hole had to be first dug down to the head of the coffin. Then holes were drilled through the box, followed by a saw to open up access to the body. After this a large hook was put under the chin of the cadaver, and then it was pulled up to the surface through the soil that was meant to have been its final resting place. The clothes or shroud were removed from the corpse and thrown back into the grave before it was carefully filled back in. Done correctly, this could be completed in only an hour and be difficult to detect if the grave was fresh and the soil already disturbed from the recent burial. In their haste that night the bodies were poorly wrapped in canvas and the hair piece fell out to be discovered the next day and used as evidence in the case.[25] The night's labor of the unhallowed workman had been discovered.

Eventually parts of the bodies were found with Doctor Sewall. He was charged with the crime of possessing the bodies, but not removing them. It seems there may not have been any precedence for a law not to dig up bodies. Doctor Sewall chose Daniel Webster as his attorney, the famous statesman who had just finished his second term in the House of Representatives. Webster had recently left political office to build up his law practice. Daniel Webster was known to be a man who could "crush his opponents with a barrage of facts,"[26] but he was still unable to win the case for his doctor friend. The doctor was found guilty, in spite of the great defense that was supplied to him by his attorney and friend Webster. Sewall was fined $800 dollars, a huge fine for the time period, and he later left Chebacco in disgrace in 1819.[27]

Earlier laws in Massachusetts concerning bodies dealt with witchcraft. These laws were enacted in 1692, during the height of the witchcraft trials. These laws concerned the use of the body or parts in pursuit of sorcery, casting charms and/or enchantment of others. The penalty for these actions was death. These Massachusetts laws were later invalidated by courts in Britain for technical reasons. As medical schools grew in New England, grave robbing became more of an issue to the public. The problem was previously confronted at Dartmouth University, and the case was likely well known to Webster who was an alumnus of that institution.

Sewall left Chebacco and went on to a successful career in Washington D.C. and helped found what has become George Washington University. He became the personal physician of three American Presidents. He remained a physician to his former attorney Daniel Webster throughout his long political career in Washington.[28]

Later Sewall became a professor of pathology, a subject he was clearly interested in. His drawings of the effects of alcohol on the stomach were the first to expose this danger to society, and these images were later used by the temperance movement throughout the rest of the century.[29] Sewall is quoted as saying:

> Alcohol is a poison, ever at war with man's nature; and in all its forms and degrees of strength, produces irritation of the stomach, which is liable to result in inflammation, ulceration, mortification, a thickening, and induration of its coats, and finally, schirrhus cancer, and other organic affections. * * * No one who indulges habitually in the use of alcoholics, whether in the form of wine or more ardent spirits, possesses a healthy stomach.[30]

Alcohol continues to be a problem in many peoples lives and stops them from becoming immortal like Abraham. Dr. Sewall's disturbing images of the ravages of alcohol on the stomach fueled the temperance movement that eventually led to the passing of the 19th Amendment and the start of Prohibition in the United States during the following century. It is unknown if Sewall ever collected his bill from Abraham and Dudley Choate; he was lucky to have escaped the village alive. Perhaps Dr. Sewall advised Abraham to put aside his rum ration and avoid alcohol which led to his long life. Maybe everyone should heed the advice of the grave robbing yet wise physician. Perhaps those reading these words can "resurrect" themselves from the evils of alcohol.

The victims of these grave robberies must have suffered horribly and felt violated by the theft of their young children's bodies and the crimes committed against their remains. Can a parent today imagine the grief of first losing a child and then the horror of them being dug up after burial? Back then it may have conflicted with religious ideals of the body being needed for the spirit to be resurrected. Religious principles often conflicted with the need for scientific advancement. Are arguments against cloning or genetically altered food in the modern day a new example of this? In the same year as the event, Mary Shelley's book Frankenstein was first published. A book about a doctor who oversteps the bounds of science through his hubris and assembles body parts to create a new life. Shelly described 1816, the year without a summer, in the introduction of her story as a, "wet, ungenial summer and incessant rain often confined us for days to the house."[31]

Interestingly enough, many years later in 1841, Abraham's last born son, Charles Stewart Channell, married Mary Ann Webster, a relative of Daniel Webster. Webster later rose to the position of Secretary of State and twice turned down the offer to become Vice President of the United States. In each case the president died in office. Talk about a missed opportunity. Not just for Webster, but for the country, he might have made a fine president.

Daniel Websters Law Office, Photo by Author.

Abraham's Tavern Stand

Up in the tavern stand in Lower Canada Abraham's wife Wealthy gave birth to another son on April 25, 1818. The sixty-nine-year-old Abraham named him Leon Lalanne Channell, after his friend the notary public. Abraham was fortunate that most of his many children survived to adulthood, with the exception of the one twin girl who had passed away in Chebacco. He also should be credited with them all being literate in a time of high illiteracy rates. In spite of his many travels and hardships he managed to see to it that his children were able to read and write. Abraham also needed to be highly literate to keep the record books in good shape at his new career as a tavern keeper. This career placed him at the center of business, transportation, and entertainment in the village.

To keep a tavern, an old sailor like Abraham certainly kept a supply of rum in the house to serve his patrons. Rum was a staple from his time in the British Navy. Abraham had likely been served grog, hot water mixed with rum, to treat scurvy in his year of service in the wooden world of the *Milford*. This beverage might do wonders to warm cold travelers as they came in off the stagecoach. One of the most popular drinks of the day was flip, a mix of strong beer with a bit of rum, and whatever other strange ingredients the mixer felt like putting in which might have included molasses and pumpkin. This was followed by dipping a red hot fireplace poker into the mix to heat it.

The ale that they brewed did not resemble the beer of today; many ingredients including the bark of trees may have been used to brew them. The ale was dark and flavorful, in some cases it tasted good, in other cases not. This varied from batch to batch. If fresh water was wanted, there was also a never ending supply of it on the property. Digging deep into the earth with great effort and care one could tap into this precious resource. The lure of the tavern is told in this poem:

> The days are short, the weather's cold,\By tavern fires tales are told. Some ask for dram when first come in, Others with flip and bounce begin.[1]

In order to be a successful tavern owner, Abraham must have been a social and friendly man. The more comfort and hospitality they enjoyed, the more money his patrons spent. The longer they stayed, the more he earned. Abraham likely learned the workings and the operation of taverns by staying in many of them while he traveled as a tailor. Everyone in the area knew him and his hospitality may have been discussed in far away cities such as Montreal and Quebec. No one in the small community was unaware of the aging yet still vital man.

The tavern was not just used for overnight visits and entertainment. Without other public buildings in the village it also served as a location for legal hearings. Abraham's friend Ralph Merry, his companion when they saw the lake monster, wrote that his father was commencing three suites against his friends, that his father claimed owed him debts, and that Ralph had to stand witness in the tavern. Other notary and land agents used Abraham's tavern for weekly stops to conduct their business as well. In this, the tavern served as a temporary town hall, courthouse, or town clerk office. So Abraham definitely knew all too well what was going on in the village.

A tavern in that sparsely settled area had to be largely self sufficient. Abraham also had his family on the western side of the lake to supply him with the bounty from their farms. Abraham probably served fish caught from the lake. The species found there off the shore included longe, trout, and salmon. The earliest settlers may not have even survived without this rich food source. Certainly not during 1816. Local game such as deer, rabbit, and pheasant may also have been served. The game, first hung outside the kitchen window, was later brought in to be dressed and made into delicious meals by Wealthy. The innkeeper Abraham certainly raised chickens, pigs, cows and other livestock near the tavern. He likely had served cheese, bread, and may have sold cigars or tobacco that he acquired in the cities from the stagecoach drivers, or from the smugglers that traveled past his inn on the lake. Johnny cakes and some other type of waffle or pancake was served in order to pour the freshly made maple syrup over that they produced when the maple sap ran out of the taps and filled the buckets in the spring.

Wealthy baked apple and blackberry pies, and made pudding to serve to their weary guests. Apples grew on the farm and dense thickets of blackberries grew along the lake. Pies were sometimes served for breakfast, along with, "beef-steak, mutton-chops eggs and often roast chicken. Keeping poultry was a large item in tavern economy."[2] Along with the drinking and eating, the guests who traveled by horse needed these animals cared for and needed provender (food), for them to eat. Abraham also arranged for shoeing the patrons horses when needed. Abraham probably kept a couple guns or a club around. There was no law enforcement in town, so Abraham would have to deal with any rowdy patrons who had ingested too much rum or ale. Any problems or arguments would receive some retribution and shipboard justice that Abraham had learned to administer from his time on board the privateer.

Along with the amenities required of a public house, other visitors saw the tavern as an opportunity to entertain or sell their wares. Nathaniel Hawthorne wrote of a visit of one of these men to a tavern he stopped at:

> After supper, as the sun was setting, a man passed by the door
> with a hand-organ, connected with which was a row of figures,
> such as dancers, pirouetting and turning, a lady playing on a
> piano, soldiers, a negro wench dancing, and opening and shutting
> a huge red mouth,—all these keeping time to the lively or slow
> tunes of the organ.[3]

Abraham welcomed these men to his tavern who entertained both his guests and his family. He may have felt sympathy for them, as he remembered his own years on the road selling his tailor services. There was little entertainment there in the rural town of Georgeville, so entertainment like the organist may have been a welcome sight and brought out money paying customers. It brought in more business and prolonged visits by his overnight guests. Songs sung by others visiting the tavern often told stories of national events or were commentaries of various political viewpoints.

Another probable guest to Abraham's tavern was the itinerant artists who traveled along the dusty rural roads of New England and Lower Canada. They set up some local advertisements and then took out a room in the tavern. They would pay for the room with funds made in their trade. Failure to attract enough customers may cause them to pay for their room with their skill. The same was true of those who sold photos from cameras in later years. It may be due to this that Abraham's likeness still exists today.

The tavern also boasted visits from touring lecturers who discussed history or the mysteries of scientific discoveries with the rural inhabitants of the local town. Some gave dancing instruction or taught locals how to play different instruments. Instruction in dancing attracted lots of visitors who then needed refreshment after their exercise. Abraham may have had a fiddler's throne installed in the tavern to have the artist perform from. Here the musician could rise above his audience and be seen and heard more clearly. Other activities such as magic shows, board games, and card games may have helped passed the long winter nights at the tavern. Adding to the friendship and camaraderie that Abraham enjoyed.

It seems unfair to speak so much of Abraham's hand in running the tavern when so much of the work was shared by his wife Wealthy. There were no days off with bedding and clothes to wash. She looked after the workers in the tavern and prepared and planned the meals. With luck she might be able to get to church on Sunday and get in her prayers. Many parishioners may have followed her back to the tavern during the noon time break to enjoy a meal at her table. Wealthy may have been a quick study of human nature and entertained herself with trying to understand the guests past life and reason for travel. She was not just a loving wife, but a skilled yet unheralded business partner. A no nonsense woman who kept the tavern running for her outgoing and friendly husband.

The couple's tavern was 36'x80' and had nine lodging rooms located within it. The main room was called the sitting room, where the guests could relax and read or discuss the events of the day. This room had a clock, two tables, six sitting chairs, and a rocking chair. Over by the window was a looking glass for taking in panoramic views of the lake. Brushes and brooms sat in the corner for cleaning up. Directly over the sitting room the guest chamber had a bed, work table, and four chairs. The bedding and a bedstead were also stored in the room.

A looking glass was supplied in the room for enjoying the view out the window. Adjoining that room, a smaller bedroom had a bed, light stand, and chair. In a room known as the square chamber there was bed and bedding, six chairs, a rocking chair, a wash stand, and a fire set. In a small adjoining room was a bed, washstand, and floor rug. There was one more small room at the head of the stairs with a bed and light stand.[4]

In the dining room were two tables, a bureau, and seven chairs, to sit and feed hungry patrons at. A looking glass was supplied in this room as well. A person has to wonder what Abraham hoped to see again out on that lake. With all the telescopes he supplied his guests may have hoped to see the same creature he had seen. Every time the ferry crossed the lake or the stagecoach arrived out front there was an opportunity for more guests to arrive. When he neared town the stage driver sounded a long coach horn to alert the tavern owner to their arrival. He also sounded it to warn people off the road ahead.[5]

The car horns of today are descended from those long slender horns. In a stagecoach without brakes descending down mountain terrain, these horns were a safety necessity. Others moving livestock or walking to town needed to be warned out of harms way of the approaching coach. The ride between Stanstead and Georgeville is a hilly ride that provided a thrill equal to almost any modern day roller coaster.

All the rooms of Abraham's tavern were supplied with curtains to block the cold winter winds that blew off the lake and through the thin window sashes. There was a large wood burning cooking stove and cupboard in the kitchen where meals were prepared. The bar was supplied with a table, chairs, and a bunk for guests who had enjoyed too much flip or hard cider.

The tavern also boasted two hundred sugaring buckets for catching the maple sap when it ran in the spring. This usually occurred the first day of April, when the trees reached forty degrees. The men then had to snowshoe through 3-4' of heavy spring snow to gather the buckets full of sap. The sap was then poured into troughs and boiled until it evaporated down to syrup. Later in the season the inn used the harrow, plow, and cart to grow crops and carry the produce back to the inn. The inn had over one hundred acres that included twenty acres set aside for wood. The tools were kept in either the barn or stable, as the inn had both, along with other outbuildings and an outhouse.

The front of the tavern stand was very impressive. Large stone flags spread out at angles away from the front entrance. On these were long wide benches, painted red, in order to sit, smoke, and indulge in conversation with Abraham or the other guests. The cool mountain air could be enjoyed there as it blew across the lake on a warm summer afternoon. They may have enjoyed tales of the Revolution and life on board a British ship. At the end of these benches were rings mounted on posts to tie horses up to.

One of these posts rose high up into the air where a sign hung advertising the Channell tavern stand, with Abraham's name proudly displayed upon it as the proprietor. There was no doubt that this was a building where travelers were welcome and felt at home. Very few of these ancient tavern signs survive today. The signs often had a painted visual image so the illiterate could understand what the services were. Three men were needed to create a sign such as this; blacksmith, joiner, and painter. The painters were said to be travelers who traded painting the sign for a few days lodging. The images in New England before the Revolution often consisted of lions and crowns; after the war they had patriotic symbolism. Abraham's sign might have offered "entertainment for man and Horse."[6] Entertainment had a different meaning then; it would have meant that the horse and man would be cared for and fed.

Alongside the building stood a line of tall evergreens that cast shade on the lawn on a hot summer day. Under the trees guests could rest and breath in the fresh mountain air as it blew over the mountains and across the lake. Visitors could walk along the lake shore and take in the views. Down on the shore they could spend time fishing and enjoying a picnic. Maybe they could try their hand at skipping a stone across the surface. There are far worse places to spend an afternoon than where the land meets the rocky shore in Georgeville.

In the fall of 1819, it was decided that a post office was needed back in Chebacco, Massachusetts. The village was now incorporated as the new town of Essex. It was decided that Abraham's son-in-law Dudley Choate, would be a, "suitable person for post-master, and conveniently situated near the meeting house." From the description it appears Dudley now lived in Abraham's old home.[7] Dudley attached a small room addition to the house to conduct the business of the post office in. He had previously been involved in shipbuilding like many of the men who lived in Chebacco.

About the same time this was occurring on October 4, 1819; Dudley's wife Sally Choate decided to bring a lawsuit against her father Abraham for the money he had borrowed in 1815. she was likely urged to do so by her husband. In December she attached his local real estate and on April 17, 1820, she received a judgment for $101.76 from Judge Minot. Because her father was in default and out of the country, it was ordered that if he paid back a portion within a year part of the additional money owed would be nullified, otherwise the judgment remained in effect.

Not to be left out Sally's brother Robert Channell and her brother in law Elisha Tucker sued Abraham for their money as well. Robert wanted $200 and Tucker was looking for $300. They were awarded less money than they asked for, and if Abraham had paid them back he would have received a better settlement. After being given an extension because he was out of the country, it seems he failed to pay and on August 14, 1820, the decision was made in Abraham's children's favor. How Abraham was to come up with this money is not known. A lack of money did not stop some people in the townships from having cash, because some were adept at printing their own.

Counterfeiters, Competition and Capitalism

In 1820, King George IV took the throne, the third King George to rule in Britain during Abraham's lifetime. In the United States the Missouri compromise passed, which allowed Missouri to join the Union as a slave state, with Maine being accepted as a free state to keep a political balance in the country. George Ramsay took over as the Governor-In-Chief of Canada. On March 3, 1820, Abraham, now seventy-one, had a new son born he named Charles Stuart Channell. Charles was the third child born to him from his fourth wife Wealthy Cox.

On June 22, 1822, Abraham sat down in his tavern with Leon Lalanne and together they drew up a last will and testament. Abraham was now approaching his mid-seventies and was concerned with the future of his wife and children if anything were to happen to him. Abraham had built a two-story house across from the tavern in the center of the settlement. Abraham was specific about which rooms Wealthy would live in within the house, and what items she would be supplied with. Wealthy was much younger than Abraham and he likely assumed she would far outlive him. He had already far outlived the life expectancy usually attributed to men born at the time, but with scanty records even this is difficult to determine accurately. Lalanne stated in the will that Abraham,

> "….appeared to be in sound health, senses and memory, but that considering the certainty of death and the uncertainty of the time

thereof, and desirous to be prepared to leave this world whenever it should please God to call him hence."[1]

Abraham wished, "to be therein interred in a Christian like manner at the discretion of his executors to be named and appointed." These executors were his wife Wealthy, Levi Knowlton, and William Bullock. "Secondly, orders and directs that all his lawful debts to be soon as possible after his decease paid and discharged."[2] Abraham showed in his will a genuine concern to pay off his debtors after his passing. After the debts were paid his property was then bequeathed to his wife, Wealthy, until the youngest of his children were twenty-one years of age, or married, if she remained his widow.

Abraham's daughters were to have "sixty pounds current money of the province,"[3] but his young sons were to have the majority of his property. The home he lived in was to be used by his wife, along with all the furniture that was inside it. If he passed away she would still have three young children to care for, and they still needed a roof over their head. Once the children were old enough or married, Wealthy would maintain use of "the two easternmost rooms upon the second floor."[4] Wealthy was also to have access to the kitchen, cellar, and garret (attic), and that his sons would support and maintain her "decently and comfortably as becometh her rank in life in sickness as well as in health."[5]

If Wealthy chose to live elsewhere, the children still had to support her. When Wealthy passed away her property was to be divided up equally among her male children. If any of his sons passed away without heirs, his share of the property was to be divided among the surviving brother's children. If all his sons died without children, the property would pass to his daughter's children. Today it is likely people would not take into account so many children and grandchildren dying at such a young age, but it was a concern of those who lived in Abraham's days. The witnesses of his will were James Lull and Sylvester Hartshorn.

Back in Essex, Abraham's son-in-law Dudley became involved in a new business venture. On June 15, 1822, Dudley and some other investors began a new company called the Essex Mill Corporation.[6] This enterprise was created at a time when farming was still a large part of New England life and what few businesses did exist were mainly single proprietor or partnerships. The business was among the early corporations of Massachusetts. This corporation was approved by the Massachusetts State Senate and House of Representatives. The company built a dam and locks on the Essex River to allow boats to pass through. The trapped river water, that had risen with the tide, could then allow power for a mill for either processing wood or carding wool as the water was released. This second use alluded to the fact that raising sheep was still an important industry in Essex. Previous to the carding machine all this had to be done at home by hand. The new carding machine greatly increased the speed and quality of wool production, and promoted this craft on hand looms in the home. Abigail Channell, Abraham's first wife, was likely well versed in this activity. The stock of the company allowed for $10,000 in capital to be raised. This was a sizable amount of money to have been raised in the early 19th century.

Unfortunately, On January 10, 1828, William Cogswell went to court to argue for damages from the river water being kept so high by the dam. He thought it had negatively impacted the grasses along the river that his animals grazed on. The corporation had been approved by the government. Since the water level was also approved by the government, it made the case an early test of the constitutionality of eminent domain. There seems to have been no thought on the part of the legislature as to whether anyone might be harmed by the water level being raised or controlled by the dam. What was in fact more important; a dam to process items for the good of the whole community or the land of one man?

It brought up the question of what a citizen can do when injured by an act of the legislature. The answer was to take the case before a jury and have it tried in common law. The corporation hired a young attorney named Rufus Choate to argue the case for them. Choate later became a senator. In one of his most famous cases he was the first attorney to free a man accused of murder by arguing that he was sleepwalking when he committed the crime.[7] He was obviously a pretty good mouthpiece for the company. The corporation seems to have survived the case. The Essex Mill Corporation did business for many years until it was later dissolved in 1892.[8] The mill was probably incapable of competing with larger mills, in a saturated industry.

Business was also on the mind of Abraham's son Robert in New Hampshire. Robert lived in an area known as Lubberland, along the shore of the Great Bay. The origin or the name Lubberland can only be guessed at. It could be that early settlers felt that there were pixies or sprites known as "lobs" that superstition told haunted the homes in the area.[9] Through the centuries the name may have evolved to Lubberland. If there were pixies in the thick forests they sure protected Robert, who lived to the ripe old age of 96. The beauty of the area can enchant visitors even today. On the farm there was fertile soil and large quantities of stone for quarrying. Robert's large farm was both in Durham and what later became Newmarket. Down the road from the farm was Lamprey River Village, located at the first fall of the Lamprey River.

Robert was a farmer, but also dabbled in pursuits such as various construction projects in the area. On February 24, 1825, Robert received a letter from B.M. Burnham in Boston thanking him for the many favors that he had done for him. Burnham wanted Robert to build him a frame so he could begin construction of a store that he wanted to start in Lamprey River. He had initially told Robert that he wanted the store to be 20x35' but he was reducing that to 20x30'. Burnham already owed Robert some money, but he hoped to be able to pay him the following week. They also appeared to have been partners in some other business because Burnham promised him "sound returns." Burnham hoped to have his "little snug store" erected quickly, because he feared someone else would beat him to it. He gave him a little news of his sister and brother-in-law Elisha Tucker, and then closed his letter.[10]

It is no wonder that Burnham was looking to build a store there because the area was rapidly expanding. In 1823, investors from Salem, Massachusetts, began plans to build a cotton mill complex on the river called the Newmarket Manufacturing Company.[11] The mills in Waltham had returned high dividends and profits for over a decade and the businessmen hoped they could repeat the accomplishment there in Newmarket.[12] This meant the delivery of baled cotton at one end of the building, and finished cloth coming out at the other end. This was an accomplishment unheard of in American manufacturing. It was not until early the next century when Henry Ford began to accomplish the same with automobiles.

The Lamprey River's flowing water seemed like an ideal spot to build a mill. Being so near to Portsmouth, New Hampshire the location offered an ocean port nearby as well. The Newmarket Manufacturing Company was one of the few companies to maintain their independence from the larger Boston investor groups.[13] A tradition has been passed down among the descendants of Robert Channell that it was Robert who had cut the stone at his farms quarry, and that he had provided the stone which built the mills. By 1832, three Waltham type cotton mills were built in Newmarket, and they employed 59 men and 613 women who worked with 18,000 spindles to produce cloth. These young working farm women lived in nearby boarding houses. A small town sprang up around the mills and the business survived into the next century.

The growth of the mill cities also led Abraham's' granddaughter Abigail George to leave Potton, across the lake from Georgeville, and move to Lowell, Massachusetts. Farm girls from all the New England States were recruited to come and work in the mills. They could not go west and settle new farmland like their brothers could, and their only prospect of otherwise escaping their parents home was marriage. Across the north the standard of living was rising and young farm girls like Abigail wanted to keep up. Most women had experience hand weaving and spinning already from their life on the farms. The revolution of cloth production had created a great increase in the available of raw material, but the production of higher quality craft goods, such as that with stripes or patterns, remained at home. It was thought that young women who were not kept busy were subject to an array of "temptations."[14] So to keep these young girls from being a burden to their parents and society, the mills of Lowell and other areas offered an alternative by employing them. Lowell paid them more than they could earn at any other type of employment, and they built the girls housing and churches to maintain their Christianity.

Abigail's Sister Fanny married in North Chelmsford, and later lived in nearby Nashua, New Hampshire. Fanny may also have traveled to the mills for employment, and then found a husband. Chelmsford also grew up as a mill town, although it never reached the fame of Lowell. Abigail sent a letter to her aunt Lydia, the wife of Abraham's son Robert on June 13, 1844.[15] Abigail wrote of how much she wanted to become more acquainted and how she had long hoped to see some of her family there. Life away from the farm had caused her to miss her family back home in Canada, and so she reached out to her closer relatives in New Hampshire. Exactly when she and her sister had arrived in the area is unknown. Women could not vote and were not recorded in the census. This makes them hard to follow through history.

The poet John Greenleaf Whittier wrote a few poetic lines about the girls he saw leaving the factory while he lived in the city:

> Acres of girlhood-beauty reckoned by the square rod, or miles by long measure!-The young, the graceful, the gay-flowers gathered from a thousand hill-sides and green vallies of New England…[16]

When the bells rang in the mills Whittier found himself in a swell of young, virtuous, well dressed women who formed the labor force of the great city of Lowell. Men who had grown up on farms were overwhelmed with the quantity of young women in the city. Their labor produced the wealth of the city, and money sent home helped their families when their own farm crops failed. Their presence created a sense of youth and energy. They formed a connection between rural and urban life.

Abigail worked in the Merrimack Company mill as a spinner, and her name appears in the Lowell Female Supplement Directory in 1836, and also in the Lowell Institute for Savings Bank Records of 1836-1840.[17] The large brick mill processed finished cloth from raw cotton from beginning to end, utilizing the power of the Merrimack River. In Lowell, throstle spinners were used. Depending on which throstle machine Abigail worked on, she would have been responsible for either one or two of these pieces of equipment. The process of spinning created yarn or thread and the machine and operator determined the final thickness of the product. After this, the yarn was sent to the weaving process machine and the cloth was made. The cloth was all one color, the technology did not exist to alternate color or create patterns. Abigail was responsible to her male overseer who watched over the work of thirty Lowell Girls.[18]

The girls worked from five in the morning until seven at night with a half hour break for breakfast and dinner. This schedule left little time for "temptation." Mill girls were paid six to ten dollars per week. Abigail's specific job paid $0.58 per day. Abigail had to pay her rent and board of $1.25 per week to the boarding house. The mill paid twenty-five cents per person to the boarding house keeper. This house keeper oversaw and took care of the young girls meals. When the mill owners later cut out this payment to the housekeeper, and the employees had to begin to pay the housekeeper themselves, the striking began.[19] The additional cut in pay to the girls was the final straw. Twelve to fifteen hundred girls "turned out," as striking was then called, and the brave young female workers then left the mill and flooded the streets of the mill city in protest.

The Lowell Mill Girls were the first American workers to stand up to the factory owners when their wages were cut and their working conditions grew unsafe. They were the daughters of freemen, and the granddaughters of the fathers of the Revolution. They found themselves in a new struggle within the American Industrial Revolution, and their rich and powerful mill owners. They had come from the hills of New England, where a primarily classless society existed. One farm not being much better off than other farms nearby. They were not afraid to stand up to the new manufacturing aristocracy of Lowell. Their attitude is apparent in the song lyrics that they chanted:

> Oh! isn't it a pity, such a pretty girl as I-
> Should be sent to the factory to pine away and die?
> Oh! I cannot be a slave, I will not be a slave,
> For I'm so fond of liberty,
> That I cannot be a slave.[20]

The girls of Lowell exhibited the same spirit and love of freedom that had won the Revolution. The tyrant they battled was capitalism. Greed had become their enemy. Slavery was a strong word considering that members of that "peculiar institution' were precisely who supplied them with the cotton they used. Opposition to slavery was a growing subject in the nearby City of Boston also.

The New England Slave-Society in 1840 was less than a decade old, yet the Abolitionist movement was growing and supported by the Liberator, a newspaper run by William Lloyd Garrison. Garrison and his friend Wendell Phillips, not only spoke out against slavery, but also against the federal Constitution. Garrison was the pen and Phillips was the voice of the movement. The rich merchants of New England were opposed to the abolitionist movement, because of their business connections to the South and their thirst for the raw material supply of cotton. Phillips, a fine orator, argued that the Constitution was a "covenant with slavery" and argued that it was better to separate politically than to be tied to evil through it. The Constitution, as he saw it, protected and provided representatives for men who enslaved others. Their criticism of the revered document led to it being burned on the 4th of July during an anti-slavery rally in Massachusetts.[21]

Now the tyrants the girls sang of, and the ones Phillips and Garrison attacked in the press and at rally's, were not the British Government but the rich industrialists who cared more about profits than people. The divide that existed between rich and poor had increased dramatically after the acceptance of the Constitution and the growth of capital in the American Industrial Revolution. The girls worked extremely long hours, and they gradually lost many of the benefits that had brought them to the area such as their inexpensive housing. Living and working in close confines did "weave" them into a tight knit group that stood together in opposition, although unsuccessfully, to the mill owners. The mill owners struck at the ringleaders and the movement failed, and wages from that point on were continually cut back as more mills were built and competition increased.

In addition to the George sisters, another immigrant group came to Lowell that had begun to swell the port in Quebec from Europe. The potato famine in Ireland caused a massive immigration to both Canada and the United States. Many of these immigrants traveled south by foot to New England in search of jobs and opportunity. Many ended up at the Lowell Mills. A New Hampshire man wrote of the procession of the masses that likely passed by Abraham's tavern on their way to the mills:

> You don't know how many Irish people there are traveling down this way every day…. I guess that there was 20-30 stopped to Uncle Herrick's [tavern] the other night. There was about 40 stayed there overnight….they slept in the stable upon some straw [-] men, women, and children all together. They looked like human misery indeed.[22]

There is no telling how Abraham treated these travelers. He may or may not have allowed them to stay in his barns. Stricken with poverty, they certainly would not have profited his tavern. One can only hope he offered them kindness and the use of his barn to escape the northern wind and the chilly night air. These immigrant workers languished in the mills in less desirable jobs than the one Abigail worked at, working as "scrubbers and waste-pickers."[23] As wages dropped Abigail seems to have returned home to Potton and marriage. The accumulation of wealth makes some men into masters, and others into slaves. Laws can be abused and wielded to keep workers in their place by stopping public gathering, and other methods of protest. The tyranny of capitalism sometimes uses the legal system and its representatives to crush all that oppose it by seeking decent pay.

Robert, at work on his farm in New Hampshire, was quite industrious in the method he used to bring his farm production to market. In successful years he had an abundance of produce to sell. He was no rich industrialist, but he was able to profit from feeding their workers in the mills and boarding houses. In a letter dated May 4, 1829, Robert's son Abraham Channell, the third one to be so named in the family, sent him a letter from Danvers, Massachusetts. An acquaintance of Robert's son Abraham, Belmour Harlow, had a small boat that he wanted to use to transport goods with. Harlow wanted to know what the prices were for "butter, cheese, fish, potatoes, and a number of other articles that he would be most likely to trade with."[24] This letter gives us a good idea of what Robert's farm was producing, and his fishing success in the Great Bay. Harlow hoped to begin sailing to Robert's area at the beginning of May.

On July 11, 1830, Robert heard from his son William P., a traveling laborer, who lived and worked in Marblehead. William was able to find work, but he was working far too cheaply. William said his wages were fair, however, and as much as anyone was then making in farming. William was sad to hear that his father had lost his horse but offered, "That it was folly to mourn much for a horse when one soul is worth more than ten thousand horses."[25] He hoped his father could replace his horse as soon as possible. William wanted him to write back and he hoped to come home soon to see how his father's crops and cattle looked. He hoped his father could read his letter because he only had a shoe knife to craft his pen with.

As the years went by and Abraham survived into his later years, his family continued to grow and seek their own future in the young nations of both Canada and the United States. As the years progressed, transportation improved, and he was able to communicate and travel with more ease. Owning a tavern allowed him to be on the main route of communication and travel that headed north. With such a large family, and being indebted to many of them still for the purchase of his tavern, Abraham had to find a way to repay the children and in-laws of his earlier marriages. Although the old tailor had once fought against King George III in the Revolution, he would soon look to the monarch's son George IV, through the kings political representatives in Lower Canada for the answer to his financial problems.

On February 5, 1823, the aging privateer petitioned his Excellency George Ramsay, the Earl of Dalhousie, who was until 1828, the "Captain General and Governor in Chief in and over the Province of Lower Canada." Ramsay was actually in charge of all of British North America. He was first sent as Lieutenant-Governor of Nova Scotia in 1816, the year after he took part in the Battle of Waterloo, which finally defeated Napoleon. Ramsay then assumed control as Governor-In-Chief of British North America in 1820. With no local representation, the only means the settlers had of expressing their need in the English speaking areas of Quebec was through petition. This is likely why Abraham used this means of communication to contact the British leader. French speaking members of the government on the other hand, did not want to support and increase the English population in the area.

In the petition Abraham stated that he had served on board the *Milford* and that he was injured four times. Due to his wounds he had been discharged in "consequence thereof."[26] He built his case by saying, "…never received land and have 56 children and grandchildren some of whom are in much distress."[27] He was seeking specific lands in a township named Dudswell. The town is to the northeast of Stanstead and Georgeville, by a distance of over fifty miles. Abraham was not entirely truthful about never receiving land before as he had petitioned and received land in Bolton and Stanstead years earlier in 1817-1820.[28]

Abraham completed his list of family members and sent it off to the Earl on November 8, 1823. It seems the leader and military veteran respected Abraham's service to the King and granted his wish for the land. The governor obviously did not know of his subsequent service in the American Massachusetts Militia and his time on board American privateers during the Revolution. Abraham had by that time reached a family of over fifty descendants, which is amazing when compared to most families in the modern era. The governor may have expected

Abraham to settle his family in the area, but his family was already well settled in various areas of Lower Canada and New England. He specifically asked for Lots seven, eight and nine in the tenth range, a total of over twelve hundred acres, which is roughly two square miles of land. By any account this was and is a large piece of property.

Yet again one can only guess at the interest that Abraham held for the land in Dudswell. He may have had inside information that a road was being planned that would offer a direct route to Quebec City from the American border. Once this road was built his land there would have increased dramatically in value. The area of Dudswell was very sparsely populated then, and had only 166 people living there.[29] Without roads to get to the land the value of it would remain small. On March 14, 1829, the money to build a road in the area was approved by the legislature in Quebec. The land then likely increased greatly in value. It was not that the French politicians in the legislature were suddenly interested in helping the English settlers in the Townships. They were seeking support in their own political activities, and sought to add members to their political party.

On May 12, 1823, an unfortunate event happened in Abraham's horse stable. Elisha Smith, a fifty-two-year-old industrial laborer found a barrel of spirit among the horses, and after he removed the bung Elisha proceeded to drink himself insensible with nothing but the sound of the horses to keep him company. Potato whiskey was a popular alcohol that was distilled in the local community.[30] With the difficulty of moving crops to the northern cities it became more profitable to distill them into alcohol for local sale.[31] Smith's son worked for Abraham also, and he later found his father Elisha inebriated and incoherent in the barn. Unfortunately, Elisha drank more than his share and died within a few hours. He left behind a wife and eleven children. Abraham's alcohol supply for the tavern needed to be more securely stored. But for many citizens living in the Eastern Townships alcohol consumption was becoming a growing problem and needed to be stopped. Within ten years a temperance movement began to strike at the abuse of alcohol in Georgeville and the surrounding areas.

Abraham's success with the tavern unfortunately brought jealousy from other members of the community. Some young upstarts named Joshua Copp and James Peasley decided to build their own hotel to compete with Abraham's. Joshua was the son of Moses Copp and when he was a young boy he traveled on his own to Montreal and came back with enough supplies to build and supply a small store in the village. James Peasley was equally as determined in life to succeed. When he was a young boy growing up in Weare, N.H. his father, feverish with smallpox, got up from his sick bed to throw wood in the fire and dropped dead at his son's feet. His son James later came down with the disease. James lost his arm as a result of smallpox after he developed a horrible infection. James stubbornly clung onto his life, but his lower jaw was locked into place for the remainder of his years. In order to eat his front teeth had to be caved in. He then suffered from an abusive and cruel stepfather.

James was a brother-in-law to Abraham Jr, and a brother of his wife Sally Peasley, but this did not stop him from becoming a thorn in Abraham's side. Through the kindness given to James from other people who lived in the village, he learned to read and write so well that he eventually ended up teaching in the community's school. He saved up what little money he made teaching class and put his meager salary to good use through investments, such as the hotel that he and Joshua Copp built.[32]

Abraham, in fear of competition from the new inn, reminded people in an ad he placed in the local Colonist newspaper on August 21, 1823, that he outfitted his buildings and built the roads for not only the good of travelers in the region, but also for the use of the local people who lived in the area. He claimed responsibility for clearing the roadway through Bolton Woods at his own cost. Abraham considered himself a friend of the government and legitimately licensed for the business that he ran. He stated that he had recently put up a new barn and had fitted out excellent new stables. His stand was to be rendered "as commodious as any other in this part of the country. He has the best of pasture and water very handy, and is determined that no exertions shall be wanting to deserve the patronage of the public."[33]

Peasley and Copp's hotel was completed on October 1, 1823. They had arranged for a stagecoach line to run from a hotel down the road in Stanstead to a hotel in Montreal, after it stopped at their establishment along the way. Two earlier attempts at this service had failed, but Peasley and Copp remained determined to make it a success this time. Early in 1824, they announced winter stagecoach service that departed from the Brook Hotel in Stanstead on Friday morning, and later traveled through Georgeville to then glide across the frozen ice of Lake Memphremagog. It continued on until it reached the Smith Inn in Montreal on Saturday evening. They apparently invested in the expense of the stagecoaches and a team of four horses to pull them.

The young entrepreneur's hotel was brand new and well furnished by a man named E. Rockwood, and was to be called the Magog Hotel. On September 25, 1823, Abraham was conveniently linked in a news story with an arch counterfeiter named Morrill Magoon, a relative of his wife Wealthy. Magoon lived down the road in Stanstead. This story was possibly a bold attempt by Peasley and Copp to discredit Abraham Channell and his tavern stand. Morrill Magoon was a horse thief and counterfeiter. A black sheep of the family whose reputation Copp and Peasley would use to try to discredit Abraham and his good name in the village.

It was important for a tavern keeper to have a spotless reputation in the 19th century. A tavern owner: "was one of the most prominent individuals encountered by travelers."[34] Others wrote that he, "is often almost always a man of character; for it is difficult for any other to obtain a license to exercise the calling."[35] Tavern keepers such as Abraham often had to prove themselves to be, "men of sober conversation."[36] Without a doubt, Abraham's reputation was of great importance to him and his hospitality business.

On October 9, 1823, the Canadian Times accused Morrill Magoon's "old cronies" of passing a petition to relieve Magoon of the need to stand in the pillory.[37] A pillory is similar to standing in the stocks, the head, hands, and feet, are put through holes in wood and secured in place. Morrill Magoon was to stand in this pillory for one hour with his crime listed on the device. This may not seem like a horrendous punishment, except for the crowds that may gather and throw garbage and other objects at the prisoner. This harsh punishment device did not last much longer in human history. It is possible Magoon's family felt he may not survive it. Abraham knew this well from his time on the streets of London. Many never survived the punishments he viewed in the great city.

In the article the author Silas Dickerson stated that "rogues......are bound by no feeling but that of dependence on each other's villainy." Dickerson went on to say "….whom we have before mentioned as being on very friendly terms with the counterfeiting marauders, and a tavern keeper at the ferry named Channel."[38] Dickerson sought to tie Abraham directly with his wife's distant in-law and make him lose credibility in not only Georgeville, but all of Lower Canada. Dickerson went on to suggest that those who tried to help Magoon should also be locked up in the pillory. Magoon was locked up in the pillory and served out this initial punishment, surviving the ordeal to either be hung or sent to Bermuda as his final punishment. His final judgment has conflicting stories. Abraham was furious with all this bad press and slander rendered to his name.

If Abraham were twenty years younger he might have ridden his horse to the offices of the Canadian Times and dealt out some of the shipboard justice that he once gave William Pearl in Manchester. But brawling and street fighting pugilism are actions for younger men, and all he could do was angrily write out his own response letter to the Canadian Times. He did not agree with how he was described at all. Abraham stated, "I was burlesqued in the Canadian Times and British Colonist about the 9th of October last, for giving my name…with many others of Respectability in this place—in petitioning to his Excellency and praying that part of Morrill Magoon's sentence of sitting in the pillory might be revoked…." Abraham continued in his statement:

> Being thus abused, I am constrained to request all friends to
> Government and Officers in my native country strictly to
> inform themselves of my manner of conduct towards the
> same, as I was a faithful subject to his Majesty in the
> Revolutionary War in which I was wounded four times in his
> Majesty's service on board the ship Milford, Capt. I. Bird,
> Com.—and was regularly discharged for my faithful service. I
> defy any friend to man to prove I have ever used any means to
> corrupt any currency or sided or assisted any others so to do.
> It is well (that) the petitioners were not all Tavern Keepers! I
> am the only….Kings subject in this place. Here are four
> persons…who are endeavoring to destroy my character and
> business in order to build themselves up: not withstanding my
> endeavors to promote the public good…..Abraham F.
> Channel[39]

Abraham was fighting mad and there must have been plenty of awkward silence when Abraham passed either Peasley or Copp in the street, he surely felt they were responsible for the bad press. Tension must have been high on the dusty road in Georgeville. He was a man whose reputation was everything. At the end of the letter, in an apparent slam to Copp he gave his address as:

Union Tavern
King's Ferry
Stanstead, Jan. 10th, 1824

Abraham had called Copp's Ferry his home for years and had always used the village name. However, with the challenge given to him by Peasley and Copp and their new Magog Hotel, he became bound and determined to change the name in honor of the many King Georges' he had lived his long life under. Peasley and Copp were damned yankees to Abraham, and he considered himself the only real British citizen. None of them had come from England or even walked the streets of London. Today it is often asserted that the town was renamed after George Copp, the first white male born in the town. It makes little sense to rename a town when the name being used is already a family name. It seems certain that Abraham got the last laugh in this one when the town became known as Georgeville after the many British Kings he had been a subject of.

During the 200th anniversary of Georgeville my 5th cousin and friend Lewis Channell's wife Nancy were walking through town when Nancy came across a Copp. Her eye was caught by a woman reading her name-tag and she introduced herself. The bitter Copp descendant confronted her with the fact that it was the no good Channell that made her family lose the honor of the town being named after them. Lewis later said "that's right" when Nancy told him of the encounter and Lewis and his wife had a good laugh. The Channell family may not have a town named after us but we do have a few streets and a bay in the lake that have our name attached to them. Those Copp's can sure hold a grudge.....

As far as the rogue Magoon is concerned it was stated in the records that he was scheduled to be hung February 20, 1826.[40] It seems that everyone was condemned that year to be hung, but none ever were.[41] But what of Magoon's counterfeiting crime? At the time there was no government issued paper money. All of it came from banks and other sources. Was Magoon in reality a Canadian Robin Hood? Did he strike against the banking system in Canada? To understand Magoon one must look towards other counterfeiters in the area, and there were a lot of them. According to a respected early settler Philip Ruiter:

> [T]he counterfeiters have become exceedingly numerous
> inasmuch that a gang of them is established in almost every
> one of the newly settled Townships and emboldened by
> impunity, they have openly proceeded to the commission of
> every species of villainy and fraud…..and they are daily
> emigrating thereto to spend in drunkenness and riot the gains
> of their iniquity.[42]

Counterfeiting in the area made perfect sense, with such a long border and not much around in the way of police enforcement. There was no law against counterfeiting bank notes in Lower Canada until 1811. Even after that time enforcement was weak. With the majority of counterfeit bank notes being American, the government in Canada did not react until they were pressured by American officials to act. In 1819, Reverend Fitch Reed, a traveling minister from New York stated: "I was told that every family in Cogniac Street was concerned in the production of spurious bank bills. These bills are purported to be on the banks in the United States; the Canadian authorities troubling themselves but little about the matter, so long as their own bills were not counterfeited."[43] There is enough evidence to consider that counterfeiting was indeed a large problem in the region. The counterfeiters living and located on the street the minister mentioned became the largest producer of illegal bank notes in all of North America. In trade for these notes they took stolen horses and other ill gotten goods.[44]

Another counterfeiter who was presumably from Lower Canada was Abigail White. She was caught making notes as a member of the Stephen Trask gang. She was reported breaking out of a jail in Newfane, Vermont in September 1808. She is known today as the last woman to receive a whipping as punishment in Vermont.[45] Counterfeiting was big business at the time, and people were needed to pass the notes as well as print them. A tavern would seem like a good place to try to pass notes, and Abraham probably had to keep his eyes open for them.

The story of the counterfeiters points out the fact that the government was still growing and unsure of its banking system. Did the federal government or states hold power? Who could assume the responsibility for producing money and guaranteeing the value of it? The United States first printed paper money at the federal level when the Civil War broke out and money was needed to finance the war. Money is guaranteed by the government, without trust or faith in the government it is nothing but paper and has no value. Today most people take the value of money for granted. For Abraham and the others who lived at that time it was to be looked at closely and scrutinized before acceptance. In 1865, the Secret Service began to defend the United States against counterfeiters, and they continue to do so today.[46]

The one way we can relieve Abraham of any possible involvement with these counterfeiters is through his friendship with Leon Lalanne. Lalanne tried his best as a public servant to stop some of these activities, but seems to have been unsuccessful. This created a lot of hardship for him as can be seen with his note, "harassed six days and nights by thieves and coniackers." Coniacker was a slang term used for counterfeiters at the time. Lalanne felt that nothing could be done to stop the coniackers until it was made a capital crime.[47] Thomas McCord, the chief magistrate in Montreal told Lalanne that they did not have the money to prosecute the cases. Witnesses had to be called from the area, and their travel had to later be reimbursed. The money to pay for men to help Lalanne rid the area of these coniackers could not be found in the government coffers.[48] Fortunately, the counterfeiters later turned against one another and became less of a problem.

In 1827, the 13th Parliament of Lower Canada met. In the United States John Quincy Adams served as President of the United States. John Quincy Adams was felt to have stolen the presidency from his rival Andrew Jackson with a "corrupt bargain"; it was a heated time in Washington. Rivalry was beginning to rise in politics north of the border in Quebec as well. During the 1820's, politics were heating up in Lower Canada between the followers of Louis-Joseph Papineau, who had risen to power in 1815, and the opposing Legislative council. The legislative council was appointed by the governor and not by the people. After a trip to England to argue reform, Papineau was re-elected Speaker of the House of Assembly in 1825, upon his return.[49] Soon the movement received a new name, "*En 1826, le Parti Canadien devint le Parti Patriote.*"[50] The name was changed to the Patriot Party in the year 1826.

Families like the Channell family, who lived and worked in the Eastern Townships were poorly represented in the national government. The Legislative Council and Governor had the most political clout. In March 1829, an act was passed in England by King George the IV to divide Lower Canada into forty counties. This added more seats to the parliament and it was hoped it would pacify the citizens. The election that followed strengthened the party that politically opposed the Governor of Lower Canada, Matthew Lord Aylmer. Overall the Governor had strong support in the area of the Townships, but this was not so in Stanstead and Georgeville.

In 1828, Abraham is said to have had a birthday party thrown for him at the Inn by his friends and family. The story states it was his 75th but given the date it figures out to be his 80th. On this day he is said to have run across the tavern and to have jumped up and put the mark of his shoe as high up as his shoulder on the doorway.[51] Whatever physical exertion and display Abraham had made that day must have made quite an impression for the event to have been written down by a witness many years later. This is one man that knew how to make an impression, even if it was with his foot. Earlier that same year on July 4th the last signer of the Declaration of Independence 91-year-old Charles Carroll turned over a shovel full of dirt to begin the building of the first railroad between Baltimore and Ohio. From this time forward railroads exploded across the northeast. This method of travel was opposed by men like Abraham, who depended on stagecoaches and turnpikes for their business livelihood. The world was rapidly changing.

The year 1832, saw the outbreak of a tremendous cholera epidemic which was blamed on the new European immigrants who had recently arrived in Canada. The epidemic brought business to a standstill in the cities. French speakers began using the term *adieu*, which means "before God" to say the farewells they thought may be final. The French inhabitants who were fearing for their lives were recognizing the fact that they may never see each other again. With all the people who traveled by Abraham's tavern stand it is a wonder he did not catch the disease. There is no replacement for fresh food and water, which was less available in the cities of Montreal and Quebec. It helped that the distance of the water was safely kept away from the tavern privy at the tavern.

The Cholera epidemic was feared beyond the borders of Canada and Abraham's tavern. William P. Channell and his brothers Robert and Abraham were moving from town to town doing a variety of jobs such as farming and quarry work in the Northeastern United States. Their travels took them from Pelham, New Hampshire to Lowell, Massachusetts. There was ample work, but it was hard work, and when their employer tried to reduce their fees they left and went elsewhere. While working in Groton, Massachusetts, west of the new mill city of Lowell, William wrote of the local inhabitants of the area who were terrified of the cholera that was ravaging New York. William felt that the best way to deal with death was, "to be prepared for death and then we shall be prepared for life."[52] He ended his letter with a poetic verse:

> I hope you all remember me
> __hear my face you no more see
> An interest in your prayers I crave
> That we may meet beyond the grave.

The poetic nature of his grandmother Abigail seems to have lived on in his soul.

Back in Lower Canada, access to the roads was a major political issue for people in the Eastern Townships. Their construction and funded repair would make the land far more valuable. Promoting the construction of these roads benefited Channell and other land owners greatly. Politically, other members of Parliament may have supported funds directed at roads in the Townships to strengthen their power against the governor, and win new members over to their side. The road project did not greatly expand settlement in the area from newly arrived Europeans, they had little money, but French speakers from the cities north grew to twenty percent of the population in the Townships. This may have relieved the overcrowded cities of Montreal and Quebec. The support of the road project is one major reason Channell's son Leon and son-in-law John Carter Tuck likely supported *Le Parti Patriote*. The roads being considered were critical to their economic welfare and the growth of the tavern business.

John Carter Tuck was born in Parsonfield, Maine (then part of Massachusetts), and at the age of twenty-five married seventeen-year-old Susan Channell, daughter of Abraham and Wealthy Cox on March 22,

1834. Now in his late seventies, Abraham was probably pleased to have a young man around to help at the tavern, and Tuck seemed to have been given responsibility for the management of the business. His two sons Leon and Charles were too young to be much help other than basic farm work, and they still needed to receive an education before they could manage things.

It was not long before Abraham was willing to completely turn over the operations and job as innkeeper to Tuck. On March 22, 1834, an agreement was hashed out between them. Abraham, "desirous of being relieved of the cares and toils of managing his own affairs during the remaining period of his life [and] considering himself in a great measure incapacitated from the infirmities of old age," turned over the day to day operations of his hotel to his son-in-law John Carter Tuck. This was until his youngest son, Charles Stewart, then thirteen, was old enough to take over. Tuck needed to support Abraham and his fifty-two-year-old wife Wealthy, and feed and educate Abraham's two sons. Tuck had taken on a lot of responsibility for a young man of twenty-six.[53] His interest in the political trouble that grew in the cities of Montreal and Quebec also increased, perhaps in hope of building the tavern's business.

In Georgeville, the drinking problem previously illustrated by the death of Smith in Abraham's barn became a major issue in the area. In 1830, a temperance society was formed in Georgeville and 245 members took an oath to abstain from alcohol.[54] This did not include wine, possibly due to religious reasons. The cholera epidemics were partially thought to have been the result of a vengeful God. Drinking alcohol became seen as the cause for God's anger and alcohol abuse slowly grew as the most despicable sin in society. Religious leaders resisted the perception of the importance of this new sin that grew outside of their own teachings. Men and women who abstained from alcohol were perceived as being morally superior. This new view of abstinence toward alcohol may have in time contributed to the demise of the tavern by reducing profit from alcohol sales. It would be up to Abraham's sons and son in law to save the tavern from the many rapid changes in society.

The Rebellion of 1837

On February 1834, in a meeting of the Lower Canadian Parliament, *Patriote* party political leader Louis-Joseph Papineau distributed a radical document he supported known as the 92 Resolutions. These resolutions were a long list of grievances and problems that his party had with the unelected portion of the colonial government, known as the Legislative Council. The members of this council were chosen by the governor and not by popular vote. These resolutions sought to bring elections to the province for all officials; striking at the governors power. The resolutions, inspired and influenced by Papineau, were strongly opposed by Governor Aylmer, who enforced the decisions of the British Parliament. All of the party's problems with the current method of government were spelled out in the resolutions, and the later discussion of the issues in the Parliament of Lower Canada. The discussion began with a powerful three-hour speech by Papineau who enthusiastically pushed for the document's adoption.

Twenty-four members chose to vote against the resolution, and seventeen of these men chose not to run for re-election the following year. Papineau called those who left the party, "Tories," a term with the same definition as loyalist, a supporter of the power of the king, but with a more negative connotation from south of the border in the United States.[1] It seems more likely in this case to have referred to a supporter of British executive rule. The use of the terms Tory and Patriot borrowed and reflected on the events and terminology of the American Revolution. Papineau and his followers gave the British Parliament a not so subtle warning by using these terms. Bad crop yields and the dependence of many families on the clergy for food fed the unrest in politics in the cities and surrounding areas. People tend to support political change and radical ideas when their stomach or their wallet is empty.

The area of Stanstead, on the eastern side of Lake Memphremagog, south of the area where Abraham and his sons lived, largely supported politicians on the *Patriote* side of the political spectrum. Funding for road building continued to be an issue with the men who chose to support Papineau and his party such as the Channell family who relied on the stagecoach routes for their livelihood. The established government opposed spending money on road projects like this in the area. After the departure of the seventeen Tories, Papineau and his party found themselves fully in charge of the assembly. For the moment, they sought non-violent political change in Lower Canada. Papineau knew the Tory Party was trying to keep things the same as they had been. They safely followed the rules that were laid down from Britain, with the real power of government residing in an unelected executive branch. Old feelings of resentment toward the British as enemies arose from the French members of the party, and a new order of government was expected from the members of the party who were then so firmly in control.

Lord John Russell (1792-1878), the acting Colonial Secretary back in Britain, fired back at Papineau and his group with his own Ten-Resolutions in April, 1837. These denied, for the most part, all the items asked for in the Ninety-Two Resolutions.[2] These Ten Resolutions gave control of all the tax money to Governor Aylmer, and thus took away the only real source of power from Papineau and the other party members. The governor not only wanted to keep his own power, but reduce theirs as well. When Lord Aylmer tried to get these resolutions passed, he was strongly opposed politically by Papineau and his assembly. This left Aylmer no other resort than to dissolve the assembly.[3] When Aylmer then tried to arrest some of the ring leaders, the Rebellion broke out in full force. The streets of Montreal seethed in discontent and opposition. Abraham and his family now had to choose their own side in the conflict, and they chose to side with the Rebels. On the other side of the border in the Northern United States citizens were ready and willing to help, but no support came from the U. S. Federal Government in Washington.

President Martin Van Buren had just taken office in 1837, and had not only the Rebellion in Canada to contend with, but also the economic trouble in the United States, later known as the Panic of 1837. This was a problem he inherited from the former president, Andrew Jackson's administration and the war that "Old Hickory" had waged against the banks. Jackson supported men who had operated in a similar way to the "Hunters," the American group that supported the *Patriotes* in Canada, in Texas when taking land from Mexico. Van Buren did not support the "Hunters," whose leadership came from his political opposition the Whig party. The Democratic Party seemed to support adding land to the south, but not in the slave free north.

Leon Channell was studying as a law student, and John Carter Tuck worked at the tavern. Tuck was the husband of Susan Channell and served as an older mentor to Leon during the conflict. They joined the secret oath bound fraternal organization known as "The Hunters." The group in Montreal was called *Les Patriotes*. The Hunters organizational membership was spread out from Vermont to Michigan and across Canada. They used a similar membership structure to Freemasons. Obviously, Masonic members had begun or influenced the development of the group.

The members of the organization were divided into degrees like the fraternal organization and used signs, handshakes, and secret passwords. Their oath pledged each member, "to defend and cherish republican institutions and ideas, combat and help to destroy every power of royal origin on our continent, and never to rest till all British tyrants ceased to have any dominion in North America."[4] A strong oath for the Channells to have taken, it was an act of rebellion as strong as their fathers. The government spies from Washington that watched the group believed they numbered in the thousands.

Leon and Tuck fled the tavern to go to Swanton, Vermont, during part of the Rebellion and were involved with the men who planned raids across the border with their sympathetic American citizen members and supporters. There in Swanton, near Lake Champlain, they waited while the attack plans were made. They had likely been seen at a rally or fingered as being members by others who sought to confiscate belongings from them or the tavern. Abraham was also conveniently absent in Massachusetts during this year. Had the old Patriot been active somehow and fled himself? John and Leon were involved with Dr.

Cyrille Côté (1809-1850), and also Dr. Robert Nelson (1794-1873), the brother of another *Patriote* leader named Dr. Wolfred Nelson. Papineau sought to build an army within the United States and strike across the border at Lower Canada by utilizing the "Hunter Lodges" or *Freres Chasseurs* like the one in Swanton as a base for operations. Papineau proved, however, to be a poor military leader, and Dr. Robert Nelson became the more radical leader of the movement.

It was no secret that the intention of these lodges was to attack the British Tories in Lower Canada. It was said that the attacks were easily stopped and an armed border did more to raise tension and hostility in the area, than provide any real threat.[5] This, however, discredits the very real threat of war that existed and greatly threatened the Rush-Bagot Treaty. Peace was in jeopardy in the region; if not the entirety of North America.

On December 13, 1837, a Patriot army led by General Rensselaer Van Rensselaer of New York State, attacked under the new flag of the Canadian Republic, and proclaimed the new Canadian Republic's independence from England. Rensselaer had accepted the leadership position in hopes of making a name for himself and to liberate Canada like Sam Houston had liberated Texas.[6] The force was beaten back to Fort Schlosser in New York. Rensselaer was the son of Solomon Van Rensselaer, a tactically skillful general in the War of 1812, and a member of the Federalist Party. While Rensselaer served in the House of Representatives he had cast the deciding vote to elect John Quincy Adams over Andrew Jackson in what Jackson later called the "corrupt bargain." Rensselaer was a good friend of future president William Henry Harrison, and campaigned vigorously for him in his future presidential campaign.

Rensselaer's son, the general of the short-lived Canadian Republic, was a clerk in the U.S. ligation under William Henry Harrison, while Harrison served as ambassador to Colombia during John Quincy Adams presidency.[7] It is hard not to imagine just how much Rensselaer or William Henry Harrison may have known about the Rebellion or the "Hunters." What would have transpired in Canada if Harrison had not died a month into his presidential term? Harrison had after all once invaded Canada during the war of 1812.

Tensions rose when it was arranged for a private American ship called the *Caroline* to carry supplies to Navy Island, a Rebel held stronghold a mile up the river from Niagara Falls on the Canadian side of the border. This stronghold was run by military leaders with strong Whig Party connections.[8] This event occurred in the final days of the Jackson presidency, but Van Buren had to contend with its aftermath after he took office.

On the night of December 29, 1837, a British-Canadian raiding party operating under government orders traveled secretly across the international border and attacked the *Caroline* at her dock on the U.S. side of the border. A small skirmish broke out between the two armed groups, and the British force prevailed in the melee. This action greatly threatened the peace that existed between the two countries. The ship was eventually torched by the British group and her burning wreckage was sent over Niagara Falls. Several Americans were first reported to have been killed in the action and one of the raiders, Alexander McLeod, a deputy sheriff in Upper Canada, was captured three years later and put on trial in New York state for the murders that occurred that night.[9]

Tension grew due to the fact that the British felt the matter should be dealt with at the international level, rather than with a civil trial in an American state court. The American Government kept the case in the local court in spite of it being a violation of American sovereignty. The encounter was after all not between two nations, but between one nation and the ideals of the citizens of two nations. The British desperately wanted to get their hands on the "British rebels and American pirates," that were allowed to arm and organize in the United States that night.[10] The negotiations were in the capable hands of the American Secretary of State Daniel Webster. The United States found itself in a difficult position to control its citizens and stop them from assisting the *Patriotes* in Canada with what may have appeared to be a struggle similar to their own earlier Revolution.

Many Americans felt that the United States should extend from the tip of South America to the Aurora Borealis, the colored lights that light up the night sky at the North Pole.[11] These were the days before Manifest Destiny was a common American thought, but clearly the borders could have gone north and south as well as west. The failure to take Canada decades before had resulted from a disastrous offensive of the Revolutionary War. Could the current trouble offer an opportunity to change this? With the difficult economic times and poor job prospects many American men with time on their hands took the oath and joined the Rebel group such as the one Leon Channell and Tuck were involved with in Swanton, Vermont. Overall an estimated five hundred people fled from Lower Canada to the United States during the Rebellion.[12] The Hunter movement was said to then grow to twelve hundred lodges and over eight thousand members.[13]

On January 4, 1838, news of the *Caroline* Affair reached Washington. American General Winfield Scott had planned to dine with President Van Buren that evening, but after the event reached the presidents ears Scott was told, "Blood has been shed, you must go with all speed to Niagara."[14] Scott left with a small army to patrol the 800 mile border and to try to keep it from erupting with more bloodshed. Scott needed to recruit men from outside the area to find enough soldiers who were not sympathetic with the Hunters. This mission was successful in not allowing the situation to explode into an international incident, but raids and troubles still continued along the border.

In Montreal political protesting led the British military leader Sir John Colborne to arm the police and to ban the printing of two local newspapers.[15] The governor then replaced all the Judges that he and the Tories felt were not loyal and supportive of their political decisions.[16] These judges may have questioned the arresting and imprisonment of men without hearings or trials. Martial law was in full force. A group of loyal citizens volunteered and began militia drilling in Montreal for action if needed. All these issues led to heightened and volatile tensions in the region. When the fighting broke out, the *Patriotes* initially had some success, but later began to lose their encounters with those loyal to the British Government and the Canadian Oligarchy that wielded its royal power. Refugee Rebels then fled to Swanton and other towns where they purchased and were supplied with weapons by supportive Americans. When they grouped together and raided across the border they were soundly defeated by a superior government force, an hour or so west from Lake Memphremagog in what is today Saint Armand.

The Rebels held meetings and raised support and funds throughout the following months of December and on into January 1838. Yet part of their problem was the disappearance of their leader Papineau, who had fled deeper into New York, out of communication with the Rebels. Papineau was a great politician and orator, but proved to be a poor military leader when one was desperately needed to lead the Rebels to victory. When Papineau was contrasted with George Washington, it was written that, "one loved himself, the other loved his country."[17] His absence created a vacuum in the movement and into his place of leadership stepped Dr. Robert Nelson, a move that was not fully supported by all *Patriotes*. Leon Channell is said to have been in close proximity with Nelson, the exact details of their relationship are not known.[18] Nelson declared political independence for Lower Canada and small areas of fighting broke out near the Channell tavern, along the east coast of the lake. The action then ceased until the fall of 1838, but the buildup of threats continued to grow, boiling under the surface in the region.

Members of the group in Detroit planned an attack on Windsor, in Upper Canada, on July 4th, 1838. They tried to gain American support by using the patriotic connection to the date. This attack was foiled by the United States democratic leadership of Martin Van Buren which ordered the government to step in and to seize their steamboats, and cut off all their supplies.[19] The "Hunters" in Vermont, next to Lower Canada, hoped for better luck in their activities.

Moving toward secrecy to avoid detection, *Les Patriotes* and their secret societies called *Freres Chasseurs*, by the francophone members, planned a major invasion from the United States. The secrecy surrounding the group hides many facts from us today, but it could be that Abraham's tavern served as a *Freres Chasseurs* lodge. Thirty-five were said to exist in Lower Canada. When the day of invasion finally came on November 4, 1838, the town of Napierville was initially captured, but the Rebels were then defeated at the Battle of Odelltown. The British military force's superior numbers made victory impossible for the Rebels. One loss after another led to the ultimate failure of the *Patriotes* in this final attempt to take over the country and bring about political changes. American politicians did nothing to help those in Canada who sought the same republican liberties as the United States enjoyed. This sealed the fate of the Rebels.

The Rebels near the tavern were not ready yet to give up. There was talk and local fear a week later of another attack coming from over five hundred Rebels preparing to attack Stanstead, a town just south of Georgeville. This led Militia leaders to come quickly to the area, and the militia was promptly fired upon by *Patriotes*, hidden in the dark of the night from view. Looking to cut Loyalist communications and troop movement across Lake Memphremagog, John Carter Tuck and Leon

Channell went secretly to the lake front to sink the Copp's ferry and hinder the movement of the opposition.[20] There was probably just as much personal satisfaction as political satisfaction in the act. Roswell Bates helped them in the sinking of the ferry and loudly boasted the night before that he would go to fight in Georgeville alone if no-one would follow him. If anyone did follow him, it was not enough.

Leon Channell and his *beau-frère* John Carter Tuck must have felt that their secret involvement had gone undetected. News of the hanging and banishment that reached them in the tavern must have filled them with fear. *Patriote* leader, Dr. Jean-Baptiste-Henri Brien, feared his involvement in the Rebellion would cost him his life after he was captured and he broke his "Hunter" oath and turned in a list of fellow *Patriotes* who were in Swanton with him. That list unfortunately included both Tuck and Channell. While in prison, Brien's Attorney, General Charles Richard Ogden, left instructions that from November 16, 1838, while Brien was being held in the Montreal jail; no one was to talk to the doctor. Brien's life was spared, but he was banished from Canada. The Rebel leader Robert Nelson, fled to the United States and was never captured.

On November 12, 1838, the sound of multiple hoof beats approached the old tavern. Samuel Gilman of the Stanstead Cavalry barged in and arrested Leon Channell and John Carter Tuck in Georgeville. Members of the family and community pleaded for their innocence and immediate release to no avail. The men were bound and removed to their imprisonment. They were taken directly to jail in Sherbrooke and incarcerated for five months without legal examination of any type. This brings up the question of exactly what the status of habeas corpus was in Canada.. They were living in a state of martial law. This sure did not help help Tuck and Channell. Exactly who ran the hotel during the period of their imprisonment is not clear. The responsibility may have fallen back on Abraham, his wife Wealthy, or daughter Susan. The ownership and future of the tavern was in danger, not to mention the lives of Abraham and Wealthy's family members.

There in the jail Leon and Tuck were interred without the benefit of a trial or a hearing. They had suffered through an interrogation that was more an accusation than a questioning. They sat in their cell in the evening and outstretched their hands in the dark to feel their way about their cell. The slimy cold surface of the masonry offered no escape from their confinement. They may have gone days without food. There was little sympathy for the Rebels in this prison. The peculiar smell of human waste and unwashed bodies drifted around the cell. This added to the torment of their confinement. In the silence the sound of their heartbeat rang in their ears. Rats and vermin ran alongside the walls and cast their shadows from what little light entered the room. They slept when their agitated mind and spirit allowed them the luxury. Outside the cell it was winter, and the cold crept into the jail and caused the limbs of the men to uncontrollably shake to stay warm. There in jail their humanity was challenged by an animal need to survive. They knew and heard of men in nearby cells being hung for their crimes and hoped they would not be the next to swing. Imprisonment offered time to think, and they may have swung from the rope a thousand times in their thoughts. During these months of confinement Leon and Tuck learned what freedom truly was, and how easily it could be lost. Would they ever see Georgeville or the sparkling water of Lake Memphremagog again?

The relatively short list of Rebels provided by the Rebel leader Brien and the fact that he was working secretly in Canada may show that Tuck and Channell were involved at a high level of strategic planning. Or they may have been at the wrong place at the wrong time. Brien was a man they would have been better off not knowing. The man that shared Brien's cell, Chevalier de Lorimier, was among the few to be hung on February 15, 1839, because of Brien's betrayal.[21] Others were sent to a penal colony in Tasmania. Many Rebellion leaders were later banished to other countries and faced death if they returned.

Tuck and Channell languished a total of five winter months at the frozen prison in Sherbrooke. They were then later released at a cost of 400 pounds each. This was a considerable amount of money to come up with and then to repay to family and friends. As they left the prison they rejoiced to be alive and finally free once again. They were lucky to escape with their lives and without banishment or being sent to prison in Tasmania. Their release and the money to free them must have come from Abraham after he returned to Canada from his visit to Massachusetts. It is unknown if the old privateer was pleased or upset at his son and son-in-law for their involvement in the "Hunters." He surely was glad not to see them hung.

In time a new American president named William Henry Harrison was elected, and he named Daniel Webster to continue as his Secretary of

State. After only a month in office Harrison died and the presidency passed peacefully to his Vice President John Tyler; the first real test of the transition of power in the case of presidential death. Any plans Harrison had for Rensselaer in Canada or the "Hunters" may have died with him, or were burned up in his papers years later. His successor, President Tyler, ordered that the Hunter Lodges were to be suppressed in 1842.[22] They had ceased militarily, but may have remained active politically. Daniel Webster served under both presidents and in 1842 he ended the troubles with Canada, left over from the Rebellion and the *Caroline* Affair. In the words of Webster:

> All that can be expected from either government, in these cases, is good faith, a sincere desire to preserve peace and do justice, the use of all proper means of prevention, and that, if offenses can not, nevertheless, be always prevented, the offenders shall still be justly punished.[23]

Webster was later able to solve both the brewing problem between the two nations, and offer a legal rather than military solution to the situation.

In 1837, possibly escaping from his own involvement in the Rebellion or the troubles he saw coming, Abraham, then eighty-nine, traveled south to Massachusetts to visit his family still living there. One thing about the story of Abraham that may tarnish him is his apparent departure from the life of his Shaker daughter Susan. However, on October 3, 1837, the old tailor stepped down from his seat on the stagecoach and visited his long estranged daughter. He looked deeply into her eyes and saw in them nothing but forgiveness. How could a woman who had pledged her life to such strict Christian principles not be a forgiving soul?

Not enough of the short lived relationship between Abraham and his third wife is known to pass judgment on it. His visitation to his estranged daughter shows that he had loved her and thought of her. Shakers were allowed these visits from what they called "non believing relatives" in Harvard. If Abraham encountered his ex-wife Mary or not is unknown, it seems likely that he would have. A month before on September 2, 1837, an "aged man" had come with Mary Smith; a daughter from Mary's marriage before she met Abraham. The name of this man remains unknown. Perhaps it was the first visit from

Abraham.

The old privateer may have told his sons to watch after the property while he was in Massachusetts but they were far too busy in their radical politics to have done that. So in March of 1838, likely while the boys were in Swanton Vermont, Abraham leased out the property to be run by a man named Levi Bigelow. He had just come to town from Worcester Massachusetts. Levi Bigelow was said to be a very good hotel keeper. After his lease with Abraham ended he bought the newer hotel of Copp and Peasley, located across the street from the aging tavern keeper. Both Joshua Copp and James Peasley then moved to the United States to seek to add to their fortunes. They may have found opportunities that existed in the United States that did not exist for them in the small northern village of Georgeville. Their homes still stand in Georgeville, a record of their past presence there.

The later years of the tavern seem to have been marred in a tangled web of failure and struggles between Abraham's sons and his son in law John Tuck; reminiscent of Shakespeare's King Lear in the following line:

> Meantime we shall express our darker purpose.
> Give me the map there. Know that we have divided
> In three our kingdom: and 'tis our fast intent
> To shake all cares and business from our age;
> Conferring them on younger strengths, while we
> Unburthen'd crawl toward death.[24]

The tavern was now apparently being struggled for between Tuck, Leon Channell, and his brother Charles. This struggle is apparent in the following sales that were made to his family in 1842.

On October 5, 1842, Abraham sold half his tavern stand and farm to John Tuck, and then on October 13 the other half of the property seems to have been given to his son Leon for three hundred and fifty pounds. The agreement with Leon was that he would support his father with food and clothing while he was at home, and also during his travels to the United States to visit his family. Everything was said to be divided in half in the tavern between Tuck and Leon, but what those things were was not pointed out in any documents. These items included the tavern stand's furniture for the property that Leon now had to run. This would not have sat well with Leon. There was immediate trouble between the two family members and former rebel friends. On October 20, 1842, seven days after Leon made the arrangement with his father; Tuck filed a lawsuit against Leon. According to Leon, he knew nothing of the sale his father had made to Tuck. A deed and copy of the sale was provided from the youngest brother Charles Stewart Channell.[25] It seems he had now come of age and joined the growing problems of the tavern stand. The kingdom of Abraham now had to be divided by three. Unfortunately, there does not seem to have been enough room for more than one innkeeper.[23] John Tuck seems to have won the battle of who was going to be running the hotel; at least for now.

On August 10, 1842, Abraham wrote a letter addressed to his son Robert in Durham, New Hampshire in response to a kind letter that he had previously received from his son. It was a great pleasure for Abraham to hear from his son and family down in Northern New England. It was good to hear from family that was not arguing about ownership and operation of his property. It seems the earlier law suit problems between Abraham and his son had been solved. The letter was carried both ways by a Mr. Witne who seems to have been assisting Abraham in some of his affairs. Mr. Witne told Abraham that he should go visit his family and stay for a while in November.

Abraham planned to go down with his daughter Nabby and her husband Moses George to visit the town of Ipswich during the trip. They may have visited his granddaughter and seen the mills in Lowell that were now a worldwide attraction. The large brick factories, dormitories, and well planned streets, were at the height of their glory. They could have heard the bells and the throng of young women passing along the street. They certainly had seen the mills in Newmarket that were located so near his son Robert's farm and quarry down the street. A man in Ipswich held a paper against Abraham which he said "hurts me." But he went on to write: "I hold all in my hands and I am well able to pay my way." In spite of Abraham's age, he still had unpaid debts in another country he had to contend with. He closed the letter, "your father and friend til death, remember me to all." Abraham F.J. Channel.[26] With all the family business problems that occurred in Georgeville, Abraham must have been all too glad to leave and let things sort themselves out without him and see his older children in New England.

Robert Channell, it has been stated, worked as a truck farmer in the Lubberland section near the great Bay in New Hampshire. At the time of Abraham's visit he grew crops and carried them by wagon to industrial areas like the Newmarket Mill Company complex. The closest large port to him was Portsmouth, N.H. and when his father wrote him the letter in 1842, he may have sold crops in this city as well. Farming in the Northeast began a steady decline after 1840, when farming grew in the richer and more fertile soil in the new and rapidly settled Northwest States. As roads and transportation improved, the competition in farming became more difficult to contend with in the Northeast. But for now, farming in the region grew steadily with the rise of cities from shipping and the growth of mills. Farming became easier with the introduction of first the iron, and later the steel plow. Robert, like his father, was able to adapt economically to survive and thrive in the young nation. Unfortunately the problems at home in Georgeville continued among Abraham's youngest sons.

Whatever happened in the situation between Abraham's son Leon and his son-in-law Tuck seems to have made all the sales contracts for the tavern property become void. This assumption is due to the fact that Abraham yet again sold the property on March 10, 1843, to his youngest son Charles Stewart Channell.[27] In a far more detailed deed of sale the property was newly surveyed and the lots were laid out and marked. The deed mentions nine rows of apple trees that grew in one section of the property. The deed mentions nothing about Charles caring for his father. Abraham's youngest son Charles seems to have now become fully in charge of the property, at least as far as the hotel was concerned. While struggles continued between the Channell family over the hotel, troubles continued to brew in politics in the cities of Montreal and Quebec.

The previous Rebellion of 1837-38 was still fresh in everyone's minds and had made it clear that the government system in Canada needed change. The British sent over political leaders to Canada to look at the situation and make suggestions on how it could be fixed. The suggestions made by these men unfortunately upset one group or another. The French feared that changes would anglicize them and cause them to eventually lose their language or culture. The situation of how to deal with former rebels such as Channell and Tuck led to yet another crisis. One governor after another came to Canada and struggled through the political gauntlet there. It was felt that in order to win back those who had been treated so poorly and falsely imprisoned during the Rebellion the government should make a generous offer to them for reimbursement of their expenses. Many felt that those who were guilty were also looking for reimbursement.

Prior to this announcement, Leon and Tuck had begun to petition the government to be reimbursed for the expenses and losses they had incurred during the struggle. Many other former rebels and those who had also been accused were petitioning at the time as well. When Leon was released from prison it appears that they were unable to convict either him or Tuck and the charges against them were discharged. Leon asked the doctor who attended to him in the jail, M. Nichols, to write up a letter on March 3, 1846. In this document the doctor stated Leon's conduct was uniformly good while he was incarcerated. His behavior was respectable in spite of his having been subject to what the doctor called, "sickness and many privations."[28] Leon was looking for ninety nine pounds reimbursement, to repay the friends that had assisted him during his confinement. He also needed to repay the expense of the damage done to the hotel.

Changes now came to Canada, and these changes were welcomed by some, while they angered others. What had once been Upper and Lower Canada were now combined into one province in 1841. This angered the French, because it weakened their representation and voice in the new combined government. Upper Canada was deep in debt and those in Lower Canada did not want to pay their debts off for them. A movement grew within the political ranks of the moderate Liberals to compensate people for their losses in the previous military activities of the Rebellion. These Liberals pressed for governmental reform, but were not willing to enter again into full scale Rebellion.

The conservative Tory members of the government were infuriated by this talk of compensation. They knew many of these people had not only had sympathies towards the Rebellion but in some cases may have even taken part in it. The thought that these rebels wanted to be paid back for their crimes was unacceptable to the Tory leaders. These claims were fraught with political danger and could possibly kindle more violence in the streets yet again. While politics began to boil, Tuck sought ways to make a living in Georgeville.

John Carter Tuck set his sights on the transportation aspect of the business in addition to the hotel. Tuck, with three other men as his partners, began running a stagecoach service on the old Magog road. He also purchased and took over control of the ferry across the lake he had tried to sink during the Rebellion. On the western side of the lake he purchased an existing hotel built by Levi Knowlton. In a time just before railroads, there was still sufficient travel between the northern Canadian cities and cities of the United States in the south to support the stagecoach and hospitality businesses. After the railroad, steamships that plied the lake from Newport, Vermont became the lifeblood of the local lodging business. Tuck looked for control of the stage line coming through the village, and this stagecoach also helped support the family hotel.

The stagecoach was the life's blood of Abraham's tavern, now being run by his son Charles Stewart Channell. It brought travelers who spent money for their lodging and meals. The journey on these stagecoaches was an adventure that is lost in the modern world. Although the carriages at best averaged seven miles an hour, they did so while going through deeply rutted mud puddles, and over rocks that roughly jostled the passengers. Hopefully the travelers enjoyed the conversation of their fellow passenger, and hopefully they have bathed recently. The cabins were not heated and not overly roomy. But still it was an adventure; at least when looked at with a romantic view of the past.

Early stagecoaches were egg shaped, rather small, and offered no shock protection. These coaches were later improved upon by the Abbot-Downing Company of Concord, New Hampshire, a leading producer of coaches.[29] The firm commenced making coaches in 1828, and their business thrived and grew. The coaches were outfitted with straps that supported the cabin, and offered some shock protection from the rough country roads. These better quality coaches offered seating for nine to twelve passengers on wooden seats. Some sat inside, and the more daring sat on the roof of the coach. There was some room for travel bags and trunks, but not a tremendous amount. Stagecoaches contracted with banks to move money, and also with the postal service to move mail. Although these stagecoaches are closely associated with the west because of Hollywood cowboy movies, they were a part of everyday life in urban cities in the Northern States before and after the advent of rail service.

On July 21, 1845, municipal government began in Georgeville in Stanstead Township. Seven men were elected and sworn in as councilors in Stanstead. They were elected from a possible population of 1,400 by 231 male voters. Women did not have voting rights. The biggest item on the councilors plate were the condition of the roads. They voted that every male who owned 200 acres would spend ten days per year working on the roads passing near their property. Anyone unable or unwilling to work paid a tax of five shillings per day. To coordinate all this political wrangling they met at Abraham Channell's tavern stand from 7 a.m. until midnight for three days, six times per year. Improving these roads often encroached on personal property, and the council found they were in the same perilous position of eminent domain that Abraham's son-in-law Dudley Choate had been in years before.[30]

Tragedy struck young Leon when he lost his wife Harriett Evelyn Goodrich on May 7, 1847. Leon and his wife were both in their late twenties, and her death left Leon with a two year old daughter named Agnes. The illness of Leon's wife and the subsequent fighting over his father's property may have caused him to leave Georgeville and the tavern stand and move to Peru, New York, along the shore of Lake Champlain. Leon does not seem to have been able to leave the beautiful shores of northern lakes. He remarried Harriet L. Gibbs, and served in Peru as the town clerk. He also owned and ran a store with a post office. This left Tuck and his brother Charles to care for his father and the hotel property. Leon, the rebel son and *Patriote* was now an American.

In 1848, an election was held in Canada and the Tory's lost power. The compensation that Leon and Tuck had petitioned the government for was now being pushed for by the new political leadership in Montreal. The exception to this was in cases in which men were convicted of high treason. But some even called into question the legitimacy of the military courts that had tried them. They were after all citizens that had been tried by a military court. A new governor named Lord Elgin took office in 1848; along with the new House of Assembly.

In 1849, the majority party opened up discussions about reimbursing the Rebels, and this was strongly opposed by the opposition party of the Tories that had fought against them ten years before. These men who had fought and defeated the Rebels considered themselves to be the true loyal subjects of Britain, and were outraged that the men they had fought against would be reimbursed for their disloyalty.

On February 23, 1849, the: *Bill to provide for the Indemnification of Parties in Lower Canada whose Property was destroyed during the Rebellion in the years 1837 and 1838*, was introduced to the assembly. The bill passed through the houses and the governor then considered the bill for over a month. Governor Elgin was clearly concerned about the havoc he may create by signing the bill, but he ultimately chose to sign it. After the signing, the former loyal political party members themselves became rebellious. A new fuse of violence had been lit. The streets of the French speaking city once again burst into violence.

Crowds gathered in the streets of Montreal after the bill was signed. When Lord Elgin's carriage approached the angry mob hurled rocks and eggs at him. Later that same night the crowd of protestors grew and the violent mob walked the narrow streets of Montreal in full fury. Their anger needed an outlet, which took shape in the outline of the Parliament building. The structure within which the bill was first passed was then attacked and fire bombed. The building burned to the ground that same night. After this, the homes of the leaders of the new moderate party were attacked, and their families trembled in fear and sought escape during the long night of terror. The riot lasted for two long days within the city of Montreal, until the violence finally cleared.[31]

The long term effect was that the bill, although unpopular with Tories, became a sign that the government was now responsible to the wishes of the majority of its citizens. Power had now shifted from the former party. After the destruction of the Parliament building in Montreal, the capital was moved elsewhere, away from the ethnic and political tensions that existed in the area. The Canadian capital never returned to the old city that rests next to the Saint Lawrence River. The troubles unfortunately, did not end with the acceptance of the bill. When the established wealthy class lost their fortunes, they tried to strike back by pulling away their loyalty from the government they no longer felt supported their interests.

A group of Tories formed and wrote The Annexation Manifesto of 1849. The supporters of it wrote of their disgust with the present political and economic situation, "what but ruin or rapid decay meets the eye?" The group called upon citizens to take steps to peaceably leave Great Britain and join the United States. In ten short years they had changed from fighting to stop a Rebellion to rebelling themselves. They saw no end to the political rivalries and problems. The Tories felt that annexation to the United States would take away French political power and open up markets and investors to the sections of Canada that annexed along with them. It was hoped that free trade with the United States might bring many advantages to their markets and help them to prosper.[32]

One thing that stood in the way of annexation was that the Northern United States was in turmoil with the South over the peculiar institution of African American enslavement. Another slave free state would have strengthened the North in the senate politically, but could have brought about a war to the United States. This would come true in another twelve years. If annexation was actually seriously considered at that time by American politicians, it could have brought forth incredible trouble to the United States. In addition to the growing slave issue the United States was then also waging a war against Mexico. This war greatly increased the western area of the United States and led to problems in deciding if the areas gained were to become "free soil" or not. For whatever reason the northern area of Canada does not seem to have been yet an issue in United States politics. As the economy in Canada gradually improved, the support of the Annexation Manifesto in the townships faded away. The land that Abraham called home stayed Canadian soil.

That year Abraham's sons also put the property up for sale in the *Stanstead Journal*. On December 27, 1849, it was advertised:

> Desirable Property for Sale/That old tavern stand in Georgeville, formerly known as the Channell Stand, and now kept by J.C. Tuck, consisting of a house 36x80 feet, part brick, horse stable 40x50, new barn 30x40; new shed 20x60, large woodshed and other outbuildings. There is a never failing supply of water on the premises. Connected with the above are 100 acres of Excellent Land, 80 of which are under improvement, the remainder woodland. For further particulars application may be made to Chas. S. Channell, Georgeville, or to Leon L. Channell, Peru, Clinton Co., N.Y.[33]

The property was unfortunately not as desirable as it was thought to be by the boys, and no buyers were found for over a decade. The land being "under Improvement" meant that it was being farmed. Charles was twenty-nine and his brother Leon thirty-one when the property went up for sale. Selling must have been a difficult decision for them to make after being raised in the tavern and knowing the business so well.

In 1850, the Townships began to see fugitive slaves and other African Americans migrate to the area, although not as many as in Canada West, an area known to fugitive slaves as "Glory Land." The Fugitive Slave Act was passed as part of the Compromise of 1850, and the Underground Railroad carried refugees to Canada through the border towns in Vermont that offered safety and freedom to those poor souls who survived the trek.[34] Odd that in the land of freedom, even after slaves escaped the South and made it safely to free states, these fugitive slaves were not actually free until they touched the northern land still held by Great Britain. They could, however, live relatively safely in free African communities. The abolitionist Wendell Phillips argued that the act, protected by the federal Constitution, rebound the chains of fugitive slaves. He felt the provision in the Constitution that provided power to the representatives from the slave states, showed the document to be wrong and that the country had outgrown the need for it.[35] To Phillips, the Constitution did not free men but enslaved them.

After 1850, the people of Canada largely supported abolition. Slavery had been previously eradicated in Canada in 1833.[36] Although a border separated some of the grandchildren of Abraham from the looming crisis in the United States, It did not stop them from later acting against slavery and joining the forces of freedom to save the Union. The opinion of the Channell family may have been reflected in the Toronto Globe: "We are in the habit of calling the people of the United States 'the American,' but we too are Americans; on us, as well as on them, lies the duty of preserving the honour of the continent."[37] In time, the citizens of Canada who shared the sentiments of the Channell family assisted in ending slavery by joining their Northern Forces. Abraham's grandsons in both Canada and Massachusetts, later had to take up arms to finally bring true freedom to the United States.

All of these troubles may or may not have been known to Abraham. At the time of the riots in Montreal, the Annexation trouble, and the approach of the Civil War, Abraham had reached the age of 104. For once it does not seem that anyone in his family was involved directly in the political turmoil. Responsible government had now finally reached his area. His family could vote and have their voices heard by their own chosen representatives. Times were hard, farms and businessmen struggled, but better times lay ahead. The tavern changed managers and owners and became different in appearance from what it once was. It had a new challenger that grew in power called the iron horse. This changed the transportation system that had been in place for half a century. Progress was coming to the area, but it lagged far behind the urban centers of the United States. Stagecoaches, wagons, and sleighs were quickly replaced by this new technology in transportation. All those modes of travel would be relegated to secondary status.

The first steam powered vessel that arrived in the area were the steamships that provided transportation on the lake. The train came by land and its distance of twenty miles from the village ensured that Georgeville and the tavern stand would no longer be a main transportation stop on the way to Montreal or Quebec. At first these trains were used to carry goods between the sections of the Saint Lawrence and other rivers that had rapids which were difficult for ships to maneuver through. But gradually the trains grew in popularity and became seen as a way to carry goods to Boston and Portland, Maine, to compete with the busy and prosperous port of New York. The ports in Montreal and Quebec were frozen in the winter, which hampered overseas trade in the region.

The dream became a reality with the charter of the St. Lawrence and Atlantic Railroad. Construction of the railroad began soon after, and it overcame numerous delays and financial woes to finally open on July 18, 1853. The first trip between Montreal and Portland, Maine, was later made in its entirety.[38] The railway was later absorbed by the Grand Trunk Railway. By 1860, the Grand Trunk Railway was extended to run between Ontario and Portland, Maine. It later became the largest international rail system in the world when it linked with the Chicago part of the American rail system.[39] The railroad had a negative affect on the prosperity of Abraham's family hotel because the railroad line was too distant from the town of Georgeville to bring guests. The main route of transportation had changed away from the stagecoach. In Newport, Vermont at the south end of the lake, a large hotel known as the Memphremagog House thrived with the travelers on this new railroad. The hotels on Memphremagog did not offer travelers so much a place to rest, eat, and imbibe, but now served a new industry that had been born; tourism.

The Camperdown

The lake did not offer the salt water or mineral springs such as those available in other early tourist areas such as Saratoga Springs in New York. Those New York springs were advertised as offering "artifice and immortality." The fact that Abraham's great age still appears on Eastern Township tourism brochures may still serve as a contradiction to this.[1] In his final years, and maybe a bit even today, Abraham's long lifespan may have been pointed out as evidence of the health that could be attained by a visit to the region. Tourism to the areas in Upstate New York grew in part to the health they advertised would be gained from their healing waters. Lake Memphremagog on the other hand, relied on fishing and the natural scenery and beauty of their crystal clear lake to attract visitors. The hotel's, taverns, and local lodging now had to offer more than just a bed to catch a quick night's sleep in.

A simple home cooked meal would not be enough either. It now took more than it once did to keep their clients happy. The hotel now had to offer comfort and amenities to a wealthier class of people who had the leisure time and financial means to enjoy a vacation. The steamships that brought tourists up from the railroad and hotel stop in Newport, Vermont, slowly became the lifeblood of the lake as they took their passengers from town to town along the increasingly busy waterway. After tourists got off the steamship at the pier in Georgeville, the first building that greeted them was Abraham's old tavern and hotel. Standing there, overlooking the lake with its great deck and chairs, the inn offered a respite on a warm summer day, as well as a view of the mountains beyond. Tourists took in the same breathtaking scenery that can still be seen from the new concrete dock. After an excursion around the small town travelers may have opted to stay overnight and enjoy the food and hospitality of the Channell Tavern. While they visited they could take a boat out for a row or hire a horse to ride through the countryside. The tavern offered a quaint charm of yesteryear that the newer hotels did not have.

On May 21, 1855, Charles Stewart Channell, Abraham's youngest son, announced in the *Stanstead Journal* to the public that he "had remodelled and fitted his house in a manner suitable to the wants of Pleasure Parties and the travelling public." He then invited his old customers back. "To those of his old friends who have patronized him in the two years he has kept the house he would return his most sincere thanks, and would respectfully solicit a continuance of their patronage."[2] The advertisement shows that the tavern had many repeat visitors from year to year. They came by again year by year to enjoy the family's hospitality. Charles reminded everyone that the Stanstead and St. Johns Stage, which he was evidently now one of the proprietors of, stopped at his inn. Charles seemed to have then called the old tavern the Memphremagog House.

The announcement was advertised to prop up the failing business. Throughout the north the old tavern businesses fell on hard times. Railroads bypassed the old routes and public sentiment toward the old public houses was becoming negative. Sure the stagecoach still came by his tavern, but the real money was in the pockets of those who traveled the rails. In the same year that Charles printed his newspaper announcement, a statewide prohibition of alcohol was announced in New Hampshire. The taverns slowly began to close up their doors as the sentiment traveled north along the old turnpike. The negativity toward alcohol that slowly grew and spread cut into the bottom line of the old tavern deeply. In 1869, the Nashua Telegraph, along the route that led to Georgeville, wrote "the era or railroads stripped the public houses...of three-fourths of their importance and patronage."[3]

As the business failed, Abraham's sons desperately sought a buyer for the property. They tried to attract more customers by doing small repairs and improvements to the old tavern stand. They lacked the business savvy and ability to adapt that their father had possessed. Like many family businesses the tavern would not survive the next generation of ownership and management.

In 1862, Tuck purchased the old pine hill lodge in Potton across the lake from the tavern stand. He began a new lodging venture at Knowlton's landing. The brick house became known as Tuck's Hotel. Tuck and his son and namesake John, Abraham's grandson, ran the hotel for decades after. This hotel was built from bricks made from local ingredients rumored to have been found along the shore of the lake. This inn survives on the same spot today. In 1862, his brother-in-law Charles Stuart Channell became employed in the customs office as Surveyor of Customs, and then later became the collector in Stanstead. This helped lead Tuck to his own career in a new capacity as an officer aboard the steamships, in spite of his rebel past.

John Tuck took full advantage of the steamboat industry when he found employment working on board one as a government customs officer. He may have once been arrested as an enemy of the government, but now he worked for it. Tuck and the hotel he now ran in Potton were described in *Harper's Ferry New Monthly Magazine* in 1874. In the magazine the author wrote, "Tuck is a very useful member of society. He is hotel-keeper, store-keeper, postmaster, and her Majesty's customs preventive officer all in one, and his little corner room at the brick hotel is a curiosity shop."[4] At varying times the dock at the hotel was known as either Knowlton's or Tucks landing. Tuck's hotel, the Pine Lodge built by Levi Knowlton, has been located there since the 1820's, in the town known today as Potton, Quebec.

The traveler wrote about the meal he enjoyed there; a plate of fresh trout at Tuck's amiable table. In a cupboard there were three bottles that represented Tuck's sparsely stocked bar. Above the bar rested a sign that stated, "I am as dry as a fish." This statement of thirst, if recited aloud by the visitor was immediately answered with a request to treat all those present to a drink. Tuck does not seem to have shared the temperance views of others. Near the bar were six "pigeon holes" that represented the post office.

The mail was carried across the lake by a young boy who apparently was so distracted by his fishing that by the time he crossed the water the mail was usually late. The mail that was carried from the cities in the north came by buggy and was transported by a man known as "old Coons." Old Coons often stopped to talk when he traveled his route and he was not any more expedient than his younger counterpart the fishing boy. Neither of them are so different from my own mail carrier in the modern world who stops and gossips at every house along his route. The paragraphs that were written about the hotel seem to wish to prevail upon the reader a sense of a slower easier time, in a world that even then in the 1870's, seemed too fast for some. Anyone who had ever reminisced about a slower time and escape from the busy cities may have enjoyed a visit to Tucks. The author seems to have been trying to paint a picture of a wonderful rural setting that someone may like to plan a vacation to. The author later crossed the lake and chose to stay at the Elephantis Hotel, rather than the new hotel that stood on the ground once occupied by Abraham's old hotel then known as the Camperdown.

Tuck was not always the amiable tavern keeper that the article painted him out to be. Like his father-in-law Abraham had been. Tuck's customs activities turned violent at times on the steamboat. On June 24, 1869, a man named John T. Tibbetts put a box of nails on the boat that he intended to send to Magog Village to sell for boat building. Officer Tuck, in this case, asked for the boxes to be detained in Georgeville. He believed the men were

Tuck's Hotel from Harpers Magazine

trying to smuggle silver. Another officer, McGowan, disagreed with Tuck and allowed them to be put on board. When a man named John Taylor stooped over to pick them up Tuck struck him on the head with his cane. Taylor stood back up and struck Tuck back with his fist and knocked him down on the wharf. The boat immediately left and most of the passengers sided with Taylor. The High Constable disagreed and felt Tuck was obstructed in his duty and the men were held at a bail of eight hundred dollars each. This must have been quite a brawl, as that was a lot of money. Tuck may have been on to something hidden by Taylor after all.[5]

Many of the travelers visiting the area were now tourists and the tavern property needed to cater to this new industry rather than the previous one that was just passing through. Abraham had always been able to adapt and survive to business threats throughout his life. From tailor to sailor, from farmer to innkeeper, Abraham knew what his customers wanted, and his children had failed to achieve this. Family businesses often fail to survive from the time of their founder to the next generation and the old tavern suffered the same fate. Stuffed with a false sense of pride from ownership of a business they did not create; and empty of the talent that the original entrepreneur had to adapt and survive, the tavern business gasped its last breath.

Camperdown 1860's, courtesy Stanstead Historical Society.

New owners with the vision to promote the Channell property in railroad and fishing publications now surfaced and tried to continue where Abraham had left off. In addition to the hotel property being sold, wealthy urbanites began to come from the cities of Montreal and Quebec to buy up the farms surrounding the lake to build grand vacation homes. The farmers began to move to the western United States to find better farmland. Some of Abraham's descendants moved to western Massachusetts on the railroad. My own Channell ancestors were among them. Many have remained in Massachusetts ever since, while other members of the family have spread out across the continent. Chasing the same dreams Abraham once had. In 1861, the old property was sold to Thomas Macduff, and Macduff changed the name to the Camperdown. Tuck had been running the hotel, and after the sale he chose to cross the lake and purchase and run his own small tavern.

After many decades of Abraham's stable presence the property quickly went from manager to manager and owner to owner during the following thirty years. One person mentioned to be running the hotel after Abraham Channell and his son Charles final ownership was A. Hamilton. A later owner of the tavern property was W.E. Tuck, and an image of the property exists from 1881, that shows a greatly expanded hotel with a commanding view of the lake. The travelers, however, missed the old Camperdown and its quaint charm that the new larger structure just did not have. It was later said to be, "a hotel so large no one wants it."[6] The hotel was too large for the small, quaint village and was compared to a "conspicious patch upon an old gown."[7]

Camperdown Hotel circa 1880, courtesy of Stanstead Historical Society.

The new owners of Abraham's old tavern were responding to competition in the lodging business that began in 1858, the final year of Abraham's life. Across the lake that year the Mountain House opened for business, described as being, "like an eastern temple embowered in its sacred grove."[8] The Mountain House boasted a reading room and beautiful dining area. The boat landing area had a Chinese summerhouse to welcome guests and perhaps influence their decision to stay at their accommodations rather than the aging Channell tavern.[9] Later owners of the property perhaps felt a challenge of needing to make their own property larger and grander than the businesses that threatened to take away their customers.

Camperdown Hotel circa 1880, courtesy of Stanstead Historical Society.

The new construction led unfortunately to the inevitable failure of the hotel and the Camperdown Hotel Company was found insolvent in court in 1882. The new Camperdown had rooms furnished with the most expensive of furnishings, and had telephones installed in every room so guests could call for room service.[10] In addition, a new sewer system was put in place to supplant the old privy. This gave the hotel modern plumbing for the first time. The quaint magic of Abraham's property was lost with the new design. The hotel at that time appears to have been owned by Arthur J. Cleveland.[11] For a time the hotel was revived by C.A. Jenkins, and was recommended in a fishing journal as a fine spot that offered boats and guides who could lead you to the good fishing spots on the lake and in the local ponds.[12] Travelers had first come to the lake for the scenery, but they now found that fishing was a fine way to pass the day.

Tourist brochures promised visitors to the lake that speckled trout could be caught which weighed ten to fifteen pounds, but that locals could catch trout weighing up to forty pounds.[13] This statement supported and promoted the employment of local guides to help find these fish for them. If all this failed to prove true, the trout could always be ordered on the hotel menu and arrive on the dinner plate. This new pastime of sport fishing was in great contrast to the need of the early settlers to fish for survival; and those who challenged the sea to fish for their livelihood back in Essex when Abraham had first come to Massachusetts. The fishing on the lake did, however, have a short season. It could only add the visits of patrons during a small time of the year. Winter comes early and leaves late at Memphremagog. June and September were recommended as the best months to fish. There was no mention of ice fishing, a popular activity in some northern locales today. The incredible cost of heating the hulking hotel property during the winter season would have been a challenge also.

Elias George Merrick may have been the one responsible for greatly expanding the size of the Camperdown. Merrick grew up in the hotel business and later learned carpentry and bought and expanded other hotels in New Hampshire after he left Georgeville in 1885. He was mentioned as the owner in an article in the *Boston Journal* printed September 3, 1884. At the time of the article the hotel could accommodate one hundred and fifty guests and stated that even with that many rooms it was overflowing, and they had to accommodate more guests with cots.

The hotel was over twice the size of most of the other properties located nearby in Vermont or on the Canadian side of the lake. The Memphremagog House in Newport was the largest on the lake with two hundred and fifty three rooms.[15] The Memphremagog also had the proximity of the railroad in its favor. Most importantly, the Memphremagog House served as a gateway to the lake from the United States. The steamship traveled across the border, and from there zigzagged back and forth across the Canadian side of the lake.

Whether or not it was true that the new hotel overflowed with customers, or was just an attempt to get more tourists to come and visit and fish on the lake cannot be ascertained. What is known is that the days of Merrick running the hotel soon came to an end. Not long after the property was built the guests would not arrive abundantly enough to support the new large structure, and the doors to the Camperdown shut permanently. In the year 1888, the Camperdown remained closed for the season.[16] The downfall of the hotel has been blamed on the construction through Magog of a new railroad line which made Magog a far better place to own a hotel. The grand hotel in Georgeville then sat largely empty, except for a small dress making shop that was run on the first floor. The final days of the hotel were approaching.

On July 18, 1898, a kerosene lamp was dropped in the Elephantis Hotel, which stood across the street from the hulking ghost of the Camperdown. The fire quickly spread through the hotel and flames quickly leaped across the street and ignited the Camperdown. The fire consumed the structure and several other buildings in the town. The fire lit up the sky for miles and reflected and sparkled off the lake that Abraham had so long called home. The empty descendant of the Inn that had once been so well run by Abraham and lost by his sons was now only ashes and memories.[17]

The Final days of Immortality

One day Abraham had to confront the fact that his legs could no longer carry him as far as they once did. The eyes that once searched the sky for signs of distant sails now struggled to see loved ones clearly. He had to move in close to hear the tender words of his loving wife. He had so many thoughts and memories that were trapped inside his mind; some good, and some bad. It was a struggle to push aside the bad memories and bring the good ones forward. What is the point of life, if all these things are forgotten? He thought: "If a man could only live forever, then there would be a point to live." Changes could be made to not repeat unfortunate mistakes. Luck may change with time, but when time runs out, so does luck, and time no longer allows one to go back and make amends. But live on Abraham did, beyond the age of anyone that people in the village could remember having lived.

In 1850, he walked with careful deliberation downtown to hear the brass band play on the waterfront in Georgeville. It was a rare time of community celebration. The *Mountain Maid*, the first steamer on the lake was going to be launched. When Captain Fogg's wife broke the bottle across the stern of the craft Abraham thought of the many schooner launches he had seen in Chebacco on the banks of the Essex River. Those were ships that depended on the wind, not on steam such as this one. Steam power replaced the need for tall masts and canvas sails to catch the wind. The undependable nature of wind and the impatience

234

this created made men seek other methods of propulsion. Abraham enjoyed one or more rides on the craft as he steamed along the lake during his final years. There was little need for the knot tying skills he had learned on the *Milford*. That is if his hands and fingers could still perform the function. The steady hand of his younger wife Wealthy was always held tightly in his hand in order to keep his balance stable on the boat. Abraham had lived at the center of the community for so long in the village, it did not seem like an event unless he made his noble appearance. Age had made him an even greater celebrity than his larger than life tavern keeper persona had made him. He was a living testimony to how healthy a place the lake really was. A final survivor to a lost but treasured generation.

When people gathered around Abraham he talked of the past as if it were the present. He was asked again and again by his sons and friends to describe how he received the many scars that could be seen on the surface of his head. Most everyone else who could share memories of the events of the American Revolution that occurred so long ago were now gone.

The leaders of the time like General Washington were now the stuff of legends and had become larger than life. At least this phenomenon was true south of the Canadian border. These men were put upon pedestals in the search for American identity. Heaven is for heroes and Hell is reserved for the foolish and Abraham would not cast judgment on himself for the group he may have felt he belonged to. At one time or another he had been both.

He remained one of the few, if not the last survivor of the American Revolution in the area. He may well have been the last man standing who had seen the conflict from both sides. Whichever side of the border he was on, he had a reason to hold his head high for his service. He could claim the title of Patriot on either side of the border.

Unlike Washington and the rest of the founding fathers, Abraham was still alive. He still enjoyed the feel of the sun on his face and the warm breeze of summer as it swept across the lake. Sweet air still filled his lungs. Abraham lived in a new world that the obsolescence of nature may have never intended him to see. Why was he chosen to still be here after so many of his friends and loved ones had left the warmth of the Earth long ago? Why had the shadow of death passed him over? One of life's great mystery is the selection process of who dies and when. Had Abraham been forgotten and overlooked? Would he ever discover the final mystery? Age brings with it too much time to think.

On July 4, 1856, the steamship *Mountain Maid* departed from Newport, Vermont, on a special evening run to entertain the Americans that were on board the vessel. An orchestra played patriotic American songs and lit off a fireworks display in honor of the holiday. The paddle ship had an American and Canadian flag on either end to celebrate the dual citizenship of the lake. As Abraham sat on the hotel veranda that night; what thoughts may have entered his mind as the fireworks lit up the night sky? One thing that is almost certain is that no-one who viewed the fireworks that night had been witness to the real sparks and fireworks of the American Revolution other than Abraham. The old tavern keeper was one of the final living witnesses to the birth of freedom. One of the final souls to appreciate what freedom costs. Yet in five short years after the countries seventy-fifth birthday many more would find out the cost of freedom after the election of another Abraham to the presidency.

When Abraham spoke of the past he brought forth the departed as if they were still alive. No historian could ever be able to recreate the events as well as they were spoken by Abraham. He was either blessed or cursed by his clear memory, depending on how long you may feel memories should be kept. The good ones put a smile upon his face, and the memories he regretted ran over again and again in his mind, and haunted him as he tried to sleep. These memories can haunt you in the twilight time between consciousness and dreams. A time of questioning actions that time no longer allowed the freedom to change. The frustration of not being able to act things out differently cannot stop a person from wanting to do so. Abraham often sat alone on the porch of the tavern and he remained a defiant challenger to the tolls of time.

When Abraham was asked by visitors to the tavern what the secret was to his eternal life, he laughed inside and said, "Keep breathing." But in truth he believed it was the love of his family that kept him going for so many years. Not just his family, but the whole community at the tavern. He also had a large amount of friends and remained active in social groups and local religious organizations. It is thought that these habits create an extension in the lives of those who live to be one hundred or more. Being isolated and alone is bad for your health and shortens your lifespan. Life and happiness are contagious and spread goodwill to those that can find it. Abraham was rarely alone; there were always new and repeat visitors to the tavern that kept him company on the porch while he spun yarns and told his tales of adventure.

There were no wonders of modern medicine that could claim to have extended Abraham's life. His medicine was a life of good fresh food, exercise, and his good mental health. The long walks Abraham took around his land and in the village of Georgeville surely did wonders for extending his life. In his many travels between the seacoast of New Hampshire and the Canadian mountains there is no accounting for the miles he may have logged while he walked these routes. It is a well known fact that men who walk farther in their later years live much longer lives than those who do not. Even as Abraham slowly lost his eyesight and hearing he never lost his cheerful spirit and positive outlook on life. People who see doom around every corner do not live long lives. Worrying a little can help stop a person from making bad decisions. Worrying a lot can kill you before your time has come. Everyone asked Abraham about life, everyone was afraid to ask him about death. And why discuss death? They will discover it all too soon themselves without Abraham needing to explain it to them. Abraham did not fear the reaper.

The food Abraham enjoyed was not processed by a factory and it did not have to travel a great distance to reach him. It held no preservatives or additives and received no food coloring to be attractive to the eye. His food came from the land and the lake. Game food came from the forests that surrounded the tavern. Animals raised on the farm supported the tavern with fresh unpasteurized milk and eggs that were gathered daily for food. These animals received no growth hormones and enjoyed enough freedom in the fields to live healthy lives themselves. When their time came they were killed humanely and with regret by those who had cared for them. Bread came from the fields and was then ground in the local mill, brown and whole grained. Vegetables were raised in the garden near the house. Exercise came from the gathering, cultivation, and nurturing, of all these food sources. Abraham did not over-eat this healthy food. Most people in the modern world know obesity is a potential killer, or a trigger to other diseases like diabetes. For some reason this does not seem to stop them from doing it.

The water that Abraham drank came from deep below the earth. It passed through permeable rock, layers of sand, and rich minerals and became purified naturally. The water naturally absorbed these minerals from the Earth which the body needs to survive. Fresh cold water refreshes the body and quenches the thirst. Only as much water as was needed for that day was bottled for later use, or for cooking. Part of the benefit that Abraham received from the water was the exercise he got by going out to get it. Pumping the well and carrying the bucket in all took effort. Today a trip from the couch to the refrigerator is a lot shorter journey than the trip out to fetch water. A trip to the bathroom is also a lot shorter trip than going out to the privy at the tavern. It should be clear that more exercise and benefit is received from the method that Abraham went through to drink. If Abraham had not been impressed and stayed in London with its polluted urban lifestyle and less healthy sources of food and water he likely would not have reached the age he did. As his later descendants left the farm and moved back to the cities, their life expectancies dropped significantly. None of Abraham's family descendants has ever reached his great age since, only his children came close, because they lived very much the same lifestyle.

I remember staying at a cabin in Maine by a lake as a young boy of six. I recall pouring water down the well pump and using all my strength to pump the steel handle and get the water to come out. This was serious exercise, but fun. Years later I visited my wife's family cabin on a lake in Massachusetts. There along the lake we dropped a bucket down a well and scooped up the cold water and heaved it up with a rope. Water never tasted better than it did in those times. I think I understand what that fresh water tasted like to Abraham; some experiences are timeless and universal. Water sources like this can still be found; as we know by the Shaker spring that bubbles up unused today in its woodland hiding place. All a person has to do is look for the source and bring a glass bottle to fill up with them when they find it.

The tavern was often filled with laughter, music, and dancing was a natural companion to both. A few surviving taverns in New England have floors that were specially constructed to be danced upon. Abraham was said to have danced a jig at his birthday party and had likely danced many more times before that with his wife Wealthy and his guests. Dancing is an activity that is also a habit of long lived people. Music filled the night and the laughter surrounded the tavern and echoed across the glassy lake. People made friendships and couples fell in love in

Abraham's old tavern while they danced and looked into one another's eyes.

Old age is sometimes seen as a period of decline and diminishing health. Those who survive to their "golden years" must cope with the loss of their physical abilities and the disappearance of their social world. They first begin to lose their vitality and health as their body begins to fail. This may lead them to retire from their work, and they often lose the ability to pay their own way in life. In the time of Abraham, far before any type of national retirement system in Canada, older men needed their family to support them in their later years. As the years go through the hour glass the aged lose their spouse, family, and their trusted friends whom they had always relied on, and in Abraham's case wrestled to tame a wilderness with. Sadly, in the modern world, they are often seen as "useless."

But through all the struggles and pitfalls of life there is at least one attribute of older men and women that is often overlooked but is one of the greatest of talents. One has to wonder why the young are so blind to it. Through all these struggles and pitfalls that are taken internally the aged can, through self analysis, discover the greatest of human accomplishments. The incredibly useful yet often overlooked awareness tool of wisdom. With retirement comes the ability to reflect inward and process a review of their lives without any ability to change or redirect it. Socrates said, "The unexamined life is not worth living." We need to examine what has occurred whether we can change it or not. To go through an entire life and not reflect on it shows the uselessness of having lived it. A person may have attained great wealth or fame, but what good was it if nothing came from it. The elderly have to fully confront the choices they have made and face the fact that there is no time left to try another method. Life has run out of second chances.

In these final years the past and future are absorbed into the present. Often the despair over this realization is cloaked by disgust. The famous psychologist Erik H. Erikson, said that "such disgust really signifies their contempt for themselves."[1] This disapproval often causes the young to avoid the old due to the older generation's disgust with what they perceive as poor choices being made by their younger acquaintances and family. Subconsciously they hope that the young will avoid the same pain of reflection from failure that they themselves experience in their twilight years. They know that their age yields no great and perfect people; something must come from it. They want to help those that follow them to avoid the anguish and pain that come from poor decision making. A hope for a better life for future generations.

A time together…

Abraham and Wealthy sat by the fire warming themselves during the dark, soundless night of January 9, 1858. The old couple listened to the burning wood crackle and felt the warmth that heated the space surrounding the hearth. The oil lamp burned and cast flickering shadows upon the walls of the home. Across the street, Abraham's son Charles still tended to the tavern and its visiting guests. The old fading and peeling tavern advertisement creaked back and forth as the wind began to pick up and blow against the sign. The smoke from the oil that was boiled out of the flesh of whales captured in the depths of churning oceans rose in the air and swirled and danced along the ceiling.

Outside, a blanket of snow grew deep around the foundation of the old couple's home. The drapes were drawn tight against the cold wind that sought to invade through the chilly thin panes of the window glass. The shore of the lake beyond was hidden by the deep white drifts that blew across the thick ice and gathered and collected on the shoreline. Overhead the sinuous branches of trees, frozen solid and covered with a varnish of ice from the cold air, twisted and crackled with every whisper of wind that found them. The cold corpse-like moon, an old friend, lit up the night sky and offered relief from an otherwise pale evening. The moonlit path of tracks and the distant faint light was all the sleds had to go by to find the tavern across the wintry way that night. Nearby farmers tracked through the thick snow that crackled with the weight of their snowshoes as they went out to check on the animals in the barns and outbuildings of the remote northern village. Ink in the well at the front entrance of the tavern froze thickly in spite of the door that tried in vain to shut out the elements of the northern clime.

Inside the dwelling Abraham sat in a chair heaped with warm quilts which laid across his thin lanky form. Sitting near the hearth he was able to snug sufficiently to be comfortable. He felt Wealthy take his hand in hers and felt a warming, not from her hand, but from her heart. Taking hold of the hand of another can mean both greeting and farewell, depending on the circumstances of the embrace. "That rare a true love is, true friendship is still rarer."[2] Even though the couple had been married for decades; "The most holy band is friendship."[3] It was a deep friendship that had carried the couple through all the trials and tribulations of life on the edge of civilization. His once young wife was now also in her final years, although still much younger than he. Abraham could not bare the thought of losing another wife, and erased it from his mind whenever he thought of it. Every day and night brought with it that possibility. Yet it was the will of God and not his choice to decide.

Abraham's life had been good but hard, and he had learned to deal with loss. Death, Abraham knew, always attached itself to beauty. Beauty was fleeting after all, and the shorter the item bloomed the more apparent was the intensity of its beauty. He thought of the apple orchard behind his home in Chebacco where it all began and the blossoms he hoped to see again. Death was no stranger to Abraham; they had met many times before. But living there amongst his family and friends, he had become safe from it. He looked across at Wealthy and no words needed to be said as the love they had for one another existed in the silence. Is love immortal and can it transcend death?

Even now as the death of winter had overtaken the landscape around him, it came with the promise of spring. The sun would again rise high in the sky and cast off the ice and snow of winter when the season changed. With spring there came a new beginning that burst with the immortality of nature and the promise of permanence in the everlasting cycles of birth and rebirth. The animals could again spring from their shelter and see within their young a new vitality and perpetuity that secure their tomorrows for all time. Life has to go on. Life would repeat itself once again. Life is the way, and death is the way.

Abraham lifted himself with great effort from his chair and took the lantern from his side table within his bent and crooked hand. He bid Wealthy good night and she watched him as he rose and tried to cross the room; then paused to catch his breath. He walked slowly as if it ached to move; he had sat too long and stiffness had crept in. She arose from her chair and took his arm and helped him to his feather bed. Wealthy felt him shiver and noticed his face was white and glowed like the moon from the light of the lamp. The deep wrinkles of his face were magnified by the light. She placed a thick quilt across his earthly torso and promised Abraham she would soon get to bed herself. Wealthy, in all ways was a good wife, it was said: "The woman who strengthens her body, and exercises her mind will, by managing her family and practicing various virtues, become the friend, and not the humble dependent of her husband."[4] Wealthy thought of: "The affection of her husband as one of the comforts that render her task less difficult and her life happier."[5] Abraham could not have lived so well and long without her. She went back to her fire to wait for her son Charles to come and check on them.

Abraham watched the reflection of his lantern as it diminished on the walls and the ceiling overhead. Abraham's breathing was labored from the effort of getting into bed; but not long after he closed his eyes he fell fast and deeply asleep. His soul, he dreamed, began to feel the warmth of a new beginning. It sprang his spirit from its aged shell, and into a new transition. The young tar struck down along a path curbed by green grass and bordered by tall evergreens. Free now of pain and stiffness and filled with the vigor the young take for granted, Abraham began to sprint along as birds sprang from their nests in the greenery all around him. Abraham felt a feeling of peace like none he had ever felt before. The spreading branches of the tall elm trees filtered the light and caused it to dance at his feet. He thought back to Wealthy, but he had always begun his journeys alone; as he did this transition. He would see her again in time. All people must someday leave the present and enter the door of the past.

Near the end of the path stood an orchard protected by a low fence. Abraham leaped over the fence and strode by a familiar looking well. He stopped and filled his tin, savoring the cold satisfying water that was so long denied him in London. With a bounding youthful step he approached the base of a spreading fruit tree. Abraham reached and pulled down the colorful apple tree blossom to admire. The king of the sky rose and warmed him with its morning embrace. The air was clear and fresh. The outer shell of age had now melted away and he smiled at the sight of old friends and family and the rush of love they had once shared as they approached him. Pain had left his aged body. He felt as light as air. An immortal spirit approached and he felt a loving hand caress his back. "Abraham!" The voice called. "Behold here I am."[6] the tailor replied. Spring had come again, as it always has, and always will.

The Immortal Patriot

A few days later after, a service by Minster Adams, the Earthly remains of Abraham were laid in the back of a sled and taken to the grave-site on January 11, 1858.[7] Everyone in the village turned out to say goodbye to the man who had become a legend. The end of an era had come with his passing. His wife Wealthy and family stood weeping by the grave site as they said farewell to the family patriarch. If the George, Tuck, Channell, and other family members crossed the frozen lake for the ceremony, it would have been a very crowded place. Abraham had not only been one of the first to settle the village, but the longest lived man in all the Eastern Townships. It is not clear if it was well known that he had taken part helping the United States in the Revolution, but after his obituary was printed it was.

His son Charles later moved into his new position in the customs office, and who better to serve the role than the son of a patriot who deserved the respect of both Canada and the United States governments. He may not have wanted to tarnish his or his father's reputation as a loyal British citizen with his fathers revolutionary service, but the real enemy of the United States now was its internal conflict over slavery that was threatening to erupt. Years later, when his brother Leon joined the Sons of the American Revolution, Charles and the rest of the family also followed him into the fraternal group. They took pride in being some of the only Canadian born members of the patriotic organization. Leon was now an American and he would stay that way. Abraham's tavern was a gathering place in the village for as long as anyone could remember. It had been the epicenter of change and revolt within the village. Everything that was worth knowing could be discovered in the old tavern. He had raised a great family, and by his family marrying into other families within the area there were few people who lived nearby who could not find some family connection to the old man.

The Minister wrote the record of his age as one hundred and five years, one month, and sixteen days in his record book.[8] His gravestone, however, was carved at one hundred and seven. Others place his age at one hundred and ten, the only date that is certain is his death. As I stood at his grave one hundred and fifty years after his burial I wondered who had given these various dates and if anyone would ever really know the answer. There is no denying he lived long and lived well, regardless of the actual number of years, days and minutes. It is the quality and not the quantity of years that really matters. The quiet solitude of Abraham's resting place is broken today only by the sound of the wind in the trees and the occasional sound of passing cars. Centuries of weather slowly wear at the stone that recorded his passage. Someday the stone itself will disappear. Around Abraham's grave lie his wife Wealthy, Tuck and Abraham's daughter, Susan. Many other members of the community that he once called home rest in the graveyard alongside them.

The lonesome stone markers are a remembrance of their passage; in most cases it is all that mark the lives they once lived. It was at this time that I understood that I also stood as a monument to his memory. A tribute to his eternal life. It was then that I resolved to write his story and thereby immortalize him.

Before coming to his grave site I had visited the Stanstead Historical Society Museum where the archivist took out a photograph of Abraham that they had in their collection. I had studied photographic history as an undergraduate and I questioned myself about this being a period piece. The photograph was printed on a heavy card stock, and did not appear to have come from the era he was alive. It may have been a *carte de visite*, this was invented in 1854, and became very popular. If it is a *carte de visite* it dates the photo to the very final years of his life.

Without a doubt it is an amazing find to have the photograph of your fifth-great-grandfather. Few people can claim they do. I was more familiar with daguerreotypes, small pictures protected inside a bronze colored case. A written testament by one of his grand children on the back is the only way to lend credence to the photo being genuine. The photograph also appeared through the collection of a different member of the family that had settled in California, and was copied and given to Rita. I have since found other distant relatives that have had the picture passed down through their family. These things all add up and add credence to the photographs authenticity.

Although Abraham was now long gone, his image, captured in that photograph, looked out from the past at me. When I first saw it, the image further challenged me to discover him and his secrets. I looked back at him and thought, "I know who you are; you can't hide from me." I was looking history full on in the face, and challenging it. I would write his story and by doing so raise his phantom up from the murky depths of time. Many people who see the photo feel that it is not him; an inability exists in the mind of people to see American Patriots as living and breathing men. They only exist for most people in highly idealized patriotic paintings, most of these painted far after the event. They cross icy rivers on boats, they hold up fallen martyrs on Bunker Hill. These images were created to tell of valor, courage, and the indomitable American spirit. This photograph was far more familiar than that. It was an image of an ancient man that was saved for remembrance; not to instill or inspire patriotism or create an icon. This was real.

His eyes had borne witness to the terrible events, disappointments, and fears of a life I struggled to study and discover. They stared back unblinking from his frozen countenance at me. How would his expression change if he smiled? What would he think if the modern world were revealed to these eyes? Would he respect what we have become? Would he be proud of what we built on top of what we were given? Abraham's eyes not only bore witness to the horror of war at sea, but had also seen the birth of many young children who were also my ancestors. The seed of youth that the country later sprang from. His eyes may have seen the humps of a serpent rise from a lake, and Native people pass by before the world had finished "civilizing" them. History would be far less of a mystery if we could be allowed to look through his eyes and not just at them.

At first I believed that the photograph of a Revolutionary War veteran was a rare find. Photography was after all a miraculous breakthrough in science that occurred a lifetime after the war. Photographs differ from a painting by not allowing for artistic control or interpretation. Only the finest of photographers could achieve this with their simple equipment. People appear as they did then, frozen in time. They appear as those who had lived, breathed, and loved just as we do today. I also wondered if Abraham, with his great age, was the final survivor of the conflict. Did Abraham alone survive long enough to be the only Revolutionary war veteran to have his mortal image captured in a photograph? Neither of these thoughts turned out to be true as I dug further into it.

The few photographs that survive of Revolutionary War veterans are different from the images of veterans of the Civil War. Revolutionary War soldiers are always pictured in the final years of their lives. They are crippled old men that stare out with wrinkled faces at the future; the past they had experienced forever lost to us. Better known men such as Adams, Washington, and Revere, alone are remembered. Civil War soldiers on the other hand were photographed at the prime of their lives. They usually posed with lots of weapons in their daguerreotypes and had a defiant look in their eyes. They did not then perceive the horror of the conflict that they later faced. The war they were told would soon be over; and they would return to pomp and glory. Delving deeper, there are photos that exist of the horrible aftermath of the war on the men. Photographers were not afraid to capture veterans with missing limbs and tragic wounds. Battlefield photos were taken long after the fighting was over and show dead men laying on quiet fields with their corpses swelling and decomposing in the hot southern sun. For the sake of art, the bodies and ephemera were manipulated and again posed in death by the photographers.

Images of death such as these existed in the Revolutionary War, but the technology was not there to capture them. So all we have are the patriotic paintings to judge that conflict by. The horrors of war were never painted during the Revolution; only triumphant symbolic images of victory were seen to be worth remembering. These moments were captured by men who were not even there. The true event was captured by the eyes of men like Abraham.

Abraham did not live quite long enough to have a view on the outcome of the American conflict. It did not begin until three years after his death. Some of his contemporaries did share their thoughts on the conflict. There were a few men from the Revolution who outlived Abraham to see the outbreak and outcome of the Civil War. These men may offer an idea on how he would have viewed it.

Lemuel Cook, a veteran of the Revolution who lived to 1865, stated, "It is terrible. ....But, terrible as it is, the rebellion must be put down. And, as though making an exclamation point, he brought down his cane with force upon the floor." Another long lived veteran of the Revolution, Alexander Milliner, wanted to march to town when the Civil War broke out and beat his old Revolutionary War drum to stir up recruitment at the age of 101. He did not want to see the union he helped create fall apart. Milliner was born in Quebec after the death of his Father, a British soldier, who helped defeat the French on the Plains of Abraham to end the French and Indian War.

Another of the last surviving soldiers of the Revolution, John Gray, had similar feeling about the Civil War, in spite of being born in Virginia.

"He often mourned and even wept over Virginia's wayward course in the Rebellion-for John Gray was loyal."[9] He had served in the Revolution, but was unable to vote for his beloved leader General Washington when he ran for President because Gray did not own land. His sacrifice and service had not been enough to guarantee him a vote. Gray, like Abraham, went to the frontier to find his own land, and lived out the rest of his life in Ohio.

Gray survived sixty-eight years beyond the lifetime of Washington. In his later years it was written in an interview that, "Gray detested war, except in defense of our flag; he knew what war was." The interview continued, "War is cruel, and repulsive, and hideous, and yet we admire it; we glory in it. To have killed a man in time of peace brands one with the mark of Cain forever; but in time of war, the man who kills or attempts to kill is held up as a paragon of all good."[10] In Gray's eyes, in the days that followed the Civil War we had become a "nation of assassins." Gray felt that the battlefield was "The devils rarest, choicest school."

Gray died March 29, 1866, the year after the Civil War ended. The last soldier of the Revolution received a special $500 pension that was approved in the House of Representatives for the final year of his life. He used his celebrity, fueled by the need to re-create common patriotism among the countries citizens in the dark days following the Southern Rebellion, to speak out against the horror of war in the final years of his life. He did not allow his sudden popularity to glorify the tragedy of it.

Through the actions of Abraham's family, many of whom enlisted in the service of the North, we can assume he would have felt the same as the others about the Civil War and conflicts in general. All the fathers of the United States and Patriots of the Revolution stood in their later years as relics to a lost time. They would have likely agreed to preserve the Union they had struggled to create; and anguish over the loss of life it cost to keep together. The loss of life would have been reminiscent of the lives it had cost them to give birth to the new country.

Now the most difficult task any author faces is in front of me: to end a story that has no end. It is easy to begin a story, and not too difficult to continue it, but by definition immortality has no ending. The problems that faced Abraham, still face us. His family, now numbering in the tens of thousands, is spread among many nations, and our numbers may include you: and so we all continue the saga. Heroes do not need to be flawless. They do not need to be famous. They just need to overcome. The Founding Fathers of both the United States and Canada were great men, but by no means without ego or ambition. They had the same flaws that are common to all humanity. The ambitious pursuit of wealth and power creates a trespass on the liberty and freedom of others in its pursuit.

The story of the life of Abraham stands as a reminder that freedom must be forever protected, and that its corruption must not be allowed by power brokers. Men of violence and greed will enslave us if we let them. Power is the ultimate creator of tyranny. Liberty and freedom is the most precious commodity that any of us can hold. These commodities are not given to us by government: government is meant to protect them. Governments and leaders can wither and die. True freedom and liberty is within the individual. The value of land and goods is fleeting, only six feet of land from head to foot is all that is needed to hold your mortal remains. Our spirit alone holds the freedom to move throughout time immemorial. The seed of our children alone protects our immortality into the vast and uncertain future.

Abraham FitzJohn Channell, courtesy
Stanstead Historical Society

ABOUT THE AUTHOR

Frederick Channell is a historian and genealogist in New England. He graduated Magna Cum Laude with Honors in history from Bridgewater State University in Massachusetts. Currently he is pursuing a Masters Degree in Education from the University of Massachusetts in Boston. He is licensed to teach history in the Massachusetts Public Schools. Frederick serves as the President of the South Shore Genealogical Society. He lives in Hingham, Massachusetts with his family.
Abraham Channell is his fifth great-grandfather.

Headstone of Abraham FitzJohn Channell outside Georgeville, Quebec

Notes

Welcome to the King's Navy

1. William B. Clark, ed. *Naval Documents of the American Revolution*. Vol. 1. Washington: U.S.G.P.O, 1964, 1304.

2. John A. Tilley, *The British Navy and the American Revolution*. Columbia, SC: University of South Carolina Press, 1987, 46.

3. John C. Miller, *Triumph of Freedom 1775-1783*. Boston: Little Brown and Company, 1948, 77-79.

4. Encyclopedia Britannica. "John Montagu, 4th Earl of Sandwich." http://www.britannica.com/EBchecked/topic/522257/John-Montagu-4th-Earl-of-Sandwich.

5. William B. Clark, ed. *Naval Documents of the American Revolution*. Vol. 2. Washington: U.S.G.P.O, 1966, 743.

6. David Syrett, *The Royal Navy In European Waters During The American Revolutionary War*. Columbia: University of South Carolina Press, 1998, 2.

7. William B. Clark,., ed. *Naval Documents of the American Revolution*. Vol. 3. Washington: U.S.G.P.O, 1968, 335.

8. David, Syrett, *Shipping and the American War 1775-83*. New York: Oxford University Press Inc, 1970, 123.

9. Clark, *Naval Documents of the American Revolution*. Vol. 3, 337.

10. Ibid., 333-334.

11. Syrett, *Shipping and the American War*. 1775-83, 122.

12. Charles Stuart Channell, "Sons of the American Revolution Application For Membership," National # 7071, State#57, June 27, 1896

13. Samuel Johnson, *The works of Samuel Johnson*. London: E. Blackadev, 1806, 146. Accessed October 16, 2011. http://books.google.com/books?id=qpMDAAAAQAAJ&printsec=frontcover&source=gbs_ge_summary_r&cad=0#v=onepage&q&f=false.

14. R. J. White, *The Age of George III*. Garden City, NY: Doubleday and Company Inc., 1969, 17.

15. William Stubbs, *The Constitutional History of England in its Origin and Development*, Volume 3.N.p.: Oxford, Clarendon Press, 1884, 261.

16. Osip Mandelstam, *Complete Poetry of Osip Emilevich Mandelstam*. Trans. Burton Raffel and AllaBurago.Introduction and notes.By Sidney Monas. Albany: State University of New York Press, 1973.

17. James Grant, *John Adams : Party of One*. New York: Farrar, Straus and 302 Giroux, 2005, 82-83.

18. David Garrick, "Hearts of Oak" (1759), in *Poems of the Love and Pride of England*, ed. Frederick Wedmore and Millicent Wedmore (London: Ward Lock and Company, 1897), 43, accessed June 24, 2012, http://books.google.com/booksid=P15LAAAAIAAJ&pg=PA43&dq=david+garrick+heart+of+oak&hl=en&sa=X&ei=JxPnT4jgC6ig6QHA54zgDg&ved=0CFgQ6AEwBQ#v=onepage&q&f=false.

19. James Boswell, *The life of Johnson: including their tour to the Hebrides*. London: John Murray, 1876, Page 308. Accessed October 16, 2011. http://books.google.com/books?id=po8EAQAAIAAJ&pg=PA308&dq=%22No+man+will+be+a+sailor+who+has+contrivance+enough+to+get&hl=en&ei=f_qaTu_oMaf10gGyyIyeBA&sa=X&oi=book_result&ct=result&resnum=10&ved=0CFcQ

20. *Impressment of seaman, and a few remarks on corporal punishment, taken from the private memoranda of a naval officer* (London: Roake and Varty, 1834), 11-12, accessed June 13, 2012, http://books.google.com/ books?id=KaEQAAAAYAAJ&pg=PA1&dq=%22impressment%22%22shilling%22&hl=en&sa=X&ei=zk3ZT5mmO8KI6QHn9MnKAg&ved=0CFEQ6AEwBQ#v=snippet&q=impressment&f=false.

21. Royal Naval Museum Library. "Impressment." http://www.royalnavalmuseum.org/info_sheet_impressment.htm. 5/11/2010

22. Ibid.

23. Lawrence Phillips, "The History of Pembroke Dock." Pembroke Dock Community Web Project. http://www.pembrokedock.org/h_dockyard_2.htm (2 February 2010).

24. Clark, *Naval Documents of the American Revolution*. Vol. 3, 422.

25. American War of Independence At Sea. "Yankee Hero."

http://www.awiatsea.com/Privateers/Y/Yankee%20Hero%20Massachusetts
%20Brig%20%5bThomas%20Tracy%5d.html#T000075B.

26. Clark, ed. *Naval Documents of the American Revolution*. Vol. 3, 506.

27. Zena Grant Collier, H.M.S Muster Rolls (Bedfordshire, England, 3, July, 1986).
Collier was hired by Rita Channell to research in English Archives.

28. Clark, *Naval Documents of the American Revolution*. Vol. 3, 430.

29. Collier, H.M.S Muster Rolls.

30. Ibid.

31. Clark, *Naval Documents of the American Revolution*. Vol. 3, 480.

32. Ibid., 514.

33. Ibid., 429.

34. Clark, ed. *Naval Documents of the American Revolution*. Vol. 3, 440-442. Proclamation by
the King in the London Gazette 12/19-12/23 1775

35. Nathan Miller, *Broadsides: The Age of Fighting Sail, 1775-1815*. New York: John Wiley
and Sons, Inc, 2000, 39.

Son of the Waves

1. Bartholomew James, et al., *Journal of Rear-Admiral Bartholomew James, 1752-1828*.
London: Printed for the Navy Records Society, 1896, 17-22.

2. Zena Grant Collier, H.M.S Muster Rolls (Bedfordshire, England, 3, July, 1986).

3. "Master-at-Arms."The Oxford Companion to Ships and the Sea. 2006.
Encyclopedia.com. (February 3, 2010). http://www.encyclopedia.com/doc/1O225-
masteratarms.html

4. William B. Clark, ed. *Naval Documents of the American Revolution*. Vol. 3. Washington:
U.S.G.P.O, 1968, 542.

5. Michael Pearson,*Those Damned Rebels: The American Revolution as seen through British Eyes*.
New York: G.P. Putnam's Sons, 1972, 142.

6. Ibid.

7. "The Irishman's Epistle" (1990), in *The Heath Anthology of American Literature*, ed. Paul
Lauter, 2nd ed. (Lexington, MA: D.C. Heath and Company, 1994), 1: 919-920.

8. James M. Volo, *Blue Water Patriots*. Lanham, MD: Rowman and Littlefield Publishers,
2006, 167.

9. Ibid., 152.

10. Ibid., 172.

11. Clark, 658.

12. Ibid., 1173.

13. William J. Morgan, ed. *Naval Documents of the American Revolution*. Vol. 5. Washington: U.S.G.P.O, 1968, 5. Pro Admiralty 52/1865

14. Morgan, *Naval Documents of the American Revolution*. Vol. 5, 45. Register of Letters of Agency, 1776-1781, Vice Admiralty Records, N.S. Arch.

15. Morgan, *Naval Documents of the American Revolution*. Vol. 5, 87-88. PRO, Admiralty 52/1865

16. Morgan, *Naval Documents of the American Revolution*. Vol. 5, 250. PRO, Admiralty 52/1865.

17. Thacher Island Association. "The History of Thacher Island." http://www.thacherisland.org/history/history.html (6 February 2010).

18. American War of Independence At Sea. "Yankee Hero." http://www.awiatsea.com/Privateers/Y/Yankee%20Hero%20Massachusetts %20Brig%20%5bThomas%20Tracy%5d.html#T000075B. (7 February 2010)

19. C. K. Wilbur, *Pirates and Patriots of The Revolution*. Chester, Conn.: The Globe Pequot Press, 1984, 8.

20. Marion Balderston and David Syrett. *The Lost War: Letters from British Officers During the American Revolution*. New York: Horizon Press, 1975, 91-92.

21. Morgan, *Naval Documents of the American Revolution*. Vol. 5, 508. Continental Journal, Thursday, June 13, 1776.

22. Morgan, *Naval Documents of the American Revolution*. Vol. 5, 391-92. PRO, Admiralty 52/1865

23. Northern Illinois University Libraries. "Account of the Capture of the Privateer Yankee Hero, by the British frigate Milford. ." http://lincoln.lib.niu.edu/cgi-bin/amarch/documentidx.pl?doc_id=S4-V6-P02-sp08-D0015&showfullrecord=on.

24. Morgan, *Naval Documents of the American Revolution*. Vol. 5, 446. Diary of Benjamin Marston.

The Battle to End the Blockade

1. Morgan, *Naval Documents of the American Revolution*. Vol. 5, 67.

2. "Resolves for Further Fortifying Boston Harbour." Chapter: 16 to *The Acts and Resolves, Public And Private, Of The Province of Massachusetts Bay: To Which Are Prefixed The Charters of the Province. With Historical And Explanatory Notes And An Appendix.*, 430-31. Vol. XIX. Boston, MA: Commonwealth, 1918.

3. Northern Illinois University Libraries. "Appointing a Committee of Fortification." http://lincoln.lib.niu.edu/cgibin/amarch/documentidx.pl?doc_id=S5-V1-P01-sp05D0032&showfullrecord=on.

4. William B. Clark, ed. *Naval Documents of the American Revolution*. Vol. 3. Washington: U.S.G.P.O, 1968, 535.

5. Morgan, *Naval Documents of the American Revolution*. Vol. 5, 228-29. May 1776, PRO Admiralty 1/484

6. William Bell Clark, *Naval Documents of the American Revolution* (Washington: Government Printing Office, 1969), 4: 1326.
James Warren to John Adams Warren-Adams letters 1, 237-38

7. Peter Force, ed. *American Archives: Consisting of a Collection of Authentick Records, State Papers, Debates, and Letters and Other Notices of Publick Affairs : The Whole Forming a Documentary History of the Origin...* Vol. 6. Washington: Clark and Force, 1848, 918.

8. William J. Morgan, ed. *Naval Documents of the American Revolution*. Vol. 5. Washington: U.S.G.P.O, 1968, p 545.

9. John S. Barry, The *History of Massachusetts: The Commonwealth Period 1775-1820*. Boston: Author, 1857, 127.

10. Force, 917-918.

11. Morgan, *Naval Documents of the American Revolution*. Vol. 5, 545.

12. *History of the Town of Hingham* (Hingham, MA: University Press, 1893), 1: 296.

13. Morgan, *Naval Documents of the American Revolution*. Vol. 5, 526. Milford's Log PRO Admiralty 52/1865

14. Morgan, *Naval Documents of the American Revolution*. Vol. 5, 524.

15. Ibid., 582.

16. Ibid., 526.

17. Ibid., 524.

18. Sally R. Snowman and James G. Thomson. *Boston Light: A Historical Perspective*. Plymouth, MA: Flagship Press, 1999, 14.

19. Marion Balderston and David Syrett. *The Lost War : letters from British Officers during the American Revolution*. New York: Horizon Press, 1975, 97.

20. Charles Martyn, *The life of Artemas Ward, the First Commander-in-Chief of the American Revolution*. New York: Artemus Ward, 1921, 225.

21. Ward, Artemus. "Letter from General Ward to General Washington, June 16. ." Northern Illinois University Libraries. http://lincoln.lib.niu.edu/cgibin/amarch/getdoc.pl?/var/lib/philologic/databases/amarch/.17398.

22. Morgan, *Naval Documents of the American Revolution*. Vol. 5, 726. 5 Pro Admiralty 52/1865

23. John Lind, *An Answer to the Declaration of the American Congress, 4th* ed. (London: Cadell, 1776), 7, accessed March 24, 2012, http://books.google.com books? id=PrE6AAAAcAAJ&dq=john+lind&source=gbs_navlinks_s.

24. Ibid., 10.

25. Malcolm. Freiberg, "Thomas Hutchinson's Strictures upon the Declaration of the Congress at Philadelphia, In a letter to a Noble Lord." Old South Leaflets (1776), 27.

26. Ibid., 30.

27. Ibid., 29.

28. Ibid., 32.

29. Ibid., 10.

30. George William Frederick, "His Majesty's Most Gracious Speech to Both Houses of Parliament" (Speech before Parliament, October 31, 1776), from Williams College, The Founding Documents, accessed March 24, 2012, http://chapin.williams.edu/exhibits/founding.html.

31. Ibid.

32. William J. Morgan, ed. *Naval Documents of the American Revolution*. Vol. 7. Washington: U.S.G.P.O, 1976, 91-92.

33. http://lincoln.lib.niu.edu/cgi-bin/amarch/documentidx.pl?doc_id=S5-V1-P01-sp06-D1524&showfullrecord=on Title: Intelligence from Halifax, in Nova-Scotia. Citation: American Archives Series 5, Volume 1, Page 0939Author/Presenter: Type: Military dispatch; Report Themes: Military action: Ticonderoga, Canada; Military action: British forces; Military action: foraging, plunder, privateering, blockadesDate Presented: 1776-08-13 Date Composed: 1776-8-13 Where Written: Halifax, Nova-Scotia, Canada, North America Document ID: S5-V1-P01-sp06-D1524

34. Morgan, *Naval Documents of the American Revolution*. Vol. 5, 833-835. June 1776, Commodore Marriot Arbuthnot to Vice Admiral Richard Howe PRO, Colonial Office, 5/125, 28C.

35. Ibid., 833.

36. Northern Illinois University Libraries. "Intelligence from Boston." http://lincoln.lib.niu.edu/cgibin/amarch/getdoc.pl?/var/lib/philologic/databases/amarch/.21471.

37. Ibid.

38. Balderston, 97.

39. Northern Illinois University Libraries. "Letter from Winthrop Sargent to Massachusetts Council: Captain Daniel Waters retook an old coasting sloop which had been taken by the Milford frigate." http://lincoln.lib.niu.edu/cgibin/amarch/getdoc.pl?/var/lib/philologic/databases/amarch/.224 33.

40. C. K. Wilbur, *Pirates and Patriots of the Revolution*. Chester, Conn.: Globe Pequot Press, 1984, 50.

41. Gardner Weld Allen, *A Naval History of the American Revolution*. Vol. 1. New York: Riverside Press, 1913, 85.

Also Bluewater Patriots page 174.

42. Gardner Weld Allen, *A Naval History of the American Revolution*, Volume 1, ed. Gardner Weld Allen (New York: Riverside Press, 1913), 116.

43. Edmund C. Burnett, The Continental Congress: *A definitive history of the Continental Congress from its inception in 1774 to March, 1789*. New York: W.W. Norton and Company, 1964, 119.

44. Peter Force, "Preface."Northern Illinois University Libraries. http://lincoln.lib.niu.edu/cgibin/amarch/getdoc.pl?/var/lib/philologic/databases/amarch/.

45. William M. Fowler, *Rebels under Sail: The American Navy during the Revolution*. New York: Charles Scribner's Sons, 1976, 14.

46. Charles H. Lincoln, ed. *Naval Records of the American Revolution 1775-1788*. Washington: Government Printing Office, 1906, 17.

47. Naval History & Heritage Command. "Niles' Weekly Register Articles Relating to John Paul Jones." http://www.history.navy.mil/bios/jones_jp_niles.htm.

48. Evan Thomas, *John Paul Jones: Sailor, Hero, Father of the American Navy*. (New York: Simon and Schuster, 2004), 64.

49. John Paul Jones, Benjamin Walker, and James Hamilton, *Life of Rear-Admiral John Paul Jones*. (Philadelphia: Walker and Gillis, 1845), page 34, accessed March 29, 2012, http://books.google.com/books?ei=WNX7Tv2kBeHo0QGZpsWMAg&sqi=2&output=text&id=El0SAAAAYAAJ&dq=john+paul+jones+and+milford&ots=yepXCLZ_XF&q=milford#v=snippet&q=milford&f=false.

50. Zena Grant Collier, H.M.S Muster Rolls (Bedfordshire, England, 3, July, 1986).

51. William J. Morgan, ed. *Naval Documents of the American Revolution*. Vol. 7, 821.

52. Ibid., 995.

53. Thomas Beamish Atkins, *History of Halifax City*. (Halifax, Nova Scotia, Canada, 1895), page #76, accessed March 29, 2012, http://books.google.com/books?id=kakOAAAAYAAJ&pg=PA3&dq=history+of+halifax+nova+scotia&h=en&ei=

bJBHTNCPOcL8AaArqHvBA&sa=X&oi=book_result&ct=result&resnum=4&ved=0CDoQ6AEwAw#v=snippet&q=general%20howe&f=false, 76.

54. Jesse Lemisch, "Jack Tar in the Streets: Merchant Seamen in the Politics of Revolutionary America," *William and Mary Quarterly* 25, no. 3 (July 1968): 371.

55. Allan Everett Marble, *Surgeons, Smallpox, and the Poor : A History of Medicine and Social Conditions in Nova Scotia, 1749-1799* (Montreal: McGill-Queen's University Press, 1993), 103, 106,108.

56. Balderston and Syrett, *The Lost War: Letters from British Officers during the American Revolution,*75.

57. Ibid., 75.

58. David Syrett, *Shipping and the American War 1775-83*. New York: Oxford University Press Inc, 1970, 243.

59. Syrett, 130-131.

60. Ibid., 129.

61. Ibid., 127.

62. Balderston and Syrett, *The Lost War : letters from British Officers during the American Revolution*, 81.

63. Donald B. Chidsey, *The American Privateers*. New York: Dodd, Mead and Company, 1962, 56.

64. George A. Billias, *General John Glover and his Marblehead Mariners*. New York: Henry Hold and Company, 1960, 87.

The Rhode Island Expedition

1. John C. Miller, *Triumph of Freedom 1775-1783*. Boston: Little Brown and Company, 1948, 328.

2. Secretary of the Commonwealth. *Massachusetts Soldiers and Sailors of the Revolutionary War*. Vol. 3. Boston: Wright and Potter Printing, 1897, 302.

3. C K. Wilbur, *The Revolutionary Soldier, 1775-1783: An Illustrated Sourcebook of Authentic Details about Everyday Life for Revolutionary War Soldiers*. 12th ed. Guilford, CT: Globe Pequot Press, 1993, 11.

4. Thomas Paine, "The American Crisis" (1990), in *The Heath anthology of American Literature*, ed. Paul Lauter, 2nd ed. (Lexington, MA: D.C. Heath and Company, 1994), 1: 861-868.

5. Wilbur, 71.

6. This source has changed and the document is either no longer available or difficult to find. The same is true of the other entries. This was the original URL. Consource. Accessed February 11, 2013. http://www.consource.org/index.asp?

bid=582&documentid=54124.

*Also available here: Washington, George. *The Writings of George Washington from the original Manuscript Sources, 1745-1799; prepared under the direction of the United States George Washington Bicentennial Commission and published by Authority of Congress.* Vol. 8. Washington: U.S Government Printing Office, 1932.

7. Consource. Accessed February 11, 2013. http://www.consource.org/index.asp?bid=582&documentid=51643

8. Consource. Accessed February 11, 2013. http://www.consource.org/index.asp?bid=582&documentid=51696

9. Dave R. Palmer, *George Washington and Benedict Arnold.* Washington: Regnery Publishing, Inc., 2006, 204.

10. By the Great and General Court of Massachusetts Bay: A Proclamation January 23, 1776 Perez Morton. Found in the following book: Mason I. Lowance and Georgia B. Bumgardner, eds. *Massachusetts Broadsides of the American Revolution.* Amherst, MA: University of Massachusetts Press, 1976, 71.

11. William S. Pattee, *A History of old Braintree and Quincy: with a sketch of Randolph and Holbrook. Quincy, Mass.:* Green & Prescott, 1879, 586.

12. Who was who in American History: The Military. Chicago: Marquis Who's Who, 1975, 422.

13. Ibid.

14. Secretary of the Commonwealth. *Massachusetts Soldiers and Sailors of the Revolutionary War.* Vol. 11. Boston: Wright and Potter Printing, 1903, 803.

15. Edward R. Snow, *Mysterious Tales of the New England Coast.* Cornwall, N.Y.: Cornwall Press, 1961, 46.

16. Elizabeth Delmage, "Asa Waterman Papers," Rhode Island Historical Society, accessed April 2, 2012, last modified May 2007, http://www.rihs.org/mssinv/MSS786.htm.

17. Charles B. Whittlesey, *Historical Sketch of Joseph Spencer, Major-General of the Continental Troops.* Hartford, Conn.: Sons of the American Revolution, 1904.

18. *Proceedings of the Rhode Island Historical Society.* (Providence, Rhode Island: Providence Press Company, Printers, 1875), 89.

19. George Washington Greene, *The life of Nathanael Greene: Major-General in the Army of the Revolution*, Volume 1 (Cambridge: Houghton Mifflin, 1900), 539.

20. "Resolve to Prevent British Prisoners from Enlisting into the Army." Chapter: 53: *Acts and Resolves, Public and Private, of The Massachusetts Bay: To Which Are Prefixed The Charters of the Province. With Historical And Explanatory Notes, And An Appendix*, 440-

41. Vol. XX. Boston, MA: Commonwealth, 1918.

21. Ibid.

22. James Boswell, *The life of Samuel Johnson*. (London: Henry G. Bohn, 1846),5:page #s, accessed March 24, 2012, http://books.google.com/books?id=OXelxBMsHJwC&pg=PA292&dq=%22patriotism+is+the+last+refuge+of+a+scoundrel%22+boswell&hl=en&sa=X&ei=r0BuT4joKpO30QGm7aD_Bg&ved=0CDMQ6AEwAA#v=onepage&q&f=false.

23. James Boswell, *The life of Samuel Johnson, LL. D.* 3rd ed. London, England: H. Baldwin and Sons, 1799, 342.

Now Fitting for a Privateer

1. Ralph D. Paine, *Ships and Sailors of Old Salem*. (Chicago: A. C. McClurg and Company, 1912), 71.

2. Ralph D. Paine, *The Old Merchant Marine*. (Yale University Press, 1919), Chapter 3.

3. Michael Pearson, *Those Damned Rebels: The American Revolution as seen through British Eyes*. New York: G.P. Putnam's Sons, 1972, 107.

4. William J. Morgan, ed. *Naval Documents of the American Revolution*. Vol. 7. Washington: U.S.G.P.O, 1976, 825.

5. "Grand Turk," American War of Independence at Sea, accessed March 29, 2012, last modified February 4, 2011, http://www.awiatsea.com/Privateers/G/Grand%20Turk%20Massachusetts%20Ship%20%5BSimmons%20Pratt%5D.html.

6. Ralph D. Paine, *The Ships and Sailors of Old Salem*. New York: the Outing Publishing Company, 1908, 69-70.

7. C. K. Wilbur, *Pirates and Patriots of The Revolution*. Chester, Conn.: The Globe Pequot Press, 1984, 8.

8. Ibid., 25.

9. Ibid.

10. Wilbur, 26.

11. Tour of Salem with NPS July 25, 2010

12. Wilbur, *Pirates and Patriots of The Revolution*, 30.

13. Wilbur, 92.

14. Ibid.

15. R. J. White, *The Age of George III*. Garden City, NY: Doubleday and Company Inc., 1969, 146.

16. Edgar S. Maclay, *A History of American Privateers*. New York: D. Appleton and

Company, 1899, p xii.

17. "The Boarding Pike," Age of Sail, http://ageofsail.wordpress.com/2009/05/28/the-boarding-pike/.

18. Ralph D. Paine, *Ships and Sailors of Old Salem*, 68.

To My First True Love

1. Massachusetts Archives volume 96 page 509 Index to French and Indian War Muster Rolls (MA 91-99) Reel 07/Broon-Burrige RR/CAB/8

2. Carol Berkin, *Revolutionary Mothers*. New York: Alfred A. Knopf, 2005, 9.

3. Kurt Wilhelm, "Essex, Mass. - 1782 Householders," The US GenWeb Project, http://essex.essexcountyma.net/cen1782a.htm.

4. Christopher M. Jedrey, *The World Of John Cleaveland*. New York: W.W. Norton, 1979, 63.

5. Berkin, 17.

6. Berkin, 10.

7. Carl Holliday, *Woman's Life in Colonial Days*. Williamstown, Mass.: Corner House Publishers, 1922, 283.

8. Henry R Stiles, *Bundling: its Origin, Progress and Decline in America*. Albany: Author, 1871, 13.

9. *Vital Records of Ipswich, Massachusetts*, vol. 1 of *Births* (Salem, MA: Essex Institute, 1910), 81.

10. Berkin, 5-6.

11. Kurt A. Wilhelm, "Chebacco Parish/ Essex, Mass. ," Rootsweb, http://www.rootsweb.ancestry.com/~macessex/tax/1780b.htm.

12. Kurt A. Wilhelm, "Chebacco Parish/ Essex, Mass." in *1780 Chebacco Beef Tax*, accessed June 14, 2012, last modified September 27, 1999, http://essex.essexcountyma.net/tax/ 1780b.htm.

13. Davis R. Dewey, *Financial History of the United States*. 2nd ed. Cambridge: University Press, 1903, 45..

14. Dewey, 46.

15. Dewey, 46-47.

16. Dewey, 47.

17. Dewey, 49-51.

18. Jedrey, 62.

19. Charles Beard, *An Economic Interpretation of the Constitution of the United States.* (New York: Macmillan, 1921), 261.

20. Leonard L. Richards, *Shays's Rebellion: The American Revolutions Final Battle.* Philadephia: University of Pennsylvania Press, 2002, 144.

21. Richard D. Brown, *Massachusetts: A Bicentennial History.* New York: W.W. Norton and Company Inc., 1978, 115.

22. Brown, 116.

23. Springfield Technical Community College. "People Daniel Shays 1747 1825."http://shaysrebellion.stcc.edu/shaysapp/person.do? shortName=daniel_shays.

24. Richards, 144.

25. Richards, 142.

26. John M. Clapp, *Select Orations Illustrating American Political History.* New York The Macmillan Company, 1909, 70.

27. Clapp, 70.

28. Edmund S. Morgan, *The Birth of the Republic: 1763-1789.* Chicago: The University of Chicago Press, 1965, 95.

29. Benjamin Franklin, "Information to Those Who Would Remove to America," *The Founders Constitution*, accessed June 9, 2012, last modified September 1782, http://press-pubs.uchicago.edu/founders/documents/v1ch15s27.html

30. Richard Langsford of Gloucester page 253 Essex county Deeds 149:86-87

31. http://www.sacred-texts.com/chr/nep/1777/index.htm

32. Joan R. Gundersen, *To be Useful to the World: Women in Revolutionary America, 1740-1790.* Chapel Hill: Chapel Hill: University of North Carolina Press, 2006, 55.

33. Nina F. Little, *Little by Little: Six Decades of Collecting American Decorator Arts.* New York: E.D. Dutton, 1984, 143.

The Ministers Daughter

1. William Little, *The History of Weare, New Hampshire 1735-1888.* Lowell, Mass.: S.W. Huse and Co, 1888.

2. Richardson Wright, *Hawkers and Walkers in Early America.* Philadelphia: J. B. Lippincott Company, 1927, 107.

3. Wright, 24.

4. Christopher M. Jedrey, *The World of John Cleaveland.* New York: W.W. Norton, 1979.

5. Jedrey, 127.

6. D. F. Lamson, *The Magazine of American History with Notes and Queries*, ed. Martha J Lamb (New York: Historical Publication Company, 1887), 18:239-242.

7. Essex Institute Historical Collections (Salem, MA: Essex Institute, 1874), 12: 88, accessed May 18, 2012, http://books.google.com/books?id=RvkWAAAAIAAJ&pg=PA88&dq=%22abraham+Channell%22&hl=en&ei=DoJWTurBFMbUgQeX49CNDA&sa=X&oi=book_result&ct=result&resnum=2&ved=0CDEQ6AEwAQ#v=onepage&q=%22abraham%20Channell%22&f=false.

8. John Cleaveland Rev. to Elizabeth Cleaveland, November 8, 1794, MSS 204, John Cleaveland Papers, Phillips Library, Salem, MA.

9. Mary Wollstonecraft, *A Vindication of the Rights of Woman: with Strictures on Political and Moral Subjects* (London: T Fisher Unwin, 1891), 9.

10. Jedrey, 72.

11. Wollstonecraft, VI and 9.

12. *Vital Records of Ipswich, Massachusetts To the End of the Year 1849*, vol. 2, *Marriages and Deaths* (Salem. MA: Essex Institute, 1910), 91.

13. Wollstonecraft, 28.

14. Deed of Sale from James Hogg to Abraham Channell, 20 February 1794, Weare, N.H., Book 32 Page 523 Hillsboro County registry of Deeds, Nashua, N.H.

15. Little, *History of Weare*, 317-318.

16. Albert Stillman Batchellor and Henry Harrison Metcalf, *Laws of New Hampshire: Second Constitutional Period, 1792-1801* (Concord NH: Evans Printing Company, 1917), 6:viii, http://books.google.com/books?id=zb1GAQAAIAAJ&pg=PR8&dq=first+new+hampshire+turnpike&hl=en&ei=RHsTsGGEKfz0gHi05GrAQ&sa=X&oi=book_result&ct=result&resnum=4&ved=0CDwQ6AEwAw#v=onepage&q=first%20new%20hampshire%20turnpike&f=false.

17. Timothy Dwight, *Travels in New England and New York*, ed. Barbara Miller 2:205.

18. Dave Dewitt, *The Founding Foodies: How Washington, Jefferson, and Franklin Revolutionized American Cuisine.* (Naperville, IL: Sourcebooks, 2010), 142-146.

19. Harold Wilson Fisher, *Hill Country of New England.* (New York: Columbia University Press,1936), 17.

20. Donna B. Garvin and James L. Garvin. *On the Road North of Boston: New Hampshire Taverns and Turnpikes, 1700-1900.* Concord, NH: New Hampshire Historical Society, 1988, 49.

21. Ibid., 49.

22. Ibid., 50.

23. Ibid., 49.

24. Ibid.

25. Little, *The History of Weare, New Hampshire 1735-1888*, 567.

26. John Cleaveland to John Cleaveland Rev., May 14, 1795, MSS 204, John Cleaveland Papers, Phillips Library, Salem, MA.

27. John Cleaveland Rev to Nehemiah Cleaveland, January 3, 1799, MSS 204, John Cleaveland Papers, Phillips Library, Salem, MA.

28. Ibid.

29. Ibid.

30. Wollstonecraft, 28.

31. John Cleaveland, "Gravestone in Old Graveyard, Essex, MA."

32. Jedrey, 169.

33. "Command To Arrest Abraham Channel," Essex County Court orders Sheriff to arrest Abraham Channel, January 3, 1800, 17-469, Court of Common Pleas, Essex County Courts (now at state archives), Salem, MA. *Court records were found by Ruth Courchaine in 1984. They are more difficult to access today.

34. Samuel Smith, "Precept," Bill for taking Abraham Channel to jail in Ipswich, January 2, 1800, 17-469, Essex County Court, Now in Massachusetts Archives, Boston, MA.

35. John Cogswell, Appear at Court of Common Pleas, April 3, 1800, 17-469, Essex County Court, Now held at Massachusetts, Archives, Boston, MA.

36. James Jackson Putnam, *A Memoir of Dr. James Jackson*. (Boston: Riverside Publishing, 1905), 104.

37. "Cleaveland versus Channel," Court case, November 1801, 236, Essex County Court, Now in Massachusetts Archives, Boston, MA.

38. Deed of Sale Abraham Channel to Obadiah Eaton, 27 February 1805, Weare, New Hampshire, Book 65, Page 56, Hillsboro County Registry of Deeds, Nashua, New Hampshire.

39. Deed of Sale from Abraham Channel to Jothan T. Tuttle, 22 March 1805, Weare, New Hampshire, Book 65 Page 331, Hillsboro County Registry of Deeds, Nashua New Hampshire.

40. Jenn Marcelais, "Byfield Parish Burying Ground ," A Very Grave Matter, accessed June 5, 2012,http://gravematter.smugmug.com/Massachusetts/Byfield/Byfield-Parish-Burying-Ground/ 1414837_NNfSk/11/70097161_Lu3fB/Medium.

41. Joan R. Gundersen, *To be Useful to the World: Women in Revolutionary America, 1740-1790*. Chapel Hill: Chapel Hill: University of North Carolina Press, 2006, 48.

Austin and the Quakers

1. Society of Friends. *Christian Faith and Practice in the Experience of the Society of Friends.* Richmond, Ind.: Friends United Press, 1973, line 57.

2. J. I. Little, *Loyalties in Conflict: A Canadian Borderland in War and Rebellion 1812-1840.* Toronto: University of Toronto Press, 2008, 4.

3. McInnis, Edgar. Canada: *A Political and Social History.* Toronto: Holt, Rhinehart and Winston of Canada Limited, 1969, 200.

4. Bishops University."Landscape." http://www.ubishops.ca/geoh/landscap/bound.htm.

5. Ibid.

6. The Automobile Blue Book (New York: The Automobile Blue Book Publishing Company, 1918), 2:755.

7. Appalachian Mountain Club, Appalachia (Boston: Appalachian Mountain Club, 1920), 15:123.

8. Society of Friends, line 570.

9. Harry B. Shufelt, *Nicholas Austin the Quaker and the Township of Bolton. Knowlton*, Canada: Brome County Historical Society, 1971, 27.

10. Wentworth, Sir John, (Dictionary of Canadian Biography Online, 2000), s.v. "John Wentworth" by Judith Fingard, accessed March 26, 2012, http://www.biographi.ca/009004-119.01-e.php?&id_nbr=2710.

11. Thomas Paine, *Common Sense; Addressed to the Inhabitants of America* (Philadelphia, PA: R. Bell, 1776), 72.

12. William Little, *The History of Weare, New Hampshire 1735-1888.* Lowell, Mass.: S.W. Huse and Co, 1888, 204.

13. John C. Miller, *Triumph of Freedom: 1775/1783.* Boston: Little, Brown and Company, 1948, 55.

14. Donna B. Garvin and James L. Garvin. *On the Road North of Boston: New Hampshire Taverns and Turnpikes, 1700-1900.* Concord, NH: New Hampshire Historical Society, 1988, 46-47.

15. Benjamin Franklin Parker, *History of Wolfeborough.* (New Hampshire) (Wolfeborough, NH, 1905), 85.

16. R. J. White, *The Age of George III.* Garden City, NY: Doubleday and Company Inc., 1969, 177.

17. Shufelt, 17.

Pearl and the Embargo

1. Jane F. Fiske, ed. *The New England Historical and Genealogical Register Index of Persons A-C*. Vol. 51-148. Boston: New England Historical and Genealogical Society, 1907, 346.

2. "Joshua Burnham to Abraham Channel," Land deed, May 3, 1802, Book 169, Page 269, Essex County Registry of Deeds, Salem, Massachusetts.

3. Documents of the City of Boston (Boston: City Council, 1902), 4: 497.

4. *Vital Records of Ipswich, Massachusetts To the End of the Year 1849*, vol. 2, *Marriages and Deaths* (Salem. MA: Essex Institute, 1910), 91.

5. Ben L. Edwards, "An Original Article – The Massachusetts Centinel – Oct. 28, 1789 (Part 3)," Teach History, accessed May 21, 2012, http://teachhistory.com/2010/06/26/president-washington-visits-boston-%E2%80%93-eyewitness-press-accounts/washington3-2/.

6. The Massachusetts Centinel – Oct. 28, 1789

7. Obituary, New York Daily Times (New York), July 23, 1855, ProQuest Historical Newspapers.

8. "Court of Common Pleas." May 5, 1808. Book 25 Pages 453-454. County of Essex Superior Court. Salem.

9. Richard D. Brown, *Massachusetts: A Bicentennial History*. New York: W.W. Norton and Company Inc., 1978, 132.

10. John Bach McMaster, *A History of the People of the United States, From the Revolution to the Civil War*, vol. 3 of 1803-1812 (New York: D. Appleton and Company, 1914), 292.

11. McMaster, 297.

12. Paul E. Rivard, *A New Order of Things: How the Textile Industry Transformed New England*. Hanover, NH: University Press of New England, 2002, 34.

13. New England Historic and Genealogical Register Vol 125 page 222 1971 Published by the Society 101 Newbury Street.

14. Abraham Channel, Power of attorney to Abraham Savage, July 10, 1810, Rita Channell collection.

15. This came from papers from the Brome County Historical Society in Knowlton Quebec that were sent to me on 10/25/2011

16. Deed Jonathan Weare to Abraham Channel Lot no. 28 in the 10th range 18th August 1810.

17. Donald Fryson, *Magistrates, Police and People: Everyday Criminal Justice in Quebec and Lower Canada*. (Toronto: University of Toronto Press, 2006), 133.

18. Catherine M. May, *History of the Eastern Townships, province of Quebec, Dominion of Canada:* Civil and Descriptive in Three Parts. Montreal: John Lovell, 1869, 268.

19. B F. Hubbard, *Forests and Clearings: The History of Stanstead County,* Province of Quebec. Bowie, MD: Heritage Books, Inc., 1988, 45.

20. "1790 US Census," Ancestry, accessed June 15, 2012, www.ancestry.com.

21. Clarke Garrett, *Origins of the Shakers: From the Old World to the New World.* (Baltimore, Md: John Hopkins University Press, 1998), 186.

22. Shaker Town: A More Perfect Order. Films Media Group, 2008. Films On Demand.Flash, http://digital.films.com/PortalPlaylists.aspx?aid=8470&xtid=43702. (accessed August, 18 2011).

23. Carol Weisbrod, *The Boundaries of Utopia.* New York: Pantheon Books, 1980, 37.

Shakers of Harvard

1. Canterbury Shakers. *Gentle Manners.* 1992. Front Page.

2. A. F. Joy, *We are the Shakers.* South Wellfleet, Mass.: Saturscent Publishers, 1985, 4.

3. Joy, 5.

4. Robben Campbell, "Susan Channel and her father," e-mail message to the author, June 17, 2011.

5. Carol Weisbrod, *The Boundaries of Utopia.* New York: Pantheon Books, 1980, xii.

6. Weisbrod, 71.

7. Judith A. Graham, "The New Lebanon Shaker Children's Order," *Winterthur Portfolio* 26, no. 4 (Winter 1991): 215.

8. Weisbrod, 48.

9. Ibid., 216.

10. Ibid., 220.

11. Edward R. Horgan, *The Shaker Holy Land: a Community Portrait.* Harvard, MA: Harvard Common Press, 1987, 61.

12. Weisbrod, 46.

13. *Bartleby.com,* s.v. "Elegy to the Memory of an Unfortunate Lady," by Alexander Pope, accessed June 23, 2012, last modified 2012, http://www.bartleby.com/101/441.html.

14. John Humphrey Noyes, *History of American Socialisms* (Philadelphia: J.B. Lippincott and Company, 1870), 604-607.

15. Gerard C. Wertkin, *The Four Seasons of Shaker Life: An Intimate Portrait of the Community at Sabbathday Lake* (New York: Simon & Schuster, Inc., 1986), pp.101-2.

16. From a conversation I had with Roben Campbell during a trip to visit her and the former Shaker grounds.

17. On April 12, 2011 I attended a history conference and had the pleasure of witnessing broom making and discussing it with Hammer, a re-enactor from Sturbridge Village. Hammer made a broom for me in the traditional manner using the same tools the Shakers would have used.

18. "Shaker Manuscripts," Diaries and Journals, http://www.fruitlands.org/shakermanuscripts#_V.

19. Horgan, 118.

20. "Shaker Manuscripts," Diaries and Journals, http://www.fruitlands.org/shakermanuscripts#_V.

21. Shaker Manuscripts.

22. Shaker Manuscripts.

23. Shaker Manuscripts.

24. Robben Campbell, "Susan Channel and her father," e-mail message to the author, June 17, 2011.

25. Horgan, 84.

26. "Shaker Manuscripts," Diaries and Journals, http://www.fruitlands.org/shaker-manuscripts#_V.

27. Carlene Phillips, "Beyond the grave in the town's cemeteries," *Harvard Press* (Harvard, MA), November 2, 2007, accessed June 23, 2012, http://www.harvardpress.com/Features/ALookBack/tabid/2189/ID/2688/PageID/5556/Beyond_the_graves_in_the_towns_cemeteries.aspx.

28. David Martin, "Serene Twilight of the Shakers: The Rich Legacy of a Celibate Sect Whose Believers are Nearly All Gone. How Mother Ann Brought the Faith to America." *Life Magazine*, March 17, 1967, 58-72.

Defiance on the Border in 1812

1. Charles D. Watkins, "Skinners Island." Owls Head Mountain House Lake Memphremagog, 1880 Accessed March 21, 2011. http://books.google.com/booksid=dy0TAAAAYAAJ&pg=PA39&lpg=PA39&dq=lake+memphremagog+smuggling+during+war+of+1812&source=bl&ots=_x9zLywWhY&sig=heP5Rp9MYH_hiDEjX0EICT3T3U&hl=en&ei=Fdt-TbfeNsGa0QHa8fmPC.

2. John B. McMaster, *History of the People of the United States.* Vol. 4. New York: D. Appleton and Company, 1895, 65.

3. Henry M. Burt, "Burt's Illustrated Guide of the Connecticut Valley : Containing Descriptions of Mount Holyoke, Mount Mansfield, White Mountains, Lake

Memphremagog, Lake Willoughby, Montreal, Quebec, &c."University of Connecticut Libraries. Accessed March 21, 2011, 198. http://www.archive.org/details/burtsillustrated1866burt.

4. Ibid., 15.

5. Georgeville Historic Society, Abraham Channel, Jr, Abraham Channel, Jr to Robert Channel 17, June 1813 (I received this in an email from Rita Channell and I transcribed it).

6. Channel, letter.

7. Secretary of the Commonwealth. *Massachusetts Soldiers and Sailors of the Revolutionary War.* Vol. 3. Boston: Wright and Potter Printing, 1897, 992.

8. Secretary. *Massachusetts Soldiers and Sailors*, 992.

9. William Little, *The History of Warren; a Mountain Hamlet, located among the White Hills of New Hampshire.* (Manchester, N.H.: W.E. Moore, printer, 1870), 287.

10. B F. Hubbard, *Forests and Clearings: The History of Stanstead County, Province of Quebec.* Bowie, MD: Heritage Books, Inc., 1988, 79.

11. Daniel Webster, Daniel Webster on the Draft: Text of a Speech delivered in Congress, December 9, 1814 (Washington, D.C.: American Union Against Militarism, 1917). Chapter: Speech of Daniel Webster Accessed from: http://oll.libertyfund.org/title/2070/156301 on 2012-04-02

12. Ibid.

13. Hubbard., 136.

14. Fernand Ouellet, *Lower Canada, 1791-1840 : Social Change and Nationalism*, trans. Patricia Claxton (Toronto: McClelland and Stewart, 1980), 112.

15. Oracle Think Quest. "Causes: The War of 1812." http://library.thinkquest.org/22916/excauses.html.

16. Allan Seymour Everest, *The War of 1812 in the Champlain Valley* (Syracuse, NY: Syracuse University Press, 1981), 32.

17. Wesley B. Turner, *British Generals in the War of 1812.* Montreal: McGill Queen's, 1999, 30.

18. Turner, 34.

19. Turner, 28.

20. Horst Dresler, *Farmers and Honest Men.* Woodstock, Vt.: Anything Printed, 2009, 103.

21. Parks Canada."Battle of the Châteauguay National Historic Site of Canada."http://www.pc.gc.ca/eng/lhnnhs/qc/chateauguay/natcul/natcul1/natcul1 d.aspx.

22. Ibid.

23. Allan Seymour Everest, *The War of 1812 in the Champlain Valley* (Syracuse, NY: Syracuse University Press, 1981), 135.

24. Dugdale-Pointon, TDP. (2 August 2000), Congreve Rockets, http://www.historyofwar.org/articles/weapons_congreve.html

25. Everest, 157.

Hospitality on the Lake

1. A transcription of the Lalanne deed June 22, 1815 was included in the email. John Scott, "Channells of Memphremagog/Georgeville," e-mail message to The author, February 17, 2010.

2. The Northern Conspiracy: According to the Plans of the "Essex Junto." http://books.google.com/books?id=gDBCAAAAIAAJ&printsec=titlepage#v=onepage&q&f=false

3. Jean J. Rousseau, *The Social Contract*. Translated by Maurice Cranston. New York: Penguin Books, 1968, 21.

4. Frederick J. Turner, "The Significance of the Frontier in American History." University of Virginia. http://xroads.virginia.edu/~hyper/turner/, Chapter 1.

5. P. Stansbury, *A Pedestrian Tour of Two Thousand Three Hundred Miles in North America*. New York: J.D. Myers and W. Smith, 1822, 153.

6. Stansbury, 153.

7. Ibid.

8. Ibid.

9. Isaac Weld, *Weld's Travels through the States of North America, and the Provinces of Upper and Lower Canada during the years 1795, 1796, and 1797* (Carlisle, MA: Applewood Books, 1807), 1:415, accessed March 24, 2012, http://books.google.com/booksid=Rvygrr4WeNYC&printsec=frontcover&source=gbs_ge_summary_r&cad=0#v=onepage&q=canada&f=false

10. Weld, 416.

11. Weld, 427.

Grave Robbing and Lake Monsters

1. Abraham Channel, Promissory Note to Elisha Tucker, January 10, 1815, Superior Court, Salem, MA.

2. Abraham Channel, Promissory Note to Robert Channel, October 10, 1815, Superior Court, Salem, MA.

3. Promissory Note to Sally Channel, October 11, 1815, Superior Court, Salem, MA.

4. Robert I Tilling, This Dynamic Earth: the Story of Plate Tectonics (U.S. Government Printing Office), accessed March 24, 2012, http://books.google.com/books?id=T5mZVQeigpMC&pg=PA67&dq=1815+eruption+of+mount+tambora&hl=en&ei=oTrQTfmDFIHTgQfdl4W3DA&sa=X&oi=book_result&ct=result&resnum=2&ved=0CDcQ6AEwATgK#v=onepage&q=1815%20eruption%20of%20mount%20tambora&f=false.

5. Harold Wilson Fisher, *Hill Country of New England*. (New York: Columbia University Press, 1936), 22.

6. Lesley-Ann Dupigny Giroux and Cary J Mock, *Historical Climate Variability and Impacts in North America*. (New York: Dordrecht, 2009), 113.

7. Loren Coleman and Patrick Huyghe. *The Field Guide to Lake Monsters, Sea Serpents, and Other Mystery Denizens of the Deep*. New York: Penguin Group, 2003, 6.

8. Coleman and Huyghe, 7.

9. John I. Little, *The Other Quebec: Microhistorical Essays on Nineteenth-Century Religion and Society*. Toronto: University of Toronto, 2006, 17.

10. Little, 17.

11. Coleman and Huyghe, 267.

12. Coleman and Huyghe, 68.

13. Coleman and Huyghe 9-20.

14. Coleman and Huyghe, 70-72.

15. William B. Bullock, *Beautiful Waters*. Vol. 1. Newport, Vt.: Memphremagog Press, 1926, 78-82.

16. Joseph A. Citro and Stephen R. Bissette, *The Vermont Monster Guide* (n.p.: University Press of New England, 2009), 79-82

17. Bullock, 121.

18. Citro and Bissette, 79-82.

19. Ibid.

20. W H. Blackman, *The Field Guide to North American Monsters*. New York: Three Rivers Press, 1998, 61.

21. John Scott, "Channells of Memphremagog/Georgeville," e-mail message to The author, February 17, 2010.

22. Elisha Dwyer Tucker to Sally Channel Miss, July 19, 1817, Coll. of Rita Channell.

23. Dudley Choate to Robert Channel, September 9, 1818, Collection of Rita Channell.

24. Dudley Choate to Robert Channel Mr., November 22, 1818, Collection of Rita Channell

25. Frederick C. Waite, "Grave Robbing in New England," Bulletin of the Medical Library Association 33, no. 3 (July 1945): page #s, accessed March 30, 2012, http://www.ncbi.nlm.nih.gov/pmc/articles/PMC194496/.

26. John Fitzgerald Kennedy, *Profiles in Courage* (New York: Harper Perennial, 1956), 59.

27. Suzanne M. Schultz, *Body Snatching: The Robbing of Graves for the Education of Physicians in Early Nineteenth Century America* (Jefferson, North Carolina: McFarland and Company Inc, 1992), 51-52, accessed March 29, 2012, http://books.google.com/books?id=IJPwpgQYwzEC&pg=PA52&dq=doctor+thomas+sewall+grave&hl=en&ei=la64TbZBYfTgQfPhcB9&sa=X&oi=book_result&ct=result&resnum=1&sqi=2&ved=0CEUQ6AEwAA#v=onepage&q=doctor%20thomas%20sewall%20grave&f=false.

28. Numerous letters appear between the two men. Lewis, Walker, ed. *Speak for Yourself Daniel*. Boston: Houghton Mifflin Company, 1969.

29. Daniel Dorchester, *Latest Drink Sophistries versus Total Abstinence*. Boston: Frank Wood Printer, 1883, 42.

30. John Hume, *The Seed and the Harvest*. Edinburgh: Gall and Inglis, 1850, 127.

31. Mary W. Shelley, *Frankenstein*. New York: Scholastic Book Services, 1970, preface.

Abraham's Tavern Stand

1. Alice Morse Earle, *Stage-coach and Tavern Days*. (New York: Macmillan Company, 1911), 108.

2. Frederick A. Currier, *Tavern Days and the Old Taverns of Fitchburg*; Stage Coach Days and Stage Coach Ways (Fitchburg: Sentinel Printing Co, 1897),28.

3. Nathaniel Hawthorne and Sophia Peabody Hawthorne, *Passages from the American Note-books of Nathaniel Hawthorne*. (London: Smith, Elder and Co., 1868), 1:223.

4. John Scott, "Inside the Old Camperdown: All the Best, With a Looking Glass in Most Every Room," *Georgeville Enterprise*: 3-7.

5. Donna B. Garvin and James L. Garvin. *On the Road North of Boston: New Hampshire Taverns and Turnpikes, 1700-1900*. Concord, NH: New Hampshire Historical Society, 1988, 109.

6. At the Sign of the Eagle Early American Life 58-67 Dec 2011

7. David Choate, *Town of Essex: From 1634 to 1868*. Springfield, Mass.: The Town of Essex, 1868, 294.

Frederick Channell

Counterfeiters, Competition and Capitalism

1. 1822 Last Will and Testament of Abraham Channel, June 22, 1822, received from Rita Channell, original located Archives Nationale, Sherbrooke, Quebec, Canada.

2. Ibid.

3. Ibid.

4. Ibid.

5. Ibid.

6. Robert Crowell, *History of the town of Essex : from 1634 to 1868*. Essex Mass.: 1868, 297.

7. Joseph Nielson, *Memories of Rufus Choate, with some consideration of his studies, methods, and opinions, and of his style as a speaker and writer* .(Boston: Houghton, Mifflin and Company, 1884), 7.

8. R.M. Smythe, comp. *Obsolete American Securities and Corporations*. (New York, 1904), 250.

9. Juliana Horatia Gaty Ewing, *Lob Lie-by-the-Fire: Or the Luck of Lingborough and Other Tales*. (London: G. Bell, 1874), 3-5.

10. B.M. Burnham to Robert Channel, February 24, 1825, Rita Channell Collection.

11. John S Garner, *The Company Town : Architecture and Society in the Early Industrial Age*. (New York: Oxford University Press, 1992), 117-119.

12. Paul E. Rivard, *A New Order of Things: How the Textile Industry Transformed New England*. Hanover, NH: University Press of New England, 2002, 49.

13. Rivard, 50.

14. Hannah Josephson, *The Golden Threads: New England's Mill Girls and Magnates*. New York: Russell and Russell, 1967, 23.

15. Abigail George to Robert Channel Mrs., June 13, 1844, Rita Channell Collection.

16. John Greenleaf Whittier, "The Factory Girls of Lowell," in *Voices of the True-Hearted* (Philadelphia: Merrihew & Thompson, printers, 1846), 40-41.

17. "Lowell Institute for Savings Bank Records 1836-1840," Center for Lowell History, accessed March 31, 2012, http://library.uml.edu/clh/LIS/LIS36-40.htm.

18. "What's In A Factory? Calculating A Textile System ," Smithsonian Institution, accessed March 31, 2013, last modified June 5, 1998, http://invention.smithsonian.org/centerpieces/whole_cloth/u2ei/u2materials/eiPac4.html.

19. Harriett Jane Hanson Robinson, *Loom and Spindle: Or, Life Among the Early Mill Girls. With a Sketch of "The Lowell Offering" and Some of Its Contributors* (New York: T. Y

Crowell & Company, 1898), 17.

20. Ibid., 84.

21. Richard D. Brown, *Massachusetts: A Bicentennial History*. New York: W.W. Norton and Company Inc., 1978, 178.

22. Donna B. Garvin and James L. Garvin. *On the Road North of Boston: New Hampshire Taverns and Turnpikes, 1700-1900*. Concord, NH: New Hampshire Historical Society, 1988, 105.

23. Robinson, 12.

24. Abraham F.J. Channell to Robert Channel, May 4, 1829, Rita Channell Collection.

25. William P. Channell to Robert Channel, July 11, 1830, Rita Channell Collection.

26. "Library and Archives Canada," Channel, Abraham and others Land Petition, February, 5, 1823 , Microfilm c. 2516, RG 1L3L, Vol. 58, Page 29494-29504, Lower Canada Land Papers, Collections Canada, accessed June 8, 2012, http://www.collections.gc.ca.

27. Petition of land RG1 l3 Volume 58 #29496

28."Library and Archives Canada," Channel, Abraham and others Land Petition, February, 5, 1823, Microfilm c. 2516, RG 1L3L, Vol. 58, Page 29494-29504, Lower Canada Land Papers, Collections Canada, accessed June 8, 2012, http://www.collections.gc.ca.

29. Joseph Bouchette, *The British Dominions in North America*. (London: Henry Colburn and Richard Bentley, 1831).

30. John I. Little, *The Other Quebec: Microhistorical Essays on Nineteenth-Century Religion and Society*. Toronto: University of Toronto, 2006, 129-130.

31. Ibid.

32. B F. Hubbard, *Forests and Clearings: The history of Stanstead County, Province of Quebec*. Bowie, MD: Heritage Books, Inc., 1988, 110.

33. Colonist August 21, 1823.

34. Donna B., and James L. Garvin. *On the Road North of Boston: New Hampshire Taverns and Turnpikes, 1700-1900*. Concord, NH: New Hampshire Historical Society, 1988, 112.

35. Garvin, 112.

36. Garvin, 112.

37. Silas Dickerson, "A fellow feeling makes us wondrous kind." *Canadian Times* (Sherbrooke, Quebec/Canada), October 9, 1823.

38. Ibid.

39. Information taken from a typed document that Rita Channell had collected on a visit to Canada decades before. Probably from the Georgeville or Stanstead Historical Society.

40. John Douglas *Borthwick, History and Biographical Gazetteer of Montreal to the Year 1892* (Montreal: John Lovell and Son, 1892).

41. John Douglas Borthwick, *From Darkness to Light; History of the Eight Prisons Which Have Been, Or Are Now, in Montreal, from A.D. 1760 to A.D. 1907, "Civil and Military", Containing Many Curious, Interesting and Forgotten Items of Golden Times from Authentic Sources and Records.* (Montreal: Gazette Printing Co, 1907), accessed March 30, 2012, http://archive.org/details/fromdarknesstoli00bortuoft.

42. Heather Darch, "Living on Easy Street: The Counterfeiters of Missisquoi County, Part 1," Townships Heritage Web Magazine, accessed April 2, 2012, http://townshipsheritage.com/article/living-easy-street-counterfeitersmissisquoi-county-part-1.

43. Ibid.

44. "Abigail White Whipping," Brattleboro History, accessed April 2, 2012, http://brattleborohistory.com/people/abigail-white.html.

45. "Secret Service History," United States Secret Service, accessed April 2, 2012, last modified 2010, http://www.secretservice.gov/history.shtml.

46. Stephen Mihm, *A Nation of Counterfeiters: Capitalists, Con Men, and the Making of the United States.* Cambridge: Harvard University Press, 2009, 80-81.

47. Mihm, 81.

48. Parks Canada."A Chronology of the Life of Louis-Joseph Papineau." http://www.pc.gc.ca/eng/lhn-nhs/qc/papineau/natcul/natcul1/a.aspx#Rise.

49. Welcome to Quebec. "Louis-Joseph Papineau." http://www.republiquelibre.org/cousture/PAPINO.HTM.

50. John Scott, "Inside the Old Camperdown: All the Best, With a Looking Glass in Most Every Room," *Georgeville Enterprise*: 3-7.

51. William P. Channell to Robert Channel, Unknown month, 22, 1830, Rita Channell Collection.

52. John Scott, "Channells of Memphremagog/Georgeville," e-mail message to The author, February 17, 2010.

53. Ibid.

Original record attributed as Ritchie 3677B, Oct 20, 1842 by John Scott a historian of Georgeville.

54. Little, *The Other Quebec*, 137.

The Rebellion of 1837

1. Fernand Ouellet, *Lower Canada, 1791-1840 : Social Change and Nationalism*, trans. Patricia Claxton (Toronto: McClelland and Stewart, 1980), 231-9.

2. Early Canadiana Online. "Statutes, treaties and documents of the Canadian Constitution, 1713- 1929." http://www.canadiana.org/view/9_03428/0371.

3. Paul Scherer, *Lord John Russell: A Biography*. Cranbury, N.J.: Susquehanna University Press, 1999, 109.

4. John B. McMaster, *History of the People of the United States*. Vol. 6. New York: D. Appleton and Company, 1914, 446.

5. Richard J. Walton, *Canada and the U.S.A.* New York: Parents Magazine Press, 1972, 76.

6. Albert B. Corey, *The Crisis of 1830-1840 In Canadian-American Relations*. New York: Russell and Russell, 1941, 35.

7. Shaun J. McLaughlin, *The Patriot War Along the New York-Canada Border: Raiders and Rebels*. (Charleston, NC: History Press, 2012), 24.

8. Kenneth R Stevens, *William Henry Harrison : A Bibliography* (Westport, CT: Greenwood Press, 1998), 38.

9. Maurice G. Baxter, *One and Inseparable: Daniel Webster and the Union*. Cambridge: The Belknap Press of Harvard University Press, 1984, 323.

10. Daniel Webster, *The Diplomatic and Official Papers of Daniel Webster, While Secretary of State*. (New York: Harper and Brothers, 1848), 105, 127.

11. Glyndon G. Van Deusen, *The Jacksonian Era: 1828-1848*. Long Grove, Ill.: Waveland Press, 1992, 137.

12. Jean P.Bernard, *The Rebellions of 1837 and 1838 in Lower Canada*. Ottawa: Canadian Historical Association Historical Booklet No. 55, 1996, 9.

13. John Lossing Benson, Harpers' *Popular Cyclopaedia of United States History from the Aboriginal Period to 1876: Containing Brief Sketches of Important Events and Conspicuous Actors*. (New York: Harper and Brothers, 1881), 1: 660.

14. Charles Winslow Elliott, *Winfield Scott: The Soldier and the Man*. (New York: The Macmillan Company, 1937), 339.

15. Bernard, 5.

16. Ibid, 6.

17. William Parr Greswell. *History of the Dominion of Canada*. Oxford, England: Clarendon Press, 1890, 179.

18. Aegidius, Fauteux. *Patriotes de 1837-1838*. Montreal, Canada: Les Editions Des

Dix, 1950, 160-161.

19. J. I. Little, *Loyalties in Conflict: A Canadian Borderland in War and Rebellion 1812-1840*. Toronto: University of Toronto Press, 2008, 91.

20. "Jean-Baptiste-Henri,Brien" Dictionary of Canadian Biography Online, accessed May 20, 2012, http://www.biographi.ca/009004-119.01-e.php?=&=&id_nbr=3267&interval=25.

21. Lossing, 660.

22. Webster, 106.

23. Shakespeare, William. *King Lear*. London, England: J. Darby, 1723. Accessed August 21, 2012. http://books.google.com/books?id=Z7IWAAAAQAAJ&dq=Meantime+we+shall+express+our+darker+purpose.&source=gbs_navlinks_s.

24. John Scott, "Channells of Memphremagog/Georgeville," e-mail message to the author, February 17, 2010.

25. Abraham F.J. Channel to Robert Channel, August 10, 1842, Rita Channell Collection.

26. Abraham F. Channel to Charles S. Channel, March 10, 1843, Deed of Sale, Rita Channell Collection.

27. "Library and Archives Canada," Channel, Leon L., 1846, Microfilm RG 19, Vol 5475, page 11, R200-113-0-E, Lower Canada Rebellion losses claims, Collections Canada, acquired June 29, 2011, http://www.collections.gc.ca.

28. Peter Anthony Adams, "Abbot-Downing History," Abbot-Downing Concord Coach, accessed March 29, 2012, last modified January 13, 2009, http://theconcordcoach.tripod.com/abbotdowning/index.html.

29. "21 juillet 1845: Le 'red letter day,'" Canton De Stanstead: Page d'histoire, accessed May 21, 2012, last modified 2010, http://www.cantonstanstead.ca/index.php?option=com_content&view=article&id=31&Itemid=87&lang=f.

30. Abraham Channel to Leon L. Channel, tavern sale and agreement to support, July 26, 1848

31. The Canadian Encyclopedia (2012), s.v. "Montréal Riots," by Jean Paul Bernard, accessed May 20, 2012, http://www.thecanadianencyclopedia.com/articles/montreal-riots.

32. *The Annexation Manifesto of 1849 Reprinted from the Original Pamphlet, with the Names of the Signers*. (Montreal: D. English and Co, 1881).

33. John Scott, "Channells of Memphremagog/Georgeville," e-mail message to the author, February 17, 2010.

34. Robin W. Winks, *Canada and the United States: The Civil War Years*. Baltimore, MD:

The John Hopkins Press, 1960, 7.

35. Wendell Phillips, *The Constitution a Pro-Slavery Compact or, Extracts from the Madison Papers, etc.* (New York: American Anti-Slavery Society, 1856), 201.

36. Winks, 7.

37. Winks, 9.

38. W H. Easterbrook, and Hugh G. Aitken. *Canadian Economic History.* Toronto: University of Toronto Press, 1984, 299.

39. Easterbrook and Aitken, 293.

The Camperdown

1. J. I. Little, "Scenic Tourism on the Northeastern Borderland: Lake Memphremagog's Steamboat Excursions and Resort Hotels 1850-1900," *Journal of Historical Geography* 35, no. 4 (February 2009): 721.

2. Charles S. Channell, "Memphremagog House," advertisement, *Stanstead Journal* (Stanstead, Quebec, Canada), May 21, 1855.

3. Donna B. Garvin and James L. Garvin. *On the Road North of Boston: New Hampshire Taverns and Turnpikes, 1700-1900.* Concord, NH: New Hampshire Historical Society, 1988, 171. From the diary of Matthew Patten of Bedford, N.H., 213.

4. Making of America Project, Harper's Magazine, Volume 49 (New York: Harper's Magazine Co, 1874), 343.

5. "A Century Ago," The *Stanstead Journal* (Stanstead, Quebec, Canada), June 26, 1869, accessed March 29, 2012, http://news.google.com/newspapers? nid=VnuxuLaQPLMC&dat=19690626&printsec=frontpage&hl=en.

6. Frances S Howe, *14,000 Miles: a Carriage and Two Women.* (Fitchburg, MA: Sentinel Printing, 1906), 164.

7. Samuel June Barrows and Isabel Chapin Barrows, *The Shaybacks in Camp: Ten Summers Under Canvas.* (Boston: Riverside Press, 1887), 61.

8. Little, 721.

9. Ibid.

10. Ibid., 735. (telephones mentioned may have been simply bell calls for services)

11. "Insolvent Notices," in The Legal News, Volume 9, comp. James Kirby (Montreal: The Gazette Printing Company, 1886), 9: 48.

12. William Charles Harris, *The American Angler.* (The Angler's Publishing Company, 1885), 7: 107.

13. Henry M. Burt, "Burt's Illustrated Guide of the Connecticut Valley: Containing Descriptions of Mount Holyoke, Mount Mansfield, White Mountains, Lake

Memphremagog, Lake Willoughby, Montreal, Quebec, &c."University of Connecticut Libraries. Accessed March 21, 2011. http://www.archive.org/details/burtsillustrated1866burt.

14. The Hermit of the Lake (New York: Liberty Printing Company, 1886). accessed March 30, 2012, http://books.google.com/books? id=QRYUAAAAYAAJ&pg=PA29&dq=%22camperdown %22+georgeville&hl=en&ei=NHyjTpWMBoXx0gH4pr2jBA&sa=X&oi=book_res ult&ct=result&resnum=9&ved=0CFAQ6AEwCDgK#v=onepage&q= %22camperdown%22%20georgeville&f=false.

15. Little, 736.

16. Red herring, "Georgeville-Then and Now," The *Stanstead Journal*, June 15, 1978, accessed March 27, 2012, http://news.google.com/newspapers? nid=805&dat=19780615&id=Z4IvAAAAIBAJ&sjid=SkkDAAAAIBAJ&pg=1092, 4234305.

The Final days of Immortality

1. William Crain, *Theories of Development: Concepts and Applications*, 4th ed. (Upper Saddle River, NJ: Prentice Hall, 2000), 286-287.

2. Mary Wollstonecraft, *A Vindication of the Rights of Woman: with Strictures on Political and Moral Subjects* (London: T Fisher Unwin, 1891), 31.

3. Ibid., 31.

4. Ibid., 30.

5. Ibid., 28.

6. Genesis 22.11

7. Adams, L. P. "Internment of Abram Fits Thon Chanell." January 11, 1858. Quebec, Vital and Church Records (Drouin Collection), Institut Généalogique Drouin., Montreal, Quebec, Canada. Accessed February 14, 2013. Ancestry Library Edition.

8. James M Dalzell, *John Gray of Mount Vernon: The Last Soldier of the Revolution* (Washington: Gibson Brothers Printers, 1868), 14.

9. Ibid.

BIBLIOGRAPHY

Adams, James T. *The Epic of America*. Garden City: Garden City Books, 1933.

Allen, Gardner Weld. *A Naval History of the American Revolution*, Volume 1. New York: Riverside Press,1913.

Balderston, Marion, and David Syrett. *The Lost War : Letters from British Officers during the American Revolution*. New York: Horizon Press, 1975.

Barry, John S. *The History of Massachusetts: The Commonwealth Period 1775-1820*. Boston: Author, 1857.

Baxter, Maurice G. *One and Inseparable: Daniel Webster and the Union*. Cambridge: The Belknap Press of Harvard University Press, 1984.

Beard, Charles. *An Economic Interpretation of the Constitution of the United States*. New York: Macmillan, 1921.

Berkin, Carol. *Revolutionary Mothers*. New York: Alfred A. Knopf, 2005.

Bernard, Jean P. *The Rebellions of 1837 and 1838 in Lower Canada*. Ottawa: Canadian Historical Association Historical Booklet No. 55, 1996.

Blackman, W H. *The Field Guide to North American Monsters*. New York: Three Rivers Press, 1998.

Borthwick, John Douglas. *History and Biographical Gazetteer of Montreal to the Year 1892*. Montreal: John Lovell and Son, 1892.

___. John Douglas. *From Darkness to Light; History of the Eight Prisons which have been, or are now, in Montreal, from A.D. 1760 to A.D. 1907*, "Civil and Military", Containing Many Curious, Interesting and Forgotten Items of Golden Times from Authentic Sources and Records . Montreal: Gazette Printing Co, 1907.

Boswell, James. *The life of Samuel Johnson*. Vol. 5. London: Henry G. Bohn, 1846. Accessed March 24, 2012.

Brown, Richard D. *Massachusetts: A Bicentennial History*. New York: W.W. Norton and Company Inc., 1978.

Bullock, William B. *Beautiful Waters*. Vol. 1. Newport, Vt.: Memphremagog Press, 1926.

Burnett, Edmund C. *The Continental Congress: A Definitive History of the Continental*

Congress from its Inception in 1774 to March, 1789. New York: W.W. Norton and Co, 1964.

Burt, Henry M. "Burt's Illustrated Guide of the Connecticut Valley: Containing Descriptions of Mount Holyoke, Mount Mansfield, White Mountains, Lake Memphremagog, Lake Willoughby, Montreal, Quebec,&c." University of Connecticut Libraries.

Clapp, John M. *Select Orations Illustrating American Political History*. New York: The Macmillan Company, 1909.

Coleman, Loren, and Patrick Huyghe. *The Field Guide to Lake Monsters, Sea Serpents, and Other Mystery Denizens of the Deep*. New York: Penguin Group, 2003.

Chidsey, Donald B. *The American Privateers*. New York: Dodd, Mead and Company, 1962.

Choate, David. *Town of Essex: From 1634 to 1868*. Springfield, Mass.: The Town of Essex, 1868.

Citro, Joseph A., and Stephen R. Bissette. *The Vermont Monster Guide*. N.p.: University Press of New England, 2009.

Clark, William B., ed. *Naval Documents of the American Revolution*. Vol. 1. Washington: U.S.G.P.O, 1964.

____. *Naval Documents of the American Revolution*. *Vol. 2*. Washington: U.S.G.P.O, 1966.

____. *Naval Documents of the American Revolution*. Vol. 3. Washington: U.S.G.P.O, 1968.

Crain, William. *Theories of Development: Concepts and Applications*. 4th ed. Upper Saddle River, NJ: Prentice Hall, 2000.

Dalzell, James M. *John Gray of Mount Vernon; The Last Soldier of the Revolution*. Washington: Gibson Brothers, 1868.

Dewey, Davis R. *Financial History of the United States*. 2nd Ed. Cambridge: University Press, 1903.

Dorchester, Daniel. *Latest Drink Sophistries versus Total Abstinence*. Boston: Frank Wood Printer, 1883.

Dresler, Horst, *Farmers and Honest Men*. Woodstock, Vt.: Anything Printed, 2009.

Easterbrook, W H., and Hugh G. Aitken. *Canadian Economic History*. Toronto: University of Toronto Press, 1984.

Elliott, Charles Winslow. *Winfield Scott: The Soldier and the Man*. New York: The Macmillan Company, 1937.

Everest, Allan S. *The War of 1812 in the Champlain Valley*. Syracuse, N.Y.: Syracuse University Press, 1981.

Fiske, Jane F., ed. *The New England Historical and Genealogical Register Index of Persons A-C*.

Vol. 51. Boston: New England Historical and Genealogical Society, 1907.

Force, Peter, ed. *American Archives: Consisting of a Collection of Authentick Records, State Papers, Debates, and Letters and Other Notices of Publick Affairs : The Whole Forming a Documentary History of the Origin...* Vol. 6. Washington: Clark and Force, 1848.

Fowler, William M. *Rebels under Sail: The American Navy during the Revolution.* New York: Charles Scribner's Sons, 1976.

Garvin, Donna B., and James L. Garvin. *On the Road North of Boston: New Hampshire Taverns and Turnpikes, 1700-1900.* Concord, NH: New Hampshire Historical Society, 1988. Getchell, Sylvia F. Lamprey River Village: The Early Years. Newmarket, MA: Newmarket Press, 1976.

Giroux, Lesley-Ann Dupigny, and Cary J Mock. *Historical Climate Variability and Impacts in North America.* New York: Dordrecht, 2009.

Gundersen, Joan R. *To Be Useful to the World: Women in Revolutionary America, 1740-1790.* Chapel Hill: Chapel Hill : University of North Carolina Press, 2006.

Holliday, Carl. *Woman's Life in Colonial Days.* Williamstown, Mass.: Corner House Publishers, 1922.

James, Bartholomew, John K. Laughton, and James Y. Sullivan. *Journal of Rear-Admiral Bartholomew James, 1752- 1828.* London: Printed for the Navy Records Society, 1896.

Jedrey, Christopher M. *The World of John Cleaveland.* New York: W.W. Norton, 1979.

Jones, John Paul, Benjamin Walker, and James Hamilton. *Life of Rear-Admiral John Paul Jones.* Philadelphia: Walker and Gillis, 1845.

Josephson, Hannah. *The Golden Threads: New England's Mill Girls and Magnates.* New York: Russell and Russell, 1967.

Joy, A F. *We are the Shakers.* South Wellfleet, Mass.: Saturscent Publishers, 1985.

Lewis, Walker, ed. *Speak For Yourself Daniel.* Boston: Houghton Mifflin Company,1969.

Lincoln, Charles H., ed. *Naval Records of the American Revolution 1775-1788.* Washington: Government Printing Office, 1906.

Lind, John. *An Answer to the Declaration of the American Congress.* 4th ed. London: Cadell, 1776. Accessed March 24, 2012. http://books.google.com/ books? id=PrE6AAAAcAAJ&dq=john+lind&source=gbs_navlinks_s.

Little, John I. *The Other Quebec: Microhistorical Essays on Nineteenth Century Religion and Society.* Toronto: University of Toronto, 2006.

Little, Nina F. Little by Little: *Six Decades of Collecting American Decorator Arts.* New York: E.D. Dutton, 1984.

Little, William. *The History of Weare, New Hampshire 1735- 1888*. Lowell, Mass.: S.W. Huse and Co, 1888.

Lowance, Mason I., and Georgia B. Bumgardner, eds. *Massachusetts Broadsides of the American Revolution*. Amherst, MA: University of Massachusetts Press, 1976.

Maclay, Edgar S. *A History of American Privateers*. New York: D. Appleton and Company, 1899.

Martyn, Charles. *The life of Artemas Ward, the First Commander- in-Chief of the American Revolution*. New York: Artemus Ward, 1921.

May, Catherine M. *History of the Eastern Townships, province of Quebec, Dominion of Canada: Civil and Descriptive in Three Parts*. Montreal: John Lovell, 1869.

McInnis, Edgar. Canada: *A Political and Social History*. Toronto: Holt, Rhinehart and Winston of Canada Limited, 1969.

McMaster, John B. *History of the People of the United States*. Vol. 4. New York: D. Appleton and Company, 1895.

Mihm, Stephen. *A Nation of Counterfeiters: Capitalists, Con Men, and the Making of the United States*. Cambridge: Harvard University Press, 2009.

Miller, John C. *Triumph of Freedom 1775-1783*. Boston: Little Brown and Company, 1948.

Miller, Nathan. *Broadsides: The Age of Fighting Sail, 1775-1815*. New York: John Wiley and Sons, Inc, 2000.

Morgan, Edmund S. *The Birth of the Republic: 1763-1789*. Chicago: The University of Chicago Press, 1965.

Morgan, William J., ed. *Naval Documents of the American Revolution*. Vol. 5. Washington: U.S.G.P.O, 1968.

___. *Naval Documents of the American Revolution*. Vol. 7. Washington: U.S.G.P.O,1976.

Paine, Ralph D. *The Ships and Sailors of Old Salem*. New York: The Outing Publishing Company, 1908.

Palmer, Dave R. *George Washington and Benedict Arnold*. Washington: Regnery Publishing, Inc., 2006.

Pattee, William S. *A History of Old Braintree and Quincy: with a Sketch of Randolph and Holbrook*. Quincy, Mass.: Green & Prescott, 1879.

Pearson, Michael. *Those Damned Rebels: The American Revolution as Seen Through British Eyes*. New York: G.P. Putnam's Sons, 1972.

Richards, Leonard L. *Shays's Rebellion: The American Revolutions Final Battle*. Philadephia: University of Pennsylvania Press, 2002.

Rivard, Paul E. *A New Order of Things: How the Textile Industry Transformed New England*. Hanover, NH: University Press of New England, 2002.

Rousseau, Jean J. *The Social Contract*. Translated by Maurice Cranston. New York: Penguin Books, 1968.

Scherer, Paul. *Lord John Russell: A Biography*. Cranbury, N.J.: Susquehanna University Press, 1999.

Schultz, Suzanne M. *Body Snatching: the Robbing of Graves for the Education of Physicians in Early Nineteenth Century America*. Jefferson, North Carolina: McFarland and Company Inc, 1992.

Secretary of the Commonwealth. *Massachusetts Soldiers and Sailors of the Revolutionary War*. Vol. 3. Boston: Wright and Potter Printing, 1897.

___*Massachusetts Soldiers and Sailors of the Revolutionary War*. Vol. 11. Boston: Wright and Potter Printing, 1903.

Shufelt, Harry B. *Nicholas Austin the Quaker and the Township of Bolton*. Knowlton, Canada: Brome County Historical Society, 1971.

Snow, Edward R. *Mysterious Tales of the New England Coast*. Cornwall, N.Y.: Cornwall Press, 1961.

Snowman, Sally R., and James G. Thomson. *Boston Light: A Historical Perspective*. Plymouth, MA: Flagship Press, 1999.

Stansbury, P. *A Pedestrian Tour of Two Thousand Three Hundred Miles in North America*. New York: J.D. Myers and W. Smith, 1822.

Stiles, Henry R. *Bundling: its Origin, Progress and Decline in America*. Albany: Author, 1871.

Stout, Neil R. *The Royal Navy in America, 1760-1775*. Annapolis: Naval Institute Press, 1973.

Stubbs, William. *The Constitutional History of England in its Origin and Development*. Vol. 3: Clarendon Press, 1878.

Syrett, David. *Shipping and the American War 1775-83*. New York: Oxford University Press Inc, 1970.

___. *The Royal Navy in American Waters 1775-1783*. Brookfield, VT: Gower Publishing Company, 1989.

___. *The Royal Navy In European Waters During The American Revolutionary War*. Columbia: University of South Carolina Press, 1998.

Thomas, Evan. *John Paul Jones: Sailor, Hero, Father of the American Navy*. New York: Simon and Schuster, 2004.

Tilley, John A. *The British Navy and the American Revolution*. Columbia, SC: University of South Carolina Press, 1987.

Tilling, Robert I. This Dynamic Earth: the Story of Plate Tectonics. U.S. Government Printing Office.

Turner, Frederick J. "The Significance of the Frontier in American History."University of Virginia. http://xroads.virginia.edu/~hyper/turner/. Chapter 1

Turner. Wesley B., *British Generals in the War of 1812*. Montreal: McGill Queen's, 1999.

Van Deusen, Glyndon G. *The Jacksonian Era: 1828-1848*. Long Grove, Ill.: Waveland Press, 1992.

Volo, James M. *Blue Water Patriots: The American Revolution Afloat*. Lanham, MD: Rowman and Littlefield, 2006.

Wallace, Willard M. Jonathan Dearborn: *A Novel of the War of 1812*. Boston: Little Brown and Company, 1967.

Weisbrod, Carol. *The Boundaries of Utopia*. New York: Pantheon Books, 1980.

Weld, Isaac. *Weld's Travels through the States of North America , and the Provinces of Upper and Lower Canada during the years 1795, 1796, and 1797*.Vol. 1. Carlisle, MA: Applewood Books, 1807.

White, R. J. *The Age of George III*. Garden City, NY: Doubleday and Company Inc., 1969.

Whittlesey, Charles B. Historical Sketch of Joseph Spencer, Major-General of the Continental Troops. Hartford, Conn.: Sons of the American Revolution, 1904.

Wilbur, C. K. *Pirates and Patriots of the Revolution*. Chester, Conn.: Globe Pequot Press, 1984.

___. *The Revolutionary Soldier, 1775-1783*. Guilford, CT: Globe Pequot Press ,1993.

___. *Revolutionary Medicine 1700-1800*. 2nd ed. Guilford, CT: Globe Pequot Press,1997.

Winks, Robin W. *Canada and the United States: The Civil War Years*. Baltimore, MD: The John Hopkins Press, 1960.

Wright, Richardson. *Hawkers and Walkers in Early America*. Philadelphia: J. B. Lippincott Company, 1927.

Journals and Leaflets

Freiberg, Malcolm. "Thomas Hutchinson's Strictures upon the Declaration of the Congress at Philadelphia, In a letter to a Noble Lord." Old South Leaflets (1776)

Watkins, Charles D. "Skinners Island." Owls Head Mountain House Lake Memphremagog, 1880 Accessed March 21, 2011. http://books.google.com/booksid=dy0TAAAAYAAJ&pg=PA39&lpg=PA39&dq =lake+memphremagog+smuggling+during+war+of+1812&source=bl&ots=_x9z LywWhY&sig=heP5Rp9MYH_hiDEjX0EICT3T3U&hl=en&ei=FdtTbfeNsGa0Q Ha8fmPC.

Frederick, George William, King. "His Majesty's Most Gracious Speech to Both Houses of Parliament." Speech before Parliament, October 31, 1776. From Williams College, The Founding Documents. Accessed March 24, 2012.

http://chapin.williams.edu/exhibits/founding.html.

The *Stanstead Journal* (Stanstead, Quebec, Canada). "A Century Ago." June 26, 1869. Accessed March 29, 2012. http://news.google.com/newspapersnid=VnuxuLaQPLMC&dat=19690626&printsec=frontpage&hl=en.

Index

Frederick Channell

Genealogy

Abraham FitzJohn Channell

Born: 24 Nov 1748 Place: London England
   Family tree in Cogswell Grant dates it 24, Nov 1759
Christened: Place: England
Died: 9 Jan 1858 Place: Georgeville, Quebec
Buried: 11 Jan 1858 Place: Bullock Cemetery Georgeville Quebec

First Spouse: Abigail Burnham
Married: 9 Dec 1779 Place: Chebacco Parish Ipswich, Essex County, MA

Second Spouse: Elizabeth Cleaveland
Married: 1 Jan 1795 Place: Chebacco Parish Ipswich, Essex County, MA

Third Spouse: Mary Dyer (Smith)
Married: 16 Nov 1807 Place: Boston MA

Fourth Spouse: Wealthy Cox
Married: 1 June 1814 Place: Unknown (possibly Quebec)

Abraham's father: Robert FitzJohn
Abraham's mother: Frances Hide

Abigail Burnham

Born: 17 Apr 1755 Place: Ipswich, Essex County, MA
Died: 21 Jun 1794 Place: Chebacco Parish Ipswich, Essex County, MA
Buried: Place: Old Burial Ground Essex MA

Wife's father: Nehemiah Burnham
Wife's mother: Elizabeth Burnham

<u>Children</u>

1. Abraham Channell

 Born: 1 Jun 1780 Place: Ipswich (Chebacco Parish), Essex County, MA
 Died: Place: Bolton, (Today Austin) Quebec
 Buried: 25 Dec 1874 Place: East Bolton Cemetery

First Wife: Sarah Peasley or Peaslee
Married: 28 May 1800 Place: Dunbarton, Merrimack, NH
Second Wife: Jane Taylor
Married: 1 Mar 1816 Place: Newport, VT

2. William Channell

Born: 27 Dec 1781 Place: Ipswich (Chebacco Parish), Essex, MA
Died: 19 Mar 1846 Place: Port Elizabeth, NJ
Buried: Place: Port Elizabeth Methodist Cemetery
Spouse: Phebe Hand
Married: 9 Oct 1802 Place: Port Elizabeth, NJ

3. Abigail Channell (mother of Abigail George, Lowell Mill Girl)

Born: 1782 Place: Ipswich (Chebacco Parish), Essex, MA
Died: 10 Aug 1859 Place: Potton Quebec
Buried: Place: George Cemetery Potton Quebec
Spouse: Moses Hayes George
Married: 4 May 1800 Place: Dunbarton, Merrimack, NH

4. Frances (Fanny) Channell

Born: 28 Mar 1784 Place: Ipswich (Chebacco Parish), Essex, MA
Died: 10 Apr 1882 Place: Topsfield, MA
Buried: Place: Pine Grove Cemetery Rte 97, Topsfield MA
Spouse: David Burnham Balch
Married: 11 Dec 1808 Place: Ipswich, Essex County, MA

5. Robert Channell

Born: 11 Feb 1785 Place: Ipswich (Chebacco Parish), Essex, MA
Died: 12 Feb 1881 Place: Newmarket, Rockingham, NH
Buried: Place: Spring Street Cemetery Essex, MA
Spouse: Lydia Butler
Married: 26 Nov 1807 Place: Chebacco, Ipswich, Essex County, MA

6. Betsy Channell
Born: Feb 1787 Place: Ipswich (Chebacco Parish), Essex, MA
Died: 1822 in Boston at age 35.

Frederick Channell

Buried: Unknown   Place: Unknown
Spouse: Elisha Tucker (Furniture Maker)
Married: 24 Dec 1809 Place: Boston, MA

7. Sally Channell

Born: 10 Aug 1793 Place: Ipswich(Chebacco Parish) , Essex , MA
Died: 13 Sept 1849 Place:
Buried: Place: Old Burial Ground Essex, MA
Spouse: Dudley Choate
Married: 28 Sept 1817 Place: Ipswich, Essex County, MA

Second Marriage

Husband: Abraham FitzJohn Channell

Second Wife: **Elizabeth Cleaveland**

Born: 25 Jun 1757 Place: Chebacco, Essex, MA
Died: 23 Nov 1828 Place: Rowley MA
Buried: Place: Newbury, MA, Byfield Cemetery

Other Spouse: Abraham was her first marriage
Married: 1 Jan 1795 Place: Chebacco Parish Ipswich, Essex County, MA

Wife's father: Rev. John Cleaveland
Wife's mother: Mary Dodge

Child

1. Mary Cleaveland Channell

Born: 4 Nov 1796 Place: Weare, Hillsborough, NH
Died: 26 Sept 1830 Place: Rowley, MA
Buried: Place: Byfield Cemetery Newbury, MA
Spouse: Never married

Third Marriage

Husband: Abraham FitzJohn Channell
Wife: **Mary Dyer** (Shaker)

Born: 10 Sept. 1764 Place: Boston, MA
Died: 24 Jun 1855 Place: Harvard MA
Buried: Place: Shaker Cemetery Harvard, MA

First Spouse: Stephen Smith
Married: 21 Jul 1791 Place: Boston, MA

Wife's father: John Dyer
Wife's mother: Mary Sweetster

Child

1. Susan Channell

Born: 1 Jan 1809 Place: Essex, MA
Died: 5 May 1880 Place: Harvard, MA
Buried: Place: Shaker Cemetery Harvard, MA
Spouse: Unmarried

Fourth Wife

Husband: Abraham FitzJohn Channell
Wife: **Wealthy Cox**

Married: 1815 Place: Canada, likely in Georgeville
Born: 15 Dec 1782 Place: Hanover, NH
Died: 19 Mar 1862 Place: Georgeville Quebec
Buried: Place: Bullock Cemetery Quebec

Wife's father: Jonathan Cox
Wife's mother: Naomi Smith

Children

1. Susan Channell

Born: 3 Jun 1816 Place: Georgeville Quebec
Died: 9 Jan 1877
Buried: Place: Bullock Cemetery Georgeville Quebec

Spouse: John Carter Tuck (Canadian Rebel)